Bucketfoot Al

ALSO BY CLIFTON BLUE PARKER

Big and Little Poison: Paul and Lloyd Waner, Baseball Brothers (McFarland, 2003)

Fouled Away: The Baseball Tragedy of Hack Wilson (McFarland, 2000)

Bucketfoot Al
The Baseball Life of Al Simmons

CLIFTON BLUE PARKER

McFarland & Company, Inc., Publishers
Jefferson, North Carolina, and London

LIBRARY OF CONGRESS CATALOGUING-IN-PUBLICATION DATA

Parker, Clifton Blue, 1963–
　　Bucketfoot Al : the baseball life of Al Simmons /
Clifton Blue Parker.
　　　p.　cm.
　　Includes bibliographical references and index.

　　ISBN 978-0-7864-6143-1
　　softcover : 50# alkaline paper ∞

　　1. Simmons, Al, 1992–1956.　2. Baseball players — United
States — Biography.　I. Title.
GV865.S519P37　2011
796.357092 — dc23
[B]　　　　　　　　　　　　　　　　　　　　　　2011017372

BRITISH LIBRARY CATALOGUING DATA ARE AVAILABLE

© 2011 Clifton Blue Parker. All rights reserved

No part of this book may be reproduced or transmitted in any form or by any means, electronic or mechanical, including photocopying or recording, or by any information storage and retrieval system, without permission in writing from the publisher.

On the cover: Al Simmons (National Baseball Hall of Fame Library, Cooperstown, New York). Front cover design by David Landis (Shake It Loose Graphics)

Manufactured in the United States of America

McFarland & Company, Inc., Publishers
　Box 611, Jefferson, North Carolina 28640
　www.mcfarlandpub.com

*For Caitlin Blue Parker,
daughter of dreams come true,
and for Sakue Nakano,
woman of love and gentleness.*

Contents

Acknowledgments ix
Introduction: Swaggering Shooting Star 1

One:	Sultan of the Milwaukee Sandlots	5
Two:	Bucketfoot Swings and a New Name	12
Three:	Milwaukee's Best	20
Four:	Athletic Ambitions	29
Five:	Sophomore Breakout	39
Six:	"Best Centerfielder"	45
Seven:	Ty Cobb and Long Flannel Sleeves	53
Eight:	Nurturing the Nucleus	62
Nine:	Building a Dynasty	71
Ten:	Hard Times and World Champions Again	86
Eleven:	"No Reason to Be Friendly"	101
Twelve:	Woe to White Elephants	115
Thirteen:	New Socks for the Sox	126
Fourteen:	Changes in Chicago	137
Fifteen:	Tail of the Tiger	151
Sixteen:	Mr. Simmons Leaves Washington	164
Seventeen:	Chasing Three Thousand	172
Eighteen:	Twilight Times	181

Nineteen:	Coaching the A's and Indians	191
Twenty:	Cooperstown Comes Calling	200
Twenty-One:	Analyzing Al Simmons	208

Appendix: Al Simmons Statistics 215

Notes 219

Bibliography 235

Index 239

Acknowledgments

Writing a book on baseball is a solitary act of historical imagination and diligent research — but one man does not write a book alone, it has been observed. That is especially true with this work, which stands on the shoulders of many who came before me — all the sportswriters and authors who chronicled the contemporary times of Al Simmons the ballplayer decades ago — and all the people today who opened up pathways into his life from our distant vantage point in the early twenty-first century. And so I am eternally grateful for all those who offered invaluable and selfless help in the preparing this book. This includes Tom Rathkamp of Milwaukee, notably, who generously shared a wealth of materials on which he was working; Richard Rosen and the Philadelphia Athletics Historical Society, who thoughtfully delivered content and pictures from the society; Kevin Ferenchik, who spent time tirelessly talking with me about baseball book ideas and supported my interest in Simmons; Bob Rose, the A's public relations director who positively pointed me in productive directions; Patrick and Karen Graeber, who kindly provided information about the son of Al Simmons; the National Baseball Hall of Fame, which supplied photographs; Bill Deane, the astute baseball researcher and writer who collected newspaper clippings on Simmons for my usage; Cyril Morong, who helpfully allowed me to quote from his fine sabermetric analysis of the ballplayer; Paul Tenpenny and Marion Kusnick of the City of Milwaukee Public Library, who allowed the publication of a photo; and the Society for American Baseball Research, of which I am a member and deeply appreciative of all the illumination that this group has brought to the national pastime.

I also owe a huge thank you to those in my family and close circle who lent me support, love and appreciation — Sakue Nakano, Rhiannon Parker, Caitlin Parker, Laura Stodden Parker, and her kind family, my late mother, Donna Reynolds — who gave me great maternal support early on in my writing pursuits and the understanding that it takes to keep moving forward through the ups and downs of the years. Last but not least, I owe the deepest gratitude to Al Simmons and the players like him who have made this game so fascinating in the way of culture and our personal connections to the national pastime.

A while back, I was given a ball signed by Connie Mack for my great grandfather, Raymond L. Pittman, who was instrumental in building the stadium and team for the Fayetteville minor league farm club of the A's many decades ago. I thank my father, Clifton Parker, and his wife, Anna Parker, for finding this ball in the attic of my grandmother's house and generously giving it to me. An official North Carolina League ball, Mack had signed it in the early 1950s when the A's were in Fayetteville for exhibition games with the minor league club before they headed north for the season opening. That little treasure in part sparked an inquiry in my mind about those old A's like Simmons.

I hope you enjoy the adventure as well.

Introduction: Swaggering Shooting Star

> "Names had to be chosen, therefore, that they could bear the whole weight of perpetuity ... Call a player Sycamore Flynn or Melbourne Trench and something starts to happen. He shrinks or grows, stretches or puts on muscle."—Robert Coover, from The Universal Baseball Association, Inc., J. Henry Waugh, Prop.

> "Hitters are born, not made."—Al Simmons[1]

Al Simmons burned like a swaggering shooting star across baseball's skies on the way to a Hall of Fame destiny in Cooperstown. The son of Polish immigrants from Milwaukee, he was a fiery competitor who crushed the enemy in the box score, pulverized pitchers with the loud crack of his line drives, and quashed rallies with his rifle-like throws and sharp instincts for outfield play.

Every great baseball player is different — some, like Simmons, flair brilliantly but too briefly in the larger march of time, before falling to earth for any number of reasons. Others are able to put together careers of long and distinguished import, yet without the peaks of some, like the subject of this work. Simmons, at top form in the Roaring Twenties, sparked one of baseball's greatest dynasties, the Philadelphia Athletics, to multiple championships — before becoming just another ballplayer. Why? While his achievements spoke greatness, he was not an easy man to like — for those competing against him, or even with him — and he seemed to play to the level of team expectation. Above all, one look at him told you what to expect.

Al Simmons looked frightful at the plate. He had a ghostly pale face that never seemed to tan, jet-black hair that covered a large head and thick eyebrows that crowned a gray-eyed glare — one that pitchers knew all too well. He was big, had broad shoulders and powerful arms, and a robust voice, standing six feet and weighing 200 pounds in an age when ballplayers were smaller and lighter — and when the game was rougher, harsher, and more mean-spirited.

All this suited Simmons just fine. Swinging from an unorthodox stance, the confident Simmons acquired the nickname "Bucketfoot Al" for how he kicked his leg toward third base while swinging — a dead-wrong technique in the eyes of experts. It worked for him, although it was his biggest obstacle to overcome in becoming a professional baseball player.

"Hitters are born, not made," said Simmons, who believed too many players in the decades after his career were over-coached, coddled, pampered, and as a result, not fully confident in their own abilities.[2] Doing it his way from 1924 to 1944, Simmons sprayed line drives for a career .334 lifetime average — he hit above .380 in four seasons, and finished with 307 home runs, two batting titles, and 1,827 RBIs.

How good was he? The celebrated baseball historian Bill James ranks him as the seventh best left fielder of all time, giving him an "A" as a fielder. In another tribute, Connie Mack, the A's manager for 50 years, five World Series titles, and hundreds of ballplayers, kept only one picture of a former player in his Shibe Park office — and it was of Simmons. "I wish I had nine players named Al Simmons," Mack once said about Simmons, who could play any outfield spot adroitly and thrived in big games, hitting .329 with six home runs and 17 RBIs in 19 World Series games.[3]

Simmons' intimidating presence was felt by Ted Williams, perhaps baseball's greatest hitter, who once said of him, "Big guy. Gorilla with a bat in his hand."[4] He had a boxer's brawling mentality toward baseball. He was no boxer, but some thought he looked like one out of Central Casting. Ken Smith, former director of the National Baseball Hall of Fame, said Simmons had a "back and chest like the late heavyweight champion Rocky Marciano and heavy black eyebrows. Watching him stomp to the batter's box on his heavy legs excited your expectancy. He was a window smasher, a rude, hairy-fisted character."[5]

The hairy gorilla was outspoken, whether to sportswriters or to players on the other team. Simmons had a "good, loud voice" with a "real swagger in it," John Kieran of the *New York Times* wrote in describing his relentless bench jockeying.[6] Simmons openly loathed opponents, and especially hated pitchers. He mocked the latter to their faces as he clubbed them in the box scores: "There's no reason to be friendly with a pitcher who's trying to take your bread and butter away from you. You're going to get paid off on what you hit, and those pitchers are trying to give you the works all the time. I never had any sympathy for a pitcher." The pitcher, he explained, always had the edge. "He always knows what he's going to throw, and you don't. All you have is a round bat that you're supposed to hit with. They give you that big herky-jerky motion and stall around and try to get you off stride, and play you for a chump. How are you going to feel friendly toward guys like that?"[7]

Aggression — expressed in hits — defined Al Simmons. The right-handed hitter swung away, often out of the strike zone and frequently for extra bases, and walked rarely. He was the quickest player ever to achieve 2,000 hits, doing it in 1,390 games — he is also ranked third all-time in hits per game among players starting their career in 1900 or later. And through 1931, he was third in the statistic of isolated power, trailing only Babe Ruth and Lou Gehrig.

Those are some of the statistics, but the tale of Simmons is about rising and falling, dramatically so. Though his career started furiously, it rambled in the middle and stalled toward the end. He finished just 73 hits shy of the 3,000-hit milestone — or he might be better known today.

The irascible Simmons reminded many of Ty Cobb, who became his mentor when the aging Detroit Tigers star joined the Philadelphia Athletics in 1927. Like Cobb, Simmons left a trail of prejudice in his wake. In 1978, well after Simmons' death in 1956, sportswriter Bob Broeg wrote, "It's apparent that Simmons doesn't get now the general overall recognition he would seem to merit. Was it because of questionable personal popularity?"[8]

That says a lot — but there is more to his story. Alois Szymanski — his given name — never had it easy on the way up from a south side Milwaukee Polish neighborhood where many first-generation Americans like him struggled. He also had lost a father at a young age. Perhaps his hardscrabble origins made him a vexing competitor. Or maybe he was just wired that way from the beginning, or both. Either way, he did not care about winning friends on the diamond. It was combat.

Simmons thought a mere "hello" to an opponent was a more than a betrayal to one's teammates — it was also a threat to his professional survival, as the opposition was trying to ruin him. Later as a coach, he urged his players not to talk on the field with players on other teams. As Simmons once put it, "I've got a reputation for being coarse and a little bit ornery, but believe me, enough things have happened to me in my lifetime to account for that."

And though he confessed his deep admiration of Mack, he was not unafraid to criticize the venerable A's manager. One time Mack made an on-the-field decision, and then looked at an apparently unsure Simmons and said, "Is it all right with you, Al?"[9]

Yet Simmons could display a soft touch. Outfielder George Case, taken under his wing by Simmons as a rookie in 1937, recalled that the aging veteran had an unusual patience and generosity in teaching him about the finer points of the game. "He turned out to be, under that gruff exterior, a very kindly and thoughtful man," said Case, perhaps shattering some images about his mentor.[10]

Gruff or thoughtful, Simmons had the fortune — or misfortune — to play at a time when Babe Ruth, Lou Gehrig, Mel Ott, Rogers Hornsby, and teammate Jimmie Foxx dominated the sports pages. Yet he achieved what none of them did, knocking in more than 100 RBIs in his first 11 seasons.

In that golden era, Simmons was surrounded by Hall of Fame talent on the A's — Foxx, pitcher Lefty Grove, catcher Mickey Cochrane — among other strong players. Loaded with these stars, the A's overcame the Ruth-Gehrig New York Yankees to claim the American League pennant from 1929 to 1931, winning the World Series in 1929 and 1930 before the Great Depression took its toll on the A's roster.

Simply, he was an incredible player on fantastic teams. Every now and then someone rediscovers Al Simmons and those magnificent Philadelphia A's. *Sports Illustrated* selected a photo of Simmons for its August 19, 1996, cover story, "The Team that Time Forgot," by William Nack. The article brought back to life the A's and their manhandling of the Yankees and everyone else. There are many reasons to believe those A's of Simmons' peak era were among the best teams of all time.[11]

Yet today those A's seem far away in baseball's collective memory, and the name "Al Simmons" is more commonly associated with a brawny Todd McFarlane comic book superhero with the same name — and nicknamed "Spawn." It has not helped matters that the A's have relocated their franchise twice, fracturing our sense of history and appreciation of the old-time A's. In 1954, the A's moved out of Philadelphia, their home since 1901, to Kansas City and in 1967 they moved yet again, this time farther west to Oakland.

While books have been devoted to virtually every season in the 1920s and 1930s and to the New York Yankees of that period — and some to A's teams — never has the full story of Al Simmons been told — until now.

Baseball, and hitting, is one thing. Off the field, Al Simmons found life was not as easy as hitting .300. He was quite often off the mark, in fact. Simmons had, as they say, the hot blood, and his emotions easily bowled over to anger or sentimentality, and too often in his later years sought the self-destructive kind of soul-numbing comfort. His life was bittersweet. Physically and emotionally ravaged, he died at the age of 54 — barely 12 years since his last game as a major leaguer. That is too young.

Today, contemporary accounts and other recollections give us a sense of Al Simmons the person and the ballplayer, his connections to people, his teams and how he captured the fans' imagination in his halcyon days. Not much if anything has been written about this formidable player. It is my humble hope that Al Simmons lives again in these pages, and that we finally understand who he was and what he means to the national pastime.

CHAPTER ONE

Sultan of the Milwaukee Sandlots

> *"The largest thing I've learned is the enormous grip that this game has on people, the extent to which it really is very important. It goes way down deep. It really does bind together."*—A. Bartlett Giamatti[1]

> *"It is the first game I recall playing, and today it seems as if I always played baseball."*—Al Simmons[2]

When Al Simmons was born in Milwaukee in 1902, baseball was booming across America, a country in the throes of industrialism and unrelenting change. Historians often regard the two decades ahead as the Golden Age of sports, especially in cities like Milwaukee where Simmons starred on the sandlots from a young age and other young boys dreamed of careers in baseball. To make it big, in any field, whether in business or baseball, was the American dream.

This upsurge in spectator sports reflected a liberating shift in American consciousness after the World War I horrors, the deadly 1918 influenza outbreak, and the blandness of mass production jobs. Off the diamond, the industrialization of America provided opportunity as well as dark forces — rigid standardization, rising bureaucracies, assembly line work, and cultural pressures to conform to one's social class. Baseball was seen as healthy, played outdoors and challenging physically. The game was not for the meek.

Sports like baseball offered an escape to this alternative. Americans from all backgrounds — from Polish immigrant to New England aristocrat — turned to sports for fun, health and entertainment. Baseball, based on talent, was both egalitarian and opportunistic. With enough production, anyone could climb above others and become a hero to people far and wide, especially boys and men.

In his late teens, the game changed for sluggers-to-be like Simmons, as the concept of the baseball hero ascended and America looked skyward for deliverance from the monotony of industrialism. Babe Ruth of the New York

Yankees symbolized the rise of power baseball in the American consciousness. He transformed the game forever with his long and frequent home runs. Soon, Ruth was not the only slugger in the game, and by the 1920s other stars had formed a colorful constellation of characters.

Al Simmons, from immigrant origins, was tailor-made to fit this American image of the strutting, upwardly mobile sporting man. He was born at the dawn of the twentieth century in Milwaukee, an area was settled by Native Americans hundreds of years before European settlers arrived at the mouth of the Kinnickinnic, Menomonee and Milwaukee Rivers. Indians gave the area its name, calling it "Milwaukie," which means "where the waters meet."

One of the first known whites to visit the area was Jesuit missionary Father Jacques Marquette, who camped there in 1674 and was soon followed by fur trappers. Eventually, wars drove most of the Indians out of Milwaukee by the 1840s. By the second half of the nineteenth century, Milwaukee was booming on trading in wheat and furs and the production of beer. By the end of the century, thousands of workers were employed by tanneries, foundries, packing plants, breweries and manufacturers. As industry flourished, the city's population exploded. As early as 1850, almost two-thirds of the city's residents were foreign born. In 1910, immigrants and their children accounted for three-fourths of the city's population.

Germans were among the city's first immigrants and they soon dominated the city. Other immigrants included the Irish, Czechs, Hollanders, Austrians, Norwegians, Britons and German-speaking Jews. By the end of the nineteenth century, Poles and Italians were flooding into the city — and among the new arrivals were the Polish immigrants John and Agnes Szymanski, who found work and began building a family.

On May 26, 1902, Alois Szymanski was born to John and Agnes, who lived at 772 American Avenue, now 1972 S. 15th Place, in south side Milwaukee. The Szymanski home was in a Polish neighborhood marked by "typical basement flats."[3]

The date was not 1903, as would be widely circulated throughout the career and life of Al Simmons. His birth certificate from the Milwaukee Health Department also indicated his first name was not "Aloysius" as many believed, but "Alois," and he had no middle name, despite later reports that it was "Harry." However, "Alois" is short for "Aloysius," which is of old German origin and means a "famous warrior." Now rare, the first name Alois or Aloysius was at its most popular in the U.S. from 1890 to 1910, a reflection of the large arrival of immigrants from the Old World.

Elsewhere on the birth certificate, John Szymanski's birthplace was noted as Poland and his occupation as "laborer." His mother's maiden name was Agnes Czarnecki, also from Poland.[4]

Alois, the firstborn in his Polish Catholic family, had two brothers (Walter and Anthony) and three sisters (Frances, Tillie and Anna). Not much is known about his father, other than he worked in a brush factory and was an ardent fan of the hometown Milwaukee Brewers of the American Association. He gave Alois his first bat, ball and glove, and the kid soon became a mainstay on the neighborhood fields.[5]

Simmons said, "A pair of discarded baseball shoes, a $1.50 baseball uniform — my first — which I wore all day Saturday, slept in Saturday night only to have it rain on Sunday, a steady round of drilling in the Sunday morning league on the South Side are among the treasured recollections of my early baseball life in Milwaukee."[6]

In those days, in every neighborhood, no matter how humble or poor, there was always somebody who had a bat and a ball, and enough space, somewhere, for a field of play. Played simply, baseball, for children like Alois, became a way out of potential poverty. He described himself as a "healthy kid who loved his baseball in summer and who flattened his nose against the frosty windows of Mitchell street's big stores in winter, to feast his eyes upon the tinsel and toys."[7]

Alois attended St. Hyacinth's grade school at Ninth and Becher Streets in Milwaukee. "I realize I was not much different from the more or less ragged urchins who played their baseball and marbles, and kicked a football about the streets and lots of our neighborhood," he observed.[8]

Alois said he and the other boys made use of whatever they could in getting a baseball game together. "All that is needed is a vacant lot, four stones, a bat and ball, and the game is on." Back then, south side Milwaukee was hungry for baseball, and kids played by the droves throughout the neighborhoods and corner lots. Alois was swinging a bat and throwing and catching at an early age. "I loved the game, but I was so awkward and butter-fingered I seldom got the chance to play except with boys smaller than myself," he later said, but "even in those days I had dreams of being a professional player."[9]

One day, "butter-fingered" Alois came home from school and told his father that he was going to be a professional baseball player. Though a baseball fan, his practical-minded father insisted that his son's future was in the butcher business. Eventually, Alois' rambling on about baseball got his father annoyed enough to get him spanked, according to one account. But Alois kept insisting he wanted to play baseball. Finally, his dad relented and told all, "Well, he'd better be a good one." His dad's misgivings may have origins in the fact that many saw ballplayers as louts in those days.[10]

The tale may well be an exaggeration. As noted, other accounts indicate his father was a fan of the game, and perhaps Simmons later spun the yarn of overcoming doubting parents. Besides, his father died before Simmons was old enough to legitimately pose a chance of becoming a professional ballplayer.

A vast majority of the quotes attributed to ballplayers of Simmons' era are fictitious — many sportswriters fancifully doled up the prose. This was a day and age when tape recorders were non-existent, and players and writers arguably had more access to each other, frequently traveling and even socializing together. Paul Dickson, author of *Baseball's Greatest Quotations,* estimates that 75 percent of all quotations fall into this category. "There is no question that a lot of quotes were tailored to the player in question."[11]

As a youngster, Alois' biggest hero was Ty Cobb, the Detroit Tigers star. Ironically, in later years Simmons was compared to Cobb for his temperament. Even more ironically, in 1927 and 1928 they would play together in the same Philadelphia Athletics outfield, with the aging Cobb mentoring the raw Simmons.

Another group of heroes for the young Simmons were the Chicago Cubs, the closest major league team to Milwaukee. "I always wanted to play with the Cubs," Simmons one day told writer John Kieran. "That was my ambition when I was growing up in Milwaukee. Frank Chance and those other fellows were my heroes."[12]

He also admired Oscar "Happy" Felsch, who began his career in 1915 as a fleet-footed center fielder for the Chicago White Sox. "Through all this period, Happy Felsch, then in his ascendancy, was my lodestar, and beyond him, glimmering like some unattainable paragon, was Ty Cobb. I used to follow their careers in the newspapers and wonder if I ever could be a ball player like they were. And as for ever meeting them, that was a dream which I never even dared to dream."[13] In 1920, Felsch's career came to an abrupt end when he was banned from baseball for supposedly fixing the 1919 World Series as one of the eight infamous "Black Sox."

In 1911, the world closed in tighter around the 8-year-old Alois. His father died, probably from a work accident, though it is not clear. Stunned, the Szymanskis faced upheaval. They had no life insurance and no savings. To hold the family together, mother Agnes got up at 4:00 A.M. to go to her job at a bakery, then would come around midday to make lunch for the children. If she had extra time, there was lots of housework to do. Alois had to do his part. "The poor soul never had a moment of her own except in slumber," Simmons said years afterwards. "It was a terrible struggle for her."[14]

His father's death "left us all in poor circumstance," Simmons said, but the children carried on "with our school at St. Hyacinth's where the Rev. B.E. Goral was pastor."[15] Philadelphia writer Edward "Dutch" Doyle said John Szymanski's untimely death put a terrible burden on both Agnes and Alois. "These were the days before special benefits for a widow from the government.

Al's mother had an enormous responsibility on her shoulders, and even at the tender age of eight realized that he (Alois) had to help out since he was the oldest of the children," Doyle wrote.[16]

About a year after her husband's death, another writer fancifully wrote, Agnes sat near the "flickering coal lamp" in the flat that she and her six children lived in. She despaired over the coming winter, how they would eat, and lamented that the boys needed new shoes and the girls needed heavy underwear. Agnes tore out a page from a school notebook laying near her, and figured out the bills and how much they needed. Alois, only nine at the time, reportedly spoke up. "Don't you cry, mama," the tale went. "When I get big I'm going to be rich and buy you a house. You just see if I don't."[17]

He did not forget baseball. At 12, Alois, who was always playing sandlot ball with the neighborhood kids, tried to join an organized ball team started up by a local parish priest. Still a bit small and scrawny, he settled for being the batboy.

Two years later, amid the turmoil of the Szymanski household finances, Alois quit school and got a job in a shoe factory making eight cents an hour. He kept that job for two years, playing as much baseball as he could in his spare time. "The South Side (of Milwaukee) always has been a hotbed of baseball, and was especially so in those days when vacant lots were plentiful," said Simmons. He enjoyed playing in a big vacant lot near America Avenue, Forest Home Avenue, and Rogers Street. "I loved my baseball and was playing it every second that I could," he said.[18]

During this period he joined the South Star Junior team and got to wear his first uniform and play in a decent ballpark. Some of the players were 10 years older than Simmons, who was already displaying a cocky attitude for a 14-year-old. His very own teammates often bet the opposing pitcher that he could not strike out the youngster.[19] "I hit so well that a restaurant man asked me to play with his team," he later recalled, "and that summer I played in an enclosed field for the first time. I couldn't field, but I could slug that old apple."[20]

To make more money and help his family, he left the shoe factory for work at the Wisconsin Motor Company and took on other jobs — truck driver, laborer, and cutter in a glove factory. Through it all, he kept playing ball, both high school and sandlot — and he watched others play the game. He said, "I know now that I was a baseball nut, for, during my (school) vacation periods each year, I would walk from my home, out on the South Side, away over to Athletic park on the North Side, a good six-mile hike, and try to horn in on a grass cutting job, just so I could be around the ball players and watch the game. If I got there too late, or if no work was available, I would wait outside for a ball to come over, or else climb up a ladder and watch the play that way."[21]

Another favorite ball field was located at Windlake Avenue and Becher Street. While playing the outfield for a team known as the "Connie Macks," ironically enough, the teenaged Alois pounded home runs over Becher Street into the middle of Kosciuszko Park. "There was a saloon keeper near our home whom we called 'Connie Mack,' and he had a team for which I was official bat boy, shag, and general mascot," said Simmons, before his promotion to ballplayer.[22]

A few years later, Alois joined the Quins in a city municipal league. He was building up his confidence and had his sights set high, he told writers. He soon was recognized as "sort of a neighborhood standout," so when the boys organized a club, Alois spent $1.50 for a uniform and became a regular member of the South Star Junior outfit. "Al Szymanski," he told himself, "if you amount to anything in this world, it'll be as a professional ballplayer," a writer quoted him as saying.[23]

He also spoke of the "uplifted" quality of the game in patriotic tones. "America is fortunate in having its baseball — it is simple, easy to play, and, among the poorer classes, it is a godsend," he said later.[24]

Baseball writers in the early twentieth century were especially given to portraying ballplayers as Horatio Alger heroes, the kind that prevailed against all the odds in going from rags-to-fame, if not always riches. The story of Al Simmons is no exception, as author Richard Crepeau pointed out in his book *Baseball: America's Diamond Mind,* describing how the Simmons house looked in years gone by. "In south (side) Milwaukee today there is a beautiful house on a pretty street. There are servants and, too, a big automobile in the garage. Friends, relatives and little children seem to be forever arriving or departing and there is always gay laughter and merry making. There lives the widow Szymanski, the mother of Al Simmons, mighty slugger of the Philadelphia Athletics," according to Crepeau, who quoted from *The Sporting News.*

Al Simmons: "The fundamental factor of my success in baseball was my determination to care for my mother. As a boy, my natural love for baseball prompted me to seek a career in the field of professional sport. Always ahead of me as a goal was that house which, when a little boy, I promised my mother."[25]

For Simmons, it was important to pay tribute to his mother. Years later, flushed with baseball money, Simmons spoke of the immense satisfaction it gave him to buy his mother that house where friends, relatives and children hung about, where servants now did the housework, and where automobiles filled the garage where there had been none before.

"In the days of failure when I was being kicked about the minor leagues as an awkward misfit, the mental picture of that house was a shining beacon ... I had told her many times about the fortunes paid to ballplayers," Simmons said.[26]

By 1920, Agnes Szymanski had reason to believe in her oldest son, who that year led the Right Laundry team to a Milwaukee amateur championship. The 18-year-old Szymanski, now a neighborhood celebrity, got nicknamed the "Duke of Mitchell Street," after the main thoroughfare in his Polish neighborhood. "Duke" seemed to befit Simmons, who even in his youth was a "natty dresser."[27]

He acknowledged having to "swallow a great deal of pride" in describing his humble origins and struggle to rise above them. "I know what it is to be a boy with unrequited childish desires," he said. "I know what it means to long and pray for things, but then in my neighborhood I had lots of company, so the pangs and heartaches were not so bitter that they blighted the enjoyment of what we had. Still, they left a mark upon my mind, even to this day." He added, "Some of my sportswriting friends have likened my life to the book career of a Horatio Alger hero."[28]

Maybe the strange sight of a young Alois at the plate was a bigger case of overcoming the odds. His eccentric batting stance appalled scouts, and from the outset, almost doomed him.

CHAPTER TWO

Bucketfoot Swings and a New Name

"What's in a name? That which we call a rose, by any other name would smell as sweet."
—William Shakespeare[1]

"The name of a man is a numbing blow from which he never recovers."
— Marshall McLuhan[2]

On the playing fields of Milwaukee's sandlot baseball world, it is likely no one much minded young Alois Szymanski's peculiar but natural batting stance. Of course, in the realm of coach-less anarchy, many players lacked the proper techniques and mechanics. It is not surprising he picked his own mechanics.

But when Alois took his stance into organized league play, where coaches did exist, serious doubts arose. A right-handed hitter, Alois stepped with his left leg away from the pitch toward third base, which went against conventional wisdom and training. Poor mechanics, the coaches said.

Young hitters are typically taught to drive their legs toward the oncoming ball — not away from it. Driving away from it, the thinking went, sapped the strength of the all-important leg and hip rotation, which is how a hitter usually brings his power into a swing.

Driving away from the ball also made the hitter look like he was afraid of the ball — not a welcomed perception in the machismo world of baseball. The irony is that Simmons was unafraid of pitchers — in fact, he bullied them with cold stares and choice words throughout his career. His stance was more a result of being comfortable with his personal style, bad habits or not.

For this, Alois eventually got tagged with the unflattering nickname, "Bucketfoot Al." Many aspiring ballplayers would have wilted under the "bucketfoot" moniker. Not the incorrigible Simmons. Somehow, it worked.

"I've studied movies of myself," he later said. "Though my left foot would stab out toward third base, the rest of me, from the belt up — especially my wrists, arms and shoulders — was swinging in a proper line over the plate."[3] Besides, it felt natural. "It is the only way I have ever hit," he declared.[4]

The term "bucketfoot" arose in the early twentieth century as a popular way to describe raw hitters who lacked the proper refinements. In 1912, pitcher Christy Mathewson wrote of a typical catcher talking to an unsure young batter. "Yer almost had your foot in the water-pail over by the bench that time," the backstop said in Mathewson's book *Pitching in a Pinch*.[5] Not an exact "bucketfoot" reference, but it arguably headed that direction for later variations to spring forth.

There was another usage in 1919: "Take your foot out of the water bucket, Mister Conley, says Buzz" in C.E. Loan's collection of baseball fiction, *Score by Innings*.

Evidence for the first use of "water bucket" used metaphorically, suggests author Paul Dickson, may have been derived by another popular phrase, as illustrated in this 1908 quotation: "(Pitcher George McQuillan) has sent many a Giant back hitless to the water bucket in days gone by." Thus, "water bucket" implied bad mechanics and worse, cowardice or incompetence, at the plate.[6]

It is ironic that Simmons, who cultivated one of the nastiest, meanest reputations in the game, got tagged with a nickname that suggested he was fainthearted and afraid.

While one day he would break the "bucketfoot" barrier in the major leagues, Simmons was far from alone among successful hitters employing it as an "effective, respected stance." Other notables using it to some degree included Arky Vaughan of the Pittsburgh Pirates in the 1930s, Roy Campanella of the Brooklyn Dodgers in the 1940s and 50s, and Vern Stephens of the St. Louis Browns and Boston Red Sox in the 1940s and 50s. Yet for whatever reason, they were not criticized as much for this as Simmons was.[7]

Bucketfoot swing and all, Alois attracted plenty of attention with his rocket line drives around Milwaukee. His first professional ballplaying opportunity came with the semi-professional Juneau team in the Lake Shore League. Juneau is a town less than an hour's drive northwest of Milwaukee.

An umpire, Anton "Butch" Schwender, tipped off the Juneau front office about Alois. Schwender knew him from umpiring in amateur games around Milwaukee. Signed as an outfielder for Juneau, Alois made eight dollars a game — a decent wage for a kid from the other side of the tracks in those days.

In signing with Juneau, Simmons apparently maintained he was born in 1903, not 1902 as his birth certificate reads. Of course, being a year younger in the baseball world has clear career advantages, and making these claims has continued right up to the present day. The incorrect date was likely given

Al Simmons in his batting stance. "I've studied movies of myself. Though my left foot would stab out toward third base, the rest of me, from the belt up — especially my wrists, arms and shoulders — was swinging in a proper line over the plate," he once explained. *National Baseball Hall of Fame*

when he filled out the paperwork upon signing his Juneau contract, though it could have happened — or been reaffirmed — at other upcoming minor league stops. In those days, when a player signed a contract, he had to fill out a form detailing his background, including birth date, for the Association of Professional Baseball Players.[8]

Of course, it was not Alois' age that drew looks from the other players and coaches when he first played for Juneau. Again, it was his batting stance.

Later, during Simmons' major league career, writers tried to describe his swing. *New York Times* writer Arthur Daley once wrote: "He didn't step into the pitch with his forward foot, the left one. Instead, he stabbed his foot toward third base. But somehow he contrived to level it off beautifully over the plate with wrists, arms and shoulders."[9] And writer Bob Broeg observed, "His hips and weight were going into the pitch even if the front foot wasn't."

Broeg maintained that Simmons hated the bucketfoot appellation because it questioned his courage. But the stance did not matter in the box scores.

In his first game with Juneau, Alois came to the plate as a pinch-hitter in the ninth inning. He singled home the tying run, and then in the eleventh inning he smacked a home run to win the game. Dutch Doyle reports another account that has him hitting the home run when he first entered the game as a pinch-hitter. Either way, it was a good start.

Alois' Juneau baseball days came to a sudden end only a few weeks after he had joined the team. The Lake Shore League went bankrupt, not an unusual occurrence in the 1920s when semipro leagues waged fierce competition against each other and were woefully underfinanced.[10]

After the Juneau ballclub folded, Alois signed on with the Stevens Point baseball team, which played in the Wisconsin State League and was northwest of Milwaukee. By then, he was growing into an adult's body, standing almost six feet tall and weighing around 190 pounds, which was large by the standards of that day. He had played basketball and football in school, and reportedly loved and excelled in those sports as well.

When the football coach from the Stevens Point Teachers College saw Alois on the baseball diamond, he offered him chance to play football. Alois accepted, and began training to become a two-sport player at Stevens. But controversy soon engulfed him. Alois, who had enrolled in college classes in order to play baseball, was criticized before the football season started by opposing players and coaches. They challenged his amateur status — due to his Juneau baseball wages. In any event, the gridiron experiment was short-lived. He got hurt on the first game of the season and found himself in the hospital for three weeks (though the nature of the injury was never made clear).[11]

Confined to a hospital bed, Alois had time to reflect — he did not much like college classes and had quickly suffered an injury in football. Soon, he felt drawn back to baseball. "I decided my football and college days were over," he said, "and so I went back to Milwaukee" after the hospital stay to play more baseball.[12]

He soon became a new man — in name, that is. By 1920, Alois Szymanski was growing weary of scorekeepers and newspaper writers butchering his name. It was hard to spell and had wildly appeared in box scores as "Chemanske" and "Schmanski." Alois — or his friends, or sportswriters — tried to simplify it.

Multiple variations on his name change exist. The most popular story is that after seeing a large sign advertising Simmons Hardware in Milwaukee, he adopted a new name — Al Simmons. "I'd seen the names on billboards advertising hardware," he said, "and inasmuch as it sounded like mine, I decided to adopt it."[13]

The hardware billboard sign account seems contrived. Later, Simmons told Milwaukee writer A.J. Schinner in a self-flattering story that Jack Spencer, a friend on the Connie Macks club, was in fact the orchestrator of the name change. "I opened the 1920 season with the Quins, but I must have looked good to someone, since midway in the race I was picked up by the Right Laundries of the Major AA league. That was quite a jump, but I took it without much debate. I was progressing, and if I did not notice my gradual climb, my friends of the old Connie Macks did. As usual, we used to get together on a Sunday morning and play our game of scrub or sides or whatever came to mind, and on those occasions, just before I joined the Right Laundries, Jack Spencer, who had more than a passing interest in me, questioned whether I intended to stay in baseball. I advised him that such was my ambition. Thereupon, without preamble, he advised me to get a name that would work into a box score without driving the sport writers and linotype men to distraction."

Spencer reportedly said, "Get a name that is easy to handle, kid. Al Szymanski won't do at all." Taking the advice to heart, the 18-year-old ballplayer proposed a bunch of names before hitting upon "Al Simmons." Voila, it sounded perfect to his ears, a hybrid of Old and New World appellations. "That was a happy thought — it sounded like the English cousin to my Polish name — and right then and there I was named Al Simmons, and that's how I sign my contracts today. You may question what there is in a name. Nothing, perhaps, but I have always considered the name Simmons lucky for me."[14]

It may have happened like that, but another possibility exists. A document from the American League Service Bureau in 1928 states that when Alois was 16 years old "scorers in the Wisconsin semipro circles declined to write Symansky (sic), and 'Simmons' he has been ever since.'"[15]

In Alois' Milwaukee baseball days, writer Westbrook Pegler wrote, the lineup on many teams was composed of names like "Szymanski, Cinkieviscz, Malkevelscz," all of which challenged the spelling abilities and ethnic sensibilities of Anglo-leaning sports scribes and scorekeepers. According to Pegler, the writer of a baseball notes column in the local newspaper titled "Diamond Dust" played a decisive role in renaming Alois Szymanski: "His name didn't remain Szymanski very long because the kid who runs the Diamond Dust department and the printers who set up the stuff in that little flyspeck type, which some papers use for Diamond Dust, are strong agents for the Americanization of difficult ethnic names ... the kid who runs the Diamond Dust department and the printers gave him his name then, but Al himself exploited it."[16]

"Exploited" is a fitting description of Simmons' aggressive self-promotional tendencies early on. He became, in Pegler's words, a "press agent" for himself and his team. "When the ball game was over, he was the one who was supposed to drop in at the sports department on his way home and tell a vivid story of the gripping contest to the third-string cub who wrote Diamond Dust."[17]

Simmons, in frequent contact with writers who apparently yearned to rename exotically-named Eastern European ballplayers, may have collaborated with one of them on his renaming.

Many precedents exist for such name changing in the early twentieth century. Like other Slavic ballplayers — Cass Michaels (Kwietniewski), Bingo Binks (Binkowski), Tony Piet (Pietruszka), Whitey Witt (Witkowski), Pete Appleton (Jablonowski), and Ray Mack (Mlckovsky) — Simmons sought to adopt a simpler name for integration into the American sporting mainstream.

Some name changes in those days were intriguing. According to Neal Pease, the minor league star "Bunny Brief" rose from the Polish sandlots of Michigan with a birth name of either Anthony Bordetzki or Grzeszkowski, depending on the source. A fan favorite for the Milwaukee Brewers of the American Association, Brief was nicknamed the "Babe Ruth of the bush leagues" while swatting 340 home runs before retiring in 1928, a huge power total for those days. He never established himself in the majors, despite four brief stints.[18]

Though Simmons did Anglicize his name, he always took pride in his ancestry, wrote Neal Pease. Changing his name was not an act of rejecting his ethnic heritage as a Polish Catholic. "As a veteran he made a point of offering friendly tips to a promising kid named (Stan) Musial as a gesture of ethnic fellowship," Pease said.[19]

The name change issue reflected the xenophobic unease surrounding immigrants and their offspring. With many of these ballplayers in the majors by the 1930s, *The Sporting News* actually declared that Poles and Italians were threatening to dethrone the Irish as the biggest ethnic presence in the game. Despite the publication's misgivings, the trend continued — by 1941, Polish Americans accounted for about 10 percent of major leaguers, about twice their share in the white population in the United States, according to Pease.[20]

Now Anglicized in name, Al Simmons began promoting himself to major league clubs in late 1920, just like his idol Ty Cobb, who had also waged a relentless letter-writing campaign on his own behalf. In the old days, players were typically signed by scouts or baseball insiders — but sometimes the more assertive players could draw attention to themselves with a few well-placed missives.

Simmons eyed one of baseball's most storied franchises at the time, the Philadelphia Athletics. Though they had fallen on hard times by the early 1920s, the A's had dominated the American League for several years in the 1910s when he was a teen. Simmons apparently wrote several letters to A's manager Connie Mack pleading for a tryout, such as the following letter and reply:

> Dear Mr. Mack:
>
> I am an amateur ballplayer in Milwaukee and have played for the Right Laundry, Juneau, Stevens Point and Iola teams. I would like to have a tryout with the Philadelphia Athletics because I have heard and read so much about them. If you take me south, I am sure I can make good.
>
> Al Simmons
>
> Dear Mr. Simmons:
>
> I appreciate your interest in my team and me, but it is impossible for me to give you a tryout this season. I receive about 1,000 requests every year.
>
> Connie Mack[21]

Despite the lack of encouragement by Mack, Simmons did not give up. In early 1921, he wrote a letter to Roger Bresnahan, the former major league catcher at Toledo managing a New York Giants farm club. Unimpressed — and perhaps deluged by other similar queries — Bresnahan showed no interest. Simmons was disappointed, and years later he recalled the episode with bitterness. "Like every other kid in the country, I wanted to play for John McGraw (the Hall of Fame Giants manager). So I wrote to Roger Bresnahan at Toledo, and all I asked for was expenses. It would have amounted to $150."[22]

Simmons harbored ambitions of playing for McGraw's Giants, who were in the midst of three straight pennant-winning seasons in the early 1920s. Hungry with this vision, he imagined great things for himself. "I never regretted playing for the Philadelphia Athletics," said Simmons. "But many a time

I couldn't help but wonder what would have happened had I reached the Polo Grounds." He added immodestly, "Can you imagine what a power hitter like me would have done there?"[23]

Simmons mused about the mercurial McGraw, perhaps a kindred soul. "I've often wondered how McGraw and I would have gotten along together. Don't forget I was just as hot-headed at that time as he was."[24] They probably would have fought bitterly, as McGraw tolerated no dissension. He traded star Frankie Frisch for such transgressions. Though he admired Connie Mack greatly, Simmons was outspoken with him.

After Simmons' major league career was over, New York sportswriters speculated on the rejection — with more than a touch of exaggeration. Arthur Daley said, "If Roger Bresnahan had been willing to spend $150, the course of baseball history would have been changed. The Giants would still be the darlings of the New York fans and their long run of pennants would have smothered Yankee efforts to wrest dominance from them."[25]

Indeed, one day Simmons would help knock off the mighty Yankees. But he would not do it wearing a Giants uniform.

CHAPTER THREE

Milwaukee's Best

"I was a terrible bust. The manager, the coaches and even friendly players told me I would never be a success as a player."
— Al Simmons, on his early days in the minor leagues.[1]

"We are born into a world where alienation awaits us."
— R.D. Laing[2]

Spurned by the Philadelphia A's and New York Giants in his letter-writing campaign, the striving Al Simmons eventually found some hometown opportunity in 1921, though he would gain almost as many faultfinders as believers along the way.

In the fall of that year, the 19-year-old ballplayer sent a note to Otto Borchert, the president of the hometown Milwaukee Brewers of the American Association, asking for a tryout. The story goes that Borchert flatly rebuffed Simmons on multiple attempts, not even answering him. Perturbed, the irrepressible youngster showed up one day unannounced at Borchert's office to demand a chance to prove himself. The encounter became, as they say, the stuff of legends.[3]

Otto Borchert was a pillar of Milwaukee sports, a hot-tempered entrepreneur who knew how to make profits in a variety of sports. In 1919, the Milwaukee native bought the Brewers franchise in the American Association, one of the top minor leagues in the country, and operated it until his death in 1927. Borchert is credited with developing a lot of Milwaukee baseball talent and sending several players to the big leagues. For this, the Brewers ballpark was later renamed Borchert Field in his honor.

Borchert also had connections in the right places. Connie Mack of the Philadelphia A's knew him from his days managing the Milwaukee Brewers— or "Creamers," as they were also called—from 1897 to 1899. Milwaukee was called the "Cream City" because of the unusual cream-colored brick used to construct buildings in the city.

In embellished language, Simmons later described approaching Borchert that day in 1921: "Borchert was also a fight promoter and when I walked into his office, he asked, 'Who do you want to fight?'" Borchert then asked Simmons if he was a "ham and egg fighter," which is a boxer whose modest skills keep him from winning big fights. Simmons may have looked somewhat like a boxer, but Simmons replied that he did not want to fight anyone. "I want to play ball," he said. Replied Borchert: "Beat it, I'm busy."[4]

Upset, Simmons claimed he even considered taking matters into his own hands. "I knew I could lick Borchert, so I stood there flat footed by his desk and opened fire. 'All I need is a chance to prove myself. I'll play for nothing if you just give me the chance.'" For some reason, Borchert relented. "With your nerve you ought to be good," and the Brewers owner told Simmons as he handed him a contract for next year's spring training.

Just like that. Well, maybe. In any event, Simmons hurried home to tell his mother and siblings. "I showed the contract to everyone who would read it and thought I would never live through the winter."

George Reimann of the *Milwaukee Journal* gave another account of the Simmons-Borchert encounter. He described a "tall, rawboned youngster, wearing a checkered cap and a flashy suit" sauntering out of the Milwaukee Brewers offices at 8th and Chamber streets. Borchert, on his way in after an afternoon of card-playing at a nearby bar, asked his business manager, appropriately named Louie "Bankroll" Nahin, who the cocky young man was. "That was Simmons," Nahin said, "a South Side boy who was recommended by Eddie Bodus. He had the kid up at Juneau last summer, and they say he really gives the ball a ride."[5]

Borchert did not like the uppity way Simmons dressed — his "ugly, checkered cap," as he put it. But he decided to invite him to spring training for the 1922 season, "to see if he's as good as they say he is." Beyond the contrived machismo of the tales, it is unclear if Simmons' signing was actually so spontaneous.[6]

In yet another version, it was Eddie Stumpf, a roving scout for Milwaukee, who saw Simmons playing for Juneau and recommended him to the Borchert and the Brewers. "After seeing him hit two home runs off Spencer Heath, I became interested in him," Stumpf said recollecting pitcher Heath who had put together an outstanding 18–8 season for Winnipeg in the Western Canada League in 1919, the year he faced Simmons, before making it to the majors briefly as a relief pitcher for the Chicago White Sox. Stumpf maintained that a priest — his name is never given — had reassured Simmons' very Catholic mother that a baseball career would not spiritually ruin her son. "She was afraid her son would lose his religion if he played baseball," Stumpf recalled.[7]

It's unlikely Simmons just burst into Borchert's office; the accounts of scout recommendations seem more plausible. But Simmons relished his image as a self-made man climbing up from humble origins, and maximized this perception whenever possible.

However, one newspaper account gives credence to Simmons' flirtation with boxing, though it may have occurred well after the initial Borchert meeting when he was in the minors. One scribe noted that a few "boxcar bouts with obscure heavies in and about Milwaukee purged him (Simmons) of the notion. Al is apt to be vague about the unrecorded details of his pugilistic fling. Stands mute on the query — was it in the ring he acquired his foot-in-the-bucket stance?"[8]

Whatever the true story, Simmons traveled with the Brewers to their 1922 spring training camp in Caruthersville, Missouri. One writer described him as a "husky lad, with a bat almost as long as a wagon tongue."[9]

In exhibition games, Simmons and the Brewers faced the St. Louis Cardinals major league team led by another powerful right-handed hitter, a 26-year-old second baseman named Rogers Hornsby, fresh off a .397 average the year before. It inspired the right-handed Simmons. "I got the thrill of my lifetime when I saw Rogers Hornsby come to Caruthersville with the Cardinals to play an exhibition with us. We just stood back and got our eyes full of the great Hornsby."[10]

Simmons, perhaps a bit too impressed by Hornsby, tried to imitate Hornsby's stance — Hornsby had an unusual one, too, positioning himself far back in the batter's box and standing almost upright and rigid with his feet close together. In doing so, Simmons seemed to make a tacit admission about concerns with his "bucketfoot" approach.[11]

Simmons' hitting suddenly swooned, and the Hornsby experiment flopped. His friend and fellow spring training invitee, Oscar "Ski" Melillo, convinced him to return to his natural batting style. He did, and began hitting again. The sportswriters soon dubbed him the "thumping rookie" and sent "flowery reports" back to the Milwaukee sports pages about his progress.[12] Simmons grew so optimistic, according to writer Bob Broeg, that he bragged to Melillo, "We're in, Osk, we're the two greatest prospects in the history of baseball. We should be in the majors right now."[13]

A diminutive, smooth-fielding second baseman Melillo, had played the two prior seasons in Winnipeg, notching a .291 average in both campaigns. He reached the majors in 1926 and would serve as a St. Louis Browns regular for nearly a decade. He later became a popular coach with the Indians, Red Sox, and A's.

Melillo suffered from Bright's disease, an often-fatal kidney inflammation. He followed a doctor's advice and began a prescribed diet of spinach, and only spinach, until cured. As chronicled in pitcher Elden Auker's book *Sleeper Cars and Flannel Uniforms*, Melillo also had zoophobia, which meant he had specific phobias of particular animals like rabbits, birds and snakes. His animal phobia led to countless pranks from other baseball players.

For Simmons, things were going so well that spring that Brewers manager Harry Clark asked Borchert to keep the odd-swinging rookie on the roster. "That kid will pack your ballpark," said Clark, "he'll be the best hitter in the league."[14]

But others disagreed that Clark liked him. Writer Ernest Lanigan said that Borchert wired manager Ira Thomas of the Shreveport minor league team, saying, "You can have Al Simmons. My manager Harry Clark doesn't like him and says he will never hit."[15]

In the end, Simmons finally did make the Brewers roster that spring — but not for long. He first appeared in a minor league box score on May 5, 1922, in a Milwaukee home game against Columbus. He entered the game as a pinch-hitter in the sixth inning, scoring a run after grounding into a fielder's choice. Afterwards, Simmons saw little action, and the Brewers had to make a decision.

Borchert concluded that Simmons needed more seasoning before becoming a Brewers regular. The young ballplayer was disappointed, but he faulted his fielding, not his hitting. "I was shipped back to Milwaukee because I wasn't making the grade. I was told, 'You can't field,'" recalled Simmons. "Finally, on May 15, in order to get rid of me, he sent me to Aberdeen in the South Dakota League."[16]

Aberdeen was low on the minor league food chain, a Class D team and a place where most rookies begin. Simmons predicted "they just made a little mistake," and he would be "right back" to Milwaukee.[17]

In moving to Aberdeen, South Dakota, Simmons was living outside of Wisconsin for the first time. Despite his fancy dressing around Milwaukee, he was still short of cash and largely unsophisticated. One report claims that Simmons owned only one suit of clothes — perhaps the "flashy suit" he wore to meet Borchert — and had to borrow a suitcase to make his trip to Aberdeen.[18] "That's all I owned in the way of clothing, except what I was wearing," said Simmons.[19]

Aberdeen's manager was E.B. Harkin, a former University of Michigan baseball player and an attorney who somehow found time to manage the team as a sideline job. He recognized the talent of his new player. "I never even thought about changing Simmons' batting stance," Harkin recalled. "He had tremendous power and his drives used to handcuff the opposing fielders. I was glad to have somebody who could hit a baseball like that."[20]

Hitting the baseball was just what Simmons did that season for Aberdeen.

He pounded out a .364 average with 26 doubles, 16 triples and 10 home runs — all in just 99 games. Every third hit went for extra bases. He also improved on his spotty outfield play. With home games in Aberdeen's spacious left field, he did not make an error that season, and nailed 18 runners trying to advance.

George Pardon, one of Simmons' teammates that season, recalled the widespread puzzlement about his batting stance. It did not matter, Pardon said, for Simmons was smacking balls to the fences in the spacious, nineteenth-century-style Johnson Field, Aberdeen's home park. "He would have had many more home runs in a modern park," said Pardon, a minor league journeyman who never made the majors.[21]

Simmons redeemed himself with his Aberdeen performance, and Milwaukee put him on its roster for the last couple weeks of the season. Though starting strong in his first game — a homer, triple and single — by season's end he had played in just 19 games with a .220 average and one home run in 50 at-bats. In the field for the Brewers, he made only one error and displayed a solid arm by cutting down three runners from the outfield.[22]

Al Simmons' first minor league season was both tantalizing and disappointing. He was far from being a finished product — and some thought he should be finished. Over the 1922 winter, Simmons had time to reflect on his whirlwind season spanning from North Dakota to Milwaukee. For one, he felt he could have done much better in his time with the Brewers.

It was Simmons' hitting style that worried people like Clark. Stepping away from the pitch was a mortal sin for a professional hitter. Not everyone was so pessimistic, though. Despite his performance, some major league clubs were starting to notice Simmons. Late in that 1922 season, the New York Yankees, New York Giants and the Brooklyn Dodgers all had expressed interest in him. Though nothing materialized, it signified better things to come.[23]

Borchert noticed the outside interest, and no doubt thought one day he could sell Simmons for a tidy sum. At the end of the 1922 season, the Milwaukee owner had told Simmons, "You can consider yourself very lucky. We're shy of rookies and I'm going to let you go south next spring with the team."[24]

At the Brewers spring training camp in 1923, when Simmons struggled early on, more doubts arose about his swing. Simmons said, "We trained at Troy, Alabama, and I was a terrible bust. The manager, the coaches and even friendly players told me I would never be a success as a player. They said I was too awkward and that I had an impossible stance at the plate."[25]

The confident Simmons faced the uncertainty of a make-it-or-break-it season ahead. While writer Bob Broeg described him as having "extreme self-assurance," could Simmons endure another setback?[26]

Rather than take a gamble on the cold-hitting Simmons that spring, the

Brewers ordered him to report to the Class A Shreveport "Gassers" in the Texas League. Management thought more seasoning might help him. Harry Brundidge wrote that someone told Simmons to send the Brewers a telegram once he "learned how to hit a curve ball." Perhaps someone could also finally convince Simmons to change his batting style — or so the Brewers thought.[27]

Years later, Simmons would put the best possible spin on the demotion, calling it a "gift" to get away from a team and manager (Harry Clark) who had lost faith in his abilities. Problem was, his road to the majors still had to go through Milwaukee, which had him under contract.[28]

In Shreveport, Simmons finally found a man who believed in him. Manager Ira Thomas had played 10 years in the major leagues as a soft-hitting but sure-handed catcher, mostly with the Philadelphia Athletics. Later he became one of Connie Mack's most trustworthy scouts. Thomas said, "When I took over the Shreveport club in the Texas League, I needed players so I called on my friends in baseball to help me. Otto Borchert called me and said he had a boy by the name of Al Simmons he could let me have, because his manager Clark didn't like him and said he will never hit."[29]

Watching closely, Thomas noticed Simmons actually brought his left foot back into position as the ball was nearing the plate. His mechanics were actually quite sound, the manager concluded. Also, Simmons used an unusually long bat, and could reach and make contact with balls out of the strike zone as he swung his leg toward third base.

Thomas left his swing alone. "He hit the ball hard and to all fields," the manager said. "The way he stood at the plate, the pitcher figured he couldn't hit a low curve, but when they threw it he would bounce it off the right field fence."[30]

Al Simmons: "He didn't monkey with my stance like the others had done, but said instead, 'go up there and swing like you did on the sandlots in Milwaukee.'"[31]

By now, Simmons was a strapping ballplayer whose legs were solid and muscled. His dark wavy hair crowned an intense glare. He was ready to absorb baseball knowledge like a studious sponge. Thomas taught him about the finer aspects of the game, and pumped him up confidence-wise. Simmons said, "Ira Thomas told me I had great possibilities and took me in hand. He spent hours with me, helped me with my fielding and hitting and gave me a lot of valuable information on baseball and baseball tactics."[32]

Thomas was a psychological motivator, telling Simmons and other ballplayers that a "slump is just a short circuit in your nervous system. Do not play ball on your nerves." He could also be stern. "I have no use for a so-called good loser. A sportsman, yes, but a good loser is seldom a hard fighter," Thomas believed, and that "a mediocre player who tries hard is more effective than a star who loafs." Thomas' psychology worked that season, as Simmons found his stroke early on. "I was clouting the ball to all the corners of the lot," he said.[33]

Simmons had a breakout season for the Gassers, raising eyebrows back in Milwaukee. In 144 games with Shreveport, he notched a .360 average, 36 doubles, 10 triples, 12 home runs, and 99 RBIs. Despite the success, concerns crept up again. Some among the Brewers thought he had feasted on poor pitching and the hitter-friendly atmosphere in the Texas League.

Toward the end of the 1923 season, Milwaukee called him up. The challenge facing Simmons was whether he could maintain his momentum. He did so for Milwaukee by smacking out a .398 average — but no homers — in 24 games. His fielding was nearly flawless, with only one error in 61 chances.

Still, Simmons had proved, if only briefly, that he could hit in the tougher American Association and at the Brewers' home field. The ballpark, which occupied just one city block, was built in 1888 and located in a residential district bordered by W. Chambers St., Burleigh St., and N. 7th and 8th Streets. The site is now covered by Interstate 43.

Like the Polo Grounds in New York, the most unique feature of the Brewers' ballpark was its rectangular shape. The right- and left-field fences were just 266 feet from home plate, while straightaway center was 395 feet away. This meant the power alleys in right and left were deeper than straightaway centerfield.

As for the American Association, its pitchers taught Simmons about hardball early on. "It was a knockdown league. I remember Sherry Magee and Pat Malone. Pat was pitching for Toledo. It was as good as vaudeville. Pat would whiz a fast one right at Sherry's ear, and Sherry would hit the plate with his nose... You didn't need a razor in that league. The pitcher would give you a singe and a close shave every time."[34]

Some thought Simmons had peaked, and Milwaukee wanted to sell him while his price was high.[35]

Tipped off early on about Simmons, Connie Mack had his scouts begin observing him at the end of the season. In fact, the A's had indicated their desire while he was at Shreveport.

Mack understood talent, of course, watching games and players like few baseball people ever have. Born Cornelius McGillicuddy in 1862 to Irish immigrants, the "Grand Old Man" of baseball presented a saintly, grandfatherly appearance on a tall, thin frame. Underneath it all, he had a complex personality of patience and impetuosity, kindness and stubbornness, tightfistedness and generosity.

A sixth-grade dropout, Mack played as a light-hitting catcher in the majors before becoming a manager. There he left his mark on the game by creating strategies for winning baseball and principles for managing men. The longest-serving manager in history, he was a key figure in the launching of the American League in 1901, winning six of the league's first 14 pennants — he still holds the all-time record for wins (3,731) and losses (3,948). In other words, he saw more games and ballplayers than anyone in the history of the game by the end of his own career.

Mack ordered scout Harry "Jaspar" Davis to follow Simmons. Davis himself had led the American League in home runs for four consecutive years in a career that spanned from 1895 to 1917. The hard-hitting first baseman played mostly for the A's, becoming one of Mack's confidantes. Davis sent word to Mack that Simmons was the real deal, and even suggested that Mack come to Shreveport to look him over.

"He said several scouts from the other major league teams had been giving the boy the once over," Davis said. "One day when the Athletics were in St. Louis, Connie intended to go down and look Simmons over. Before he could get away, however, he got a wire from Ira [Thomas] saying that Milwaukee had claimed Simmons and the boy was on his way north. A letter came to Connie shortly afterwards. It was from Ira. He predicted that he would be almost as great a player as Speaker or Cobb. Connie got busy that night and wrote to me. He told me to hustle out to Milwaukee and look Simmons over. The Brewers were playing a doubleheader, so I sneaked out in the grandstand where I felt nobody would recognize me. In the first game, Simmons got a single and fanned twice."[36]

Ironically, it was not Simmons stroking the single that enchanted Davis. It was how he whiffed in his other two plate appearances: "It was the cut he took at the ball when he struck out. That was the thing about the kid that I liked. He was hitting at bad ones, but he wasn't letting any good ones go by."

Davis claimed he had approached the opposing hurler, Ben Tincup, and asked the right-hander to challenge Simmons to see how he would react. Tincup, who had played in the majors, would win 20 games for Louisville that year.

Ben Tincup: "Before the game Davis came to me and said, 'Ben, do me a favor. Bear down extra hard against Simmons this afternoon.' So I brushed Al back with a hard, high inside pitch."[37]

Al Simmons: "He lets go and the ball comes right at my head. Down I went, hit the dirt hard. And down I went on the next. I thought, this guy is wild."[38]

Ben Tincup: "I wanted to scare Simmons, but he didn't scare at all. Instead, he just dug in and dared me to come back with the same pitch. I did. He didn't move an inch."[39]

Simmons had three more plate appearances, and was dusted each time.

On his final at-bat, he swung and the ball bounced softly over the first baseman's head. "I gave Tincup the last laugh," said Simmons.[40]

After the first game, Davis tracked Borchert down and began negotiations on behalf of the A's to buy Simmons. No deal was immediately made, but Mack later approached Borchert at the winter baseball meetings in Louisville to continue discussions.[41] Borchert could afford the delay, contemplating what Simmons would be worth if he increased his stock with another strong season in 1924 with the Brewers.

Ira Thomas said, "I knew that if Simmons ever played with his home town team he would be such a sensation that Borchert would ask — and get — $100,000 in cash for him. I urged Connie to make Otto a real offer."[42]

Mack made Borchert a good offer on December 15, 1923, when the A's acquired Simmons for $40,000 along with journeymen Wid Matthews, Beauty McGowan and Heine Scheer. The signing represented a hefty investment by the A's in Simmons. Around the time he brought Simmons aboard, Mack was also buying Paul Strand, a power-hitting outfielder in Salt Lake City, and an eagle-eyed second baseman, Max Bishop, from the Baltimore Orioles in the International League. "Simmons is the player whom I desired to secure above all others," Mack said. "He should add the necessary punch to our lineup."[43]

The ecstatic Simmons proclaimed, "This was the chance I had been battling for since I first played with the Connie Macks on the old lot on the South Side, and now I was with the real Connie Mack and was shortly to meet all the stars I had dreamed of in my sandlot days." He mused grandiosely, "Perhaps, I thought, some day they will write about Al Simmons as they did of Cobb, Speaker, Johnson and the rest."

While Strand did not pan out, Bishop became a key leadoff hitter for the A's, a guy that Simmons would drive across the plate for years to come. Those days were still far off in 1923, as Simmons still had to overcome critics — this time, in Philadelphia and around the majors.

CHAPTER FOUR

Athletic Ambitions

"The best game managers, generally speaking, are those who have the courage to keep their hands in their pockets, let their players play and take the inevitable flak from the fans."
— Bill James[1]

"It's hits we want, not beauty, so we left him alone."
— Connie Mack on the rookie Al Simmons[2]

In the world of Al Simmons as he began his major career in 1924, baseball was a vastly different experience for both the player and the fan than it is today. The game was more simple, accessible, and rougher.

This is not to say it was a better one — as we know, people of color were forbidden to play in the majors until 1947 and the labor rights of players were non-existent — but the game took place on a smaller scale. Many reasons exist for this: some economic, some demographic, some cultural. The overarching point is that baseball is reflective of the social period it takes place in.

The 1924 census put the country's population at 114 million. Major league baseball consisted of a 16-team system mostly confined to the northeast — New York, Boston, Chicago, Philadelphia, Pittsburgh, Cincinnati, Cleveland, and Detroit. St. Louis, on the western banks of the great Mississippi River, was the western-most major league city. Compare this to today's 30 teams scattered across the U.S. (with one outside of it), and about 308 million people living in the U.S. Talent today does not come only from America, but from Latin America, South America and Asia.

More than anything, coverage of the sport is entirely different today — the visual aspects of the game reign supreme, as portrayed in 24-hour cable channels and the Internet that now often drive coverage. Back in the 1920s, the written word and still photos drove coverage in the print newspapers of the major cities; radio was only beginning to take hold, with TV still years away.

In the 1920, teams like the Philadelphia Athletics used railroad transportation — not chartered jets like today — to travel between cities. Once there, the squads often played in ballparks oddly shaped and sometimes eccentric — only Chicago's Comiskey Park had a symmetrical outfield, a clear digression from the nuanced dimensions of Fenway Park in Boston, Forbes Field in Pittsburgh, and Baker Bowl and Shibe Park in Philadelphia, the latter being the A's home. The parks were more intimate, with seating in most in the 28,000 to 42,000 range — Yankee Stadium had the largest seating capacity of almost 70,000.

Prohibition was in full swing in 1924; until this law was repealed in 1933 after 13 years of lackluster enforcement, beer would not be served at the parks. Ticket admissions ranged from 50 cents for bleacher seats to $1.75 for field level boxes.

With no TV broadcasts of the games — no commercials — games usually took considerably less time to complete than today, usually two hours or less. There were fewer pitching changes — starting pitchers often completed about half of their games.

The reserve clause kept players hungry as they battled each other for jobs every season. Players had to work in the offseason to make ends meet. There were no guaranteed multi-million dollar salaries, retirement plans, or union benefits.

There were no pitch counts, well-manicured fields, batting helmets, body-armor elbow pads, or padded outfield walls.

Then, players had no trainers or agents to advise them on their careers, and when an injury arose, medical treatment was often hit-or-miss. Many players played hurt, and all of them played without the benefit of today's conditioning regimes, nutrition knowledge, contemporary medical science or Tommy John surgery, with careers frequently ending prematurely and sometimes tragically.[3]

In the 1920s, baseball was a harsh contest of physical and mental wits played on a diamond sharp with danger. Sometimes one literally ran into the hard outfield wall of baseball reality, breaking and bruising dreams and bones and hearts. The end, for the unlucky or less talented, was always an instant away.

Al Simmons, just 22 as he headed to the Athletics spring training camp in Montgomery, Alabama, understood the scarcity of major league jobs. His rollercoaster minor league career ensured he knew how easy it was to fall out of favor with the manager and front office. For him, there was a take-no-prisoners attitude to making the A's roster.

Expectations were high, but not only of him. Simmons was almost lost in the rookie hoopla on the A's, who were in a rebuilding mode with young talent surfacing. "The reporters and other baseball men in camp concentrated on [Paul] Strand and took little notice of this other outfielder," wrote Jerome Romanowski. "When they did notice him, many of them thought he would not make it in the major leagues because of his odd batting stance which they described as 'putting his foot in the bucket.'"[4]

Despite the awkward style, observers saw a hulking 200-pound athlete with a pale face that never seemed to tan. He must have looked like an angry ghost at the plate, as he gripped the bat and grimaced at the pitcher. Even as a rookie, Simmons' disdain for hurlers was clear. "The more intense a hitting situation or the angrier Simmons became," wrote Bob Broeg, "the whiter his face."[5] However, the sportswriters had mixed views on Simmons: "Simmons, with his bucketfoot stand at the plate, didn't impress them. And he wasn't fast as a runner, his arm only fair, so they couldn't see him as a major league player. The more they saw of Simmons they began to realize that here was a great batsman, he covered a world of ground in the outfield, and he always got the ball back to the right base."[6]

Like Thomas, Mack did not tinker with the young hitter's style. "Simmons is no flash. He couples ability with stability. He won't blow," he told writers that spring.[7] Later, in his own book, Mack said he didn't try to change Simmons hitting style: "I noticed Al's unusual batting stance the first time I saw him play. Ordinarily, I would have suggested that he try to correct it. But he did so well at batting even in spite of his unorthodox procedure that I never suggested he try to remedy it. If he can hit with 'one foot in the bucket,' or even with both feet in there, I am inclined to let him alone. A player will always do a thing better if he does it naturally than if some other technique is forced upon him. Besides, it's hits we want, not beauty."[8]

That may be revisionist history. Early on, Mack apparently felt like he made a mistake in signing Simmons. According to writer Ed Pollock writing in 1956, Mack was so worried about Simmons' stance that he asked Otto Borchert to come to spring training camp to discuss the matter. "Mack was in the mood to drop (what he paid for him) and return Simmons to Milwaukee without the additional payment if Borchert agreed," Pollock maintained. But Borchert insisted the A's keep Simmons until July — if he could not hit, Philadelphia could send him back to Milwaukee with the money returned. So, Mack agreed.[9]

Mack was widely praised by sportswriters for his intelligent and innovative managing, which earned him the nickname "the Tall Tactician." He valued intelligence and "baseball smarts," always looking for educated players — he traded away Shoeless Joe Jackson, despite his talent, because of his bad attitude and unintelligent play. Mack wanted men who were self-directed, self-disciplined, and self-motivated.

Mack also looked for players with quiet and disciplined personal lives, having seen many players destroy themselves and their teams through heavy drinking in his playing days. Mack himself reportedly never drank. However, he was not a tyrant—tough on contracts, he was an easygoing manager in other aspects, and never imposed curfews or bed checks.

Mack's strength as a manager was finding the best players, teaching them well, and letting them play. Still, he was one of the first managers to work on repositioning his fielders during the game, often directing the outfielders to move left or right, play shallow or deep, by waving his scorecard from the bench. Sometimes, he simply waved his scorecard as a feint.

In his managerial strategy, Mack generally favored a set lineup as opposed to a platoon approach; preferred young players to veterans; preferred hitters with power who got on base a lot to high-batting-average players; did not often employ the sacrifice bunt; believed in "big-inning" offense rather than small ball; and very rarely issued an intentional bases on balls.

Mack, although excited about Simmons that spring, was also hopeful about the rookie Paul Strand, for whom the A's had paid $35,000 plus a few players. For the 1924 season, the A's were gearing up for a youthful infusion that spring. In 1923, they had posted their ninth straight losing season with a 69–83 record. Though down at the time, the Philadelphia A's was a franchise steeped in history and accolades.

In the late nineteenth century, Philadelphia sports fans had come together and formed a professional baseball team named the "Athletics." The team joined the National Association in 1871, but quickly folded in 1875. Then, in 1901 when Mack was given American League team, he paid tribute to Philadelphia's first professional team by naming it the Athletics. Mack's Athletics went on to appear in the World Series in 1905 (lost), 1910 (won), 1911 (won), 1913 (won) and 1914 (lost).

The team name was typically pronounced "Ath-LET-ics," but Mack reportedly called them by the old-fashioned colloquial pronunciation, "Ath-uh-LET-ics." Sportswriters also often referred to the team as the "Mackmen" during their Philadelphia days, in honor of their manager.

Beyond A's baseball, Philadelphia in the early twentieth century was known as the "workshop of the world." Some of this translated to the baseball field, where some of Philadelphia's most memorable clashes—first against the Giants and later against the Yankees—expressed the city's aspiration to reclaim its place from New York as the nation's center and birthplace of the American Revolution. "The battle between New York and Philadelphia in baseball was symbolic of that battle for urban supremacy," says Bruce Kuklick, author of *To Every Thing a Season: Shibe Park and Urban Philadelphia*.[10]

While one might conjure up romantic visions of the Founding Fathers and the birth of the nation, by the 1920s Philadelphia was a cacophony of steam engines, whirling lathes, pounding forges, clattering looms, smoke, sweat and strain. Outside of the manufacturing, the city government was corrupt and hostile to outside influences. *Harper's Magazine* once commented, "The one thing unforgivable in Philadelphia is to be new, to be different from what has been."[11]

New and different would describe Simmons and his bucketfoot swing that spring. Wearing the A's blue and white uniform, he pounded the ball throughout training camp in his own unique style. In doing so, he received some puzzled looks from coaches and teammates, including star second baseman and future Hall of Famer, Eddie Collins, who was shocked the first time he saw Al Simmons at the plate. One of the A's coaches predicted, "That boy Simmons will never make it as a hitter. He pulls away from the plate." Pressed to explain Simmons, Mack replied, "I don't care if he stands on his head as long as he keeps hitting."[12]

It was clear to Perkins and others that Simmons had strong wrists and forearms, and could drive a ball on this alone. It also helped that he used an unusually long Hillerich and Bradsby bat, about 38 inches and 46 ounces. It gave him considerable reach to outside pitches even if one part of his body seemed to move away from the plate.

Above all, Simmons made impressions with his confidence. Catcher Cy Perkins said he had "that famous swagger as a kid. It was a swagger of confidence, of defiance." Perkins said that Simmons "wanted everybody to know that here was a kid who had just joined a big league ball club and was going to be a great star." Added Perkins, "Some called him a showboat. They were wrong. They didn't know Al as I learned to know him from that first day in Montgomery, Alabama."

Another teammate, pitcher Stan Baumgartner, who became a sportswriter after his playing days, also noticed the special talent of the rookie. "I thought I'd get a lot of attention from the boys in spring training after my big years," he said. "I was wrong. Simmons stole the show." The kid from Milwaukee "acted and talked like he had been in the majors for a long time," added Baumgartner. "There was no braggadocio about him, he just bubbled over in confidence." Baumgartner threw him a pitch one day in batting practice, and Simmons walloped it over the fence. "You should have seen him swagger and strut. That made a big hit with me. I was convinced that here was a kid who was bound to become a star—and he did."[13]

Mack defended Simmons' style with his players. "If anyone of you," Mack said, "pokes any more fun at that young man or tries to change his style at the plate, I will hit him (the critic) over the head with a bat."[14]

At the end of the exhibition season camp, Mack surprised even Simmons when he picked him to open the season in the outfield. "I'm going to place you in left field today and if you make good, you'll stay there," Mack told the rookie.[15]

As for his ungainly hitting style, Simmons would later say that many young players were "over coached" and given too many instructions, only to become confused. He advised that one should feel natural about his approach. "Nobody can change a guy all around and make a good hitter out of him. Hitters are born, not made. I'm not saying that a hitter can't improve himself with a tip here and there. But a fellow has to swing the way it feels more comfortable to him."[16]

In the field, Simmons practiced long and hard on his throws, and ran deft routes to fly balls. Proud of his errorless streak at Aberdeen, he sought to bring the same fielding consistency to the A's.

On April 15, the season opened on a beautiful spring day in Washington, and D.C. President Calvin Coolidge threw out the ceremonial first ball before a crowd of 26,000 at Griffith Stadium as the A's prepared to face the Washington Senators and their aging but powerful pitcher, Walter Johnson.

Simmons was slotted in left field and in the batting lineup's fifth spot behind first baseman Joe Hauser. Before the game, a photographer asked him to pose with his foot in a red water bucket, according to author William Kashatus. Simmons was enraged, and turned him down. When Jimmy Dykes asked him what was wrong, Simmons replied, "Oh, some cheese picture taker out there wants me to pose with my foot in a water bucket."[17] Dykes replied, "If I hit like you, I'd be willing to stand on my head."[18]

After Simmons calmed down, he got a single in four at-bats, his first major league hit. He also played the field perfectly, tracking down two hard-hit fly balls. But the Athletics lost, 4–0, as Johnson completed a four-hitter in an hour and forty-five minutes. It was the 36-year-old hurler's 99th shutout — he would toss 110 in his 417-win career. Simmons might have been unduly relaxed in that first game. Strangely, Arch Ward, writer for the *Chicago Tribune*, later claimed that Simmons took a few drinks before his debut. "The day Al Simmons was to make his big league appearance in the spring of 1924, he was so nervous he decided to take drastic action. Before entering Shibe Park, home of the Athletics, he sneaked into a nearby speakeasy and swallowed three pints of beer. This buoyed him so well that he wasn't embarrassed at all when he struck out his first trip to the plate."[19]

Three pints is a lot, and there is no other account to support Ward's claim. With the teetotaler Mack watching him closely, why would Simmons would risk so much in his rookie debut?

Pints or not, from that game on, Simmons kept up a solid attack, recording his first extra-base hit in his second game, his first stolen base (he was never a big basestealer) on April 17, and his first home run on April 25 —

against Walter Johnson, beating the Senators 6–5. His first triple came on May 4. Ironically, all of these "firsts" came against the Senators.[20]

By May 1, he was cruising at .386 after getting hits in 12 of the 13 games. He fell back to earth by the end of May with a .295 average, then got up to .299 by July 1.

Simmons, 22, was tireless, playing every game for the A's until midseason when Mack sat him on the bench for some well-deserved rest, though he did pinch hit.[21]

Away from baseball, Simmons could often be found at his rented apartment across the street from Shibe Park. From his first year with the A's through several seasons, Simmons lived with Arthur Conwell and his family at 2745 N. 20th Street.

One story goes that while living there Simmons awoke from a nightmare in which he had found his career over and that he was flat broke and out of baseball. The possibility terrified him; as the son of immigrants, he knew all too well the precariousness of existence. Now that he was making money, he was determined to never lose his newfound financial security. The next day Simmons approached pitcher George Earnshaw, an insurance salesman in the offseason who had advised his teammates, including Simmons, on investments. "Where are those papers?" Simmons asked Earnshaw. "Let me sign them. I want to start now to lay aside money for the time when I'm through as a player."[22] That's pretty farsighted for a rookie in those days. But Simmons was a man who understood the value of a dollar.

Back on the field, he entered the stretch drive in decent shape, posting a .305 average by August 27. He was not hitting for a lot of power — seven home runs by then — but home runs were not as common then and his line drives were falling in safely for other hits. Hits — that's what mattered most to Al Simmons.

In 1924, a power revolution was underway. Since 1920, when Babe Ruth first put on a Yankees uniform and swatted an otherworldly 54 home runs, offensive numbers were rising in baseball. Long gone was the "dead ball" era — baseball was evolving into more of a power game in the 1920s, and beyond.

Purists like sportswriter F.C. Lane criticized the new paradigm, declaring that "baseball, in the past few seasons, has become transformed from a scientific pastime to a contest of brute strength." But managers who adapted to the new realities, like Mack, were successful. "Inside baseball is all right," Mack once said about the dead-ball approach, "but you gotta have punch."

Punch was what Mack got more of that year. Along with signing Simmons back in December 1923, he later inked deals during 1924 for a fiery catcher named Mickey Cochrane and a young slugger named Jimmie Foxx. Along with Simmons, these acquisitions alone defined the A's offense for the next 10 years, and illustrated how the shrewd Mack had an uncanny knack for getting the most out of his players.[23]

Al Simmons: "The greatest fellow I ever knew. A strict disciplinarian. I never knew him to hurt anyone's feelings or humiliate a member of his club. If you were doing something wrong, or he had reason to find fault with your work, he would take you to one side to tell you about it. He never bawled a man out in front of his teammates. He would get himself alongside of you on the bench, where to all appearances you were having a friendly chat. And on the other hand, if you were playing extra hard, he would make a point to comment about it in the presence of everybody, using your name."[24]

While Mack was making all the right moves in acquiring Hall of Fame talent, some of it — like Al Simmons — was getting noticed around the league. Babe Ruth, for one, attempted to explain his success despite such an unorthodox batting style.

Babe Ruth: "I don't think there's another man in either league who could stand at the plate the way Al does, and still hit the size of his hat. But stepping in the bucket is Al's natural hitting form — and what is natural is generally best in baseball. Al overcomes that back step by using an exceptionally long bat — the longest in the league that I think, and just as long as the baseball law will allow. The result is that he can reach the outside corner for a curve if he has to, and at the same time he's far enough away that the inside stuff doesn't bother him ... there's no one more off form than Al, and mighty few better hitters. It all goes back to the same thing: the most important thing about hitting is to be natural, and be easy."[25]

As Ruth pointed out, Simmons generated his power from a long follow-through that allowed the bat to finish the full arc of its sweep. He timed his swing to meet the ball in front of the body, where the arms were fully extended and the sweep of the bat was at the point of its greatest power.

When the dust settled on the 1924 season, Simmons had lived up to his hot-prospect billing. He hit .308 with 8 home runs, 102 RBIs, 31 doubles, 9 triples and 183 base hits — excellent first-year numbers. On his young legs, he also stole a career high 16 bases, and mostly played center field (101 of his 152 games) with 10 errors and 17 assists.

Rather than explosiveness, Simmons' year was marked by a steady consistency. He had only one four-hit game, and only twice had four RBIs in a game. He never slumped badly and never caught fire madly, whether at the plate or in the field. He was still learning the game, under the fatherly tutelage of Mack. Simmons was seen as an intelligent if not fleet-footed center fielder. "He never threw to the wrong base," said Yankee pitcher Johnny Murphy.[26]

Although still finishing in the second division at 71–81, the A's had played much better in the second half on a burgeoning nucleus of talent. There was

Simmons, of course, rookie Max Bishop, along with Jimmy Dykes, Eddie Rommel and Bing Miller. And there was more talent coming. In July, Philadelphia had purchased 17-year-old Jimmie Foxx from the Easton Farmers, where they were cultivating him. Mickey Cochrane would soon arrive for the 1925 season. The future looked bright for Simmons, the young Polish player from Milwaukee.

One belief surrounding Jackie Robinson's breaking of the color barrier in 1947 is that baseball was a game long open to people of any ethnic background — except blacks. Yet there were other "ethnic barriers" overcome long before Robinson, though certainly Robinson suffered uglier challenges than any Polish, Italian or Jewish ballplayer did.

As historian Steven Riess has pointed out, baseball and ethnicity in early twentieth century America mirrored society in all its aspects. Then, the game was dominated by White Anglo Saxon Protestants (WASPs), and German and Irish players. Few players were from Eastern or Southern Europe. Riess stated there were only three Bohemian, Jewish or Italian ballplayers by 1920.

All this did not keep immigrants and their children from becoming smitten with the sport, however. "Many in this group loved baseball," Riess wrote, "viewing it as a means to become real Americans and a chance to embrace such values as teamwork and a respect for authority." But the path to professional ball was strewn with obstacles, as many immigrant families lived in cities that lacked ball fields. When young boys like Simmons had to drop out of school to work, the chances for interscholastic competition faded. Moreover, to the elders from the Old World, making a living playing a kid's game seemed like "loafing" compared to the practical jobs of the industrial age.[27]

Riess pointed out that some Slavic immigrants had a familiarity with an Old World ball game of sorts, the somewhat popular "palant," which was similar to "one-old-cat," a predecessor of baseball itself.[28]

Oscar Bielaski was likely the first Slav to play in a major league. An American-born outfielder of Polish extraction who learned to play baseball in the Civil War, Bielaski played a short and underwhelming career for three ballclubs in the National Association from 1872 to 1875, with one year in the National League in 1876.

For first-generation Americans like Bielaski, interest in baseball was seen as an embrace of their new culture and a rejection of strict Old World ways. He was soon followed by others, including Stan Coveleski, who emerged out of the Pennsylvania coalfields to win 215 games in the major leagues and earn a ticket to the Hall of Fame, the first Slavic player so honored. Baseball was a way out of a harsh life for Coveleski, who as a kid worked in the mines twelve hours a day, six days a week, for a nickel an hour. He told writer

Lawrence Ritter, "Most of the year I went to work in the dark and came home in the dark."[29]

The other notable Slavic player in the early twentieth century was Ed Konetchy, a huge first baseman of Czech heritage who played in the majors from 1907 to 1921. From Wisconsin like Simmons, "Big Ed" cranked out more than 2,000 hits in a career in the National and Federal Leagues.

Coveleski and Konetchy were rare cases of Slavic ballplayers in the early twentieth century. It took awhile for the urban ball fields of the immigrant neighborhoods to harvest more young talent. But the motivation was there in the Progressive Age, where social planners advocated an abundance of parks and playgrounds to teach boys about the American creed of fair play and sportsmanship. With players like Simmons emerging, the Slavic ascent on the diamond was well underway.

CHAPTER FIVE

Sophomore Breakout

In 1925, a prosperous America was sunk in conspicuous consumption and social tension. In the heartland state of Tennessee, teacher John T. Scopes was arrested for teaching the theory of evolution, which was still forbidden by state law. In Chicago, mobster Al Capone took over the Chicago bootlegging racket made possible by federal Prohibition, an ill-fated attempt to ban booze in America. On the nightclub floors around the country, a new dance called the Charleston became popular.

While Americans danced away, Europeans witnessed rising dark forces — this was the year that Adolph Hitler, a failed artist and aspiring demagogue, wrote his first volume of *Mein Kampf.* The nightmare that would convulse the world a decade or so away was just beginning.

Back in the City of Brotherly Love, Al Simmons and the A's were on the cusp of bigger, better seasons — especially after Mack in the offseason landed 25-year-old pitcher Lefty Grove from the Baltimore Orioles of the International League. Grove was so prized that Mack paid $100,500 for him, the highest amount ever paid for a minor league player at the time.

Soon, he would also bring aboard Mickey Cochrane from the Portland Beavers of the Pacific Coast League where he was grooming the young catcher. So certain was Mack of Cochrane's future greatness that he bought the Portland ballclub in order to give Mickey a place where he could hone his skills without the danger of the A's losing him. Cochrane was known as "Black Mike," because of his fiery temper.

With this talent infusion, one scribe wrote, "Connie Mack has few predictions to make. He is standing pat on the team that finished 1924 in such excellent style, but is hopeful that added strength to his battery departments will pull his club up in the race."[1]

The A's infield was set with clean-up hitter Joe Hauser at first, fresh off a 27-homer year, table-setter Max Bishop at second base, steady Chick Galloway at shortstop, and veteran Jimmy Dykes at third base. Behind the plate, the veteran Cy Perkins and newcomers Jimmie Foxx and Cochrane were all in the mix. In the outfield, Simmons was in center, solid-hitting Bing Miller in left and late–1924-sensation Bill Lamar in right.

In April, Grove made the Opening Day start for Philadelphia at Shibe Park, winning 9–8 against the Boston Red Sox in his major league debut. Simmons played center field and went hitless in five at-bats. In the season's second game, Simmons collected three hits, including a home run, as the A's went on to take three games out of four against Boston.

The first concrete-and-steel stadium in the majors, Shibe Park was completed in less than one year, opening in April 1909. The field was built on a city block along Lehigh Avenue and Somerset Street, and named after Benjamin Shibe, the half-owner of the A's along with Mack from 1901 until his death in 1922. When the American League awarded its Philadelphia franchise to Mack in 1901, he needed a local backer who would give the newcomers instant credibility and prestige. He also needed investment money. Ben Shibe was the perfect man.

Born in 1838, Shibe is credited with the invention of the machinery that made uniformed baseballs, among other innovations, like his ballpark. As William A. Phelon observed in *Baseball Magazine,* Shibe was a "wise, shrewd, a clever calculator, a great money-maker."[2] With baseball's popularity on the rise the end of the Civil War, Shibe joined his brother John and nephew Dan, who had worked for a company that made cricket balls, in founding John D. Shibe & Co., which made baseballs. Their company supplied others, such as Alfred J. Reach. Reach and Shibe were friends, and by 1882 Benjamin Shibe and A.J. Reach formed a new company, Reach & Shibe, which became A.J. Reach and Company. By 1883, the Reach factory was making 1.3 million baseballs and 100,000 bats each year.

Shibe Park was home to a few historic clouts. On September 9, 1921, Babe Ruth of the Yankees smashed a home run to deep left-center that cleared the then-single-bleacher stand, went across the street, and hit a tree, reportedly about 500 feet away.

In 1925, the A's added an upper-deck and left-field stands. That season the dimensions were left field, 334 feet; center field, 468 feet; and right field, 331 feet. Shibe Park mostly played fair, unlike the cozy Baker Bowl of Philadelphia where the Phillies enjoyed a short 280-foot right field and its 60-foot-high wall.

That spring, Simmons started strong, and on April 25 began a stretch of getting a hit in 33 out of 34 games (with 10-game and 23-game streaks). On May 12, a then-record 20 home runs were hit in the major leagues— another sign that the lively ball era was here to stay. Simmons swatted one of those in a 4–3 win over Detroit. Washington squeaked past the A's, 10–9, on

Five: Sophomore Breakout

The A's added an upper deck and left field stands to Shibe Park in 1925. Off the Shibe Park ball field, Al Simmons could often be found at this rented apartment across the street from Shibe Park. From his first year with the A's in 1924 through several seasons, Simmons lived with Arthur Conwell and his family at 2745 North 20th Street. *National Baseball Hall of Fame*

May 27 as Walter Johnson tallied his seventh win in a row. Simmons walloped one of Johnson's pitches in the fourth inning that landed on 20th street.

On June 6, Simmons found himself leading the American League with a .415 average. "He not only ran roughshod over the leaders, going from .389 to .415 in a week, but passed Ty Cobb and McManus of the Browns in scoring, and made Ken Williams of the Browns look up to him for the honors of total base hitting," noted one writer, referring to his 44 runs and 123 total bases.³ Another paper described him as "breaking loose."⁴

However, a few days later Simmons lost his hold on the batting title chase. Al Wingo of Detroit usurped him, although Wingo was only one point better than that of his player-manager, Ty Cobb.⁵

By the June trading deadline, the A's were in first place with a 23–10 record, fending off the pitching-strong defending AL champion Washington Senators who would challenge them the rest of the way. Then, on June 15, the A's staged one of baseball's all-time great comebacks in a game. Against

Cleveland, Philadelphia was down 15–4 in the eighth inning with one out. Simmons came up sixth in the inning, and singled. By the time he again came to bat in the same inning—now with two down and two on—Philadelphia had scored 10 times. Just a few days earlier against the White Sox (June 13), Simmons had struck a home run that bounced on the newly built left field roof of Shibe Park. He found the same rooftop again, this time cranking a three-run homer to give the A's a 17–15 victory, capping an amazing 13-run inning over Cleveland. Philadelphia, in first place with 34 wins and 18 losses, began a six-game winning streak.[6]

By June 18, Bucketfoot Al was hitting .394 with 11 homers and 52 RBIs. Nine days later he and George Sisler of St. Louis were the first players to reach 100 hits that season. Simmons' teammate, third baseman Sammy Hale, despite limited action, topped the charts in batting at .421.

Around this time, as Simmons seemed to be getting hits in every game, he was the subject of a profile by writer Billy Evans, who started his article by saying that a year ago, Simmons was "known as foot-in-the-bucket Al," but now he was the "sensation of the major leagues." Evans wrote, "A year ago the experts doubted whether Simmons, because of his unusual stance, would be able to hit major league pitching. Despite the fact Simmons pulled badly, he hit better than .300 his first year. Often badly out of position, and apparently much fooled by fast-breaking curves, Simmons would hit it hard to right field."

A year ago, Simmons, Evans declared, was a raw rookie. "He didn't always make the proper play. Certain experts questioned his smartness." That all changed his sophomore year. "From an unpolished busher, he stepped into the big show this year a real star," the writer observed. Evans disagreed with those who question Simmons' baseball brains, saying that his work in the field was every bit as solid as at the plate. He called him the "most improved player" in the junior circuit. "I consider Simmons a smart ballplayer," he added, one destined to be like Cobb or Tris Speaker, a "colorful player, a distinct asset to the American League."[7]

On August 10, the first-place A's came from behind in the eighth inning on a two-run Simmons' home run to beat St. Louis, 6–4. Philadelphia was riding high on strong offensive contributions from its young players—Simmons and Cochrane—as well Hale and outfielders Lamar and Miller, all of whom were hitting well over .300 as the summer progressed.

The vastly talented 17-year-old Foxx was used almost strictly as a pinch-hitter and a batting-practice catcher. He was still a bit too green for regular play, though. In late June, Mack optioned him to Providence of the International League for tutelage under manager Frank Shaughnessy—Foxx went on to hit .327 in 41 games, returning to Philadelphia in late September. "I think one of the greatest things Mr. Mack did for me was to give me confidence by allowing me to prove myself in the minors," Foxx said later.[8]

The A's boasted a considerable mound presence in Eddie Rommel, Slim Harriss, Sam Gray, Rube Walberg and Jack Quinn. However, the heralded rookie Lefty Grove was issuing a lot of walks and getting shellacked in his first major league season.

The A's attack was not enough, however, to hold off the charging Washington Senators, who took the AL league lead on August 20 as Philadelphia began a five-game losing streak that dropped them into second place.

Simmons was trying to make a charge of his own to challenge Tris Speaker for the American League batting title. He lashed out 11 hits in six games from August 18 to August 23 to raise his average to .378, behind Speaker's .392. Detroit's Harry Heilmann trailed Simmons by just one point at .377.[9]

Much was made in the press about the youthful challenge of baseball's elite by the A's newcomer. "Al Simmons, colorful star with the Philadelphia Athletics, is the youngster battling the grizzled veterans, Ty Cobb and Tris Speaker, with another veteran, Harry Heilmann, showing up around the corner," reported the Associated Press, noting that 23-year-old Simmons had played in 123 games compared to 101 for the 38-year-old Cobb.[10]

But Philadelphia stumbled badly in late August, losing 12 straight games until they overcame Washington, 6–4, at home on September 8. In the last game of the losing streak, Simmons went hitless in five trips to the plate.

Meanwhile, the 37-year-old Speaker, a player-manager for Cleveland, was sitting himself on the bench frequently and only appearing as a pinch-hitter. He wound up in only 117 games that season, though he collected his 3,000th career hit along the way (as did Eddie Collins that year). "Speaker had retired from play (that season) with an average of .389," one scribe complained.[11]

Both the A's and Simmons regrouped for the stretch, but it was, in both cases, too little, too late. The team won 15 of its last 25 games to finish in second place at 88–64 (Washington won the pennant, but lost to the Pittsburgh Pirates in the World Series). Grim and determined Simmons, in his last 14 games collected an amazing 34 hits in 65 at-bats to raise his final average to .387. However, he was disappointed to finish third in the AL behind Heilmann at .393 and Speaker at .389.

Hits, hits, hits. Simmons' torrid hitting in the last weeks gave him by season's end the highest hit total — 253 — since George Sisler had set the major league record with 257 in 1920. The 253 hits for Simmons set a major league single-season record for right-handed hitters that still stands (Rogers Hornsby is next with 250 in 1922). As such, it marked his career high, uneclipsed by his five other 200-hit seasons.

Simmons hit safely in 133 of his 153 games — a huge mark of consistency for a second-year player. He finished first in the league in total bases (392), second in slugging (.599), second in runs scored (122) and fourth in OPS (1.018); the latter was not a statistical yardstick in use back then.

With 24 home runs and 129 RBIs, Simmons put up impressive power figures, far outpacing his A's teammates on those fronts. Suddenly, he was the toast of Philadelphia. On September 26, Philadelphia fans chipped in to buy a new automobile for Simmons, the A's player chosen by the press as the team's most valuable player. Mickey Cochrane, a .331 hitter in his first year, was second in the voting.

Simmons was at his most durable during the 1925 season, playing in every A's game; he was the lone player in the American League to start and finish each game in his original position of center field.[12]

Simmons was not the only young player to wrap up a fine campaign. Lou Gehrig, of the Yankees, completed his first full season of play, swatting 20 homers with a .295 average.

But Simmons was snubbed when the Most Valuable Player accolades were handed out. He finished second to Washington's Roger Peckinpaugh in one of the more controversial choices ever. With the award voted upon by one writer from each city in the league, the selection of the shortstop Peckinpaugh was odd — he had only 429 at-bats and had sported a .294 average. American League batters collectively hit .292 that season. Perhaps a jinx was at work. Peckingpaugh, on the pennant-winning Senators, committed a record eight errors against Pittsburgh in the World Series.

Offense was up all around the league. Topped by Philadelphia at .307, three entire teams had averages over .300 (none did in 1924), and five clubs scored more than 800 runs, with Detroit leading the pack. Meanwhile, Babe Ruth had suffered injuries and posted his worst year thus far, playing in only 98 games and hitting 25 homers.

Arguably the MVP, Bucketfoot Al enjoyed a breakout season — no sophomore jinx for him. Simmons not only joined the hit parade, he was blazing the trail in the heat of the lively ball era.

CHAPTER SIX

"Best Centerfielder"

"Simmons was a testy character who was called a 'swashbuckling pirate of a man' by one contemporary. King of his league's right-handed hitters for a decade, he was an elitist who bullied rookies, manifested a chilly disdain for lesser mortals, and even on occasion questioned the wisdom of Connie Mack himself."
— Donald Honig[1]

"I love baseball. You know it doesn't have to mean anything, it's just beautiful to watch."
—Woody Allen in the movie Zelig

In 1926, America brimmed with confidence and expansion as the economy soared and people found more leisure time for sports and entertainment. This was the year that auto magnate Henry Ford introduced the 40-hour work week, when the government completed the last leg of U.S. Route 66 from Chicago to Los Angeles, and when the National Broadcasting Company was organized as the first nationwide radio broadcasting network. While spectator sports like baseball boomed, the book *Winnie the Pooh* was published to classic delight, and songs like "Bye Bye Blackbird" and "The Desert Song" hit the top of the charts.

What filled the air was not all honey and sweet sounds, though. A Roman Catholic priest in Michigan named Charles Coughlin made his first radio broadcast, beginning his 20-year career of racist polemics. Prosperity had angels and demons alike.

In Philadelphia during the offseason, Connie Mack was optimistic about his team's godsends, especially Al Simmons. "He is the best centerfielder the American League has had since Tris Speaker was in his prime," the 64-year-old manager told writers, while acknowledging that Simmons "lacks the grace" of the Grey Eagle in his outfield play, admittedly a hard standard to approach.[2]

Simmons was not the only rising talent in the A's outfield, as right fielder Walter French seemed promising. Like Simmons, he also sported an unusual swing and gave Philadelphia an "unusual spectacle of two players using stances that are entirely unorthodox." The fleet-footed French, who had hit .370 in only 100 at-bats in 1925, stood with his feet wide apart and swung without stepping into the ball. "Opposing pitchers ridicule his style," one newspaper observed.[3]

As for the A's roster, Mack was blending youth and experience. On the young side were players such as Simmons, Mickey Cochrane, Jimmie Foxx, Lefty Grove and Max Bishop. Among the veterans were Jimmy Dykes, Bill Lamar, Sammy Hale, Joe Hauser, and pitchers Eddie Rommel, Howard Ehmke and Jack Quinn.

One day during spring training, the A's received a visit from celebrity inventor Thomas Edison at their complex in Fort Myers — and Al Simmons figured in the story. "Think you could hit one?" asked coach Kid Gleason, who was pitching batting practice, to the stately Edison. Edison grinned and nodded. Then he took off his Panama hat and white suit jacket, and looked around for a bat. He grabbed Al Simmons' heavy, long bat, and ambled up to the plate. "Let's go," said the inventor. Gleason's first pitch sailed past a flailing Edison. "Strike one," someone shouted. The next pitch came in too low — a curve ball. But Edison swung away anyhow. "Edison stepped into it and connected clearly," wrote Edison biographer Neil Baldwin. "With a crack, the ball sailed out of the infield for a Texas leaguer over first base."[4]

Edison was not a big fan of baseball, but he apparently knew who Simmons was — kind of. When Mack introduced Edison to Simmons, Edison asked, "What is your position, Mr. Simmons." Simmons replied, "I'm an outfielder, Mr. Edison." "Is that so," Edison said. "I thought you were a batter."

Writers started having fun with the gruff but youthful Simmons. That year 21-year-old Shirley Povich's first baseball column appeared in the *Washington Post*. Two years earlier the Maine native had arrived in Washington and found work as a copyboy for the *Post* while studying law at Georgetown. He was still a student when he became sports editor, beginning a storied career. His column, "This Morning," became a mainstay in the baseball world, appearing from 1926 to his retirement in 1974, except for time he spent as a war correspondent. Simmons was one of his favorite subjects.

Shirley Povich: "When he strode up there with a bat in his hands, Simmons hated all pitchers. He was impatient with young hitters who took their strikeouts casually, and would say, 'You gotta hate those pitchers.' ... He accepted the fact that most pitchers hated the hitters, too, or they should, he said."[5]

Simmons that spring was high on teammate Sammy Gray, a 28-year right-handed pitcher coming off a 16–8 season that would have been even better had he not broken his thumb. "There is the toughest man in the American League to hit," he told writers, brashly predicting a 25-win season for Gray on behalf of the "White Elephants" of Philadelphia (Gray would only post a 11–12 record in 1926).

The White Elephant nickname of the A's originated back in the 1905 World Series when Philadelphia faced the New York Giants. Then, Giants manager John McGraw told reporters that owner Benjamin Shibe had a "white elephant on his hands." Afterwards, Mack defiantly adopted the white elephant as the team mascot — it made its first appearance on a uniform in 1918, and it is still there today.

As the A's gathered for spring training in 1926, they wore uniforms with that white elephant on the front — with no "Philadelphia" or "A's" anywhere. Their home uniforms were white with black trim, with ball caps that were white with black trim. Their road uniforms were gray with black caps and gray trim. Mack's ball cap designs usually employed a variation of black or medium blue as the accent color. It was not until 1963 that the A's (then in Kansas City) used green and gold uniforms. Until 1954, when the uniforms had "Athletics" spelled out in script across the front, the team's name never appeared on either home or road uniforms. Not once did "Philadelphia" appear on the uniform, nor did the letter "P" appear on the cap or the uniform. In most years, the typical Philadelphia uniform had only an "A" on the left front, and likewise the cap usually had the same "A" on it.

Al Simmons in his early days as a major leaguer with the Philadelphia A's. *National Baseball Hall of Fame*

On Opening Day April 13, Washington Senators ace Walter Johnson and Philadelphia Athletics knuckleballer Eddie Rommel locked horns in one of the greatest season-opening pitchers' duels in history. After going head-to-head for 15 grueling innings, Johnson emerged the 1–0 victor after fanning 12 batters. Simmons went 1-for-5 in the game.

Even at age 38, Johnson was a tough pitcher. It was especially satisfying for a young hitter like Simmons to belt a home run off of him, which he did four times in his career. One shot came May 23 that year in Washington when Simmons powered a long drive off Johnson. One writer described it colorfully—"Al Simmons, foot in the water bucket and all, got one in the fourth with a home run that dropped through one of the entrance gangways in the bleachers." The A's went on to beat the Big Train, 5–3, behind the pitching of Slim Harriss.[6]

Simmons was learning how to hit, especially in placing his line drives. Writer Billy Evans observed progress in the youngster. "Due to his habit of pulling, Simmons last year was regarded as a dead left-field hitter," Evans wrote. "He has overcome that habit and now hits to all fields." The writer was impressed when he saw Simmons knock the ball through the vacant hole left by the second baseman covering the hit-and-run. "This greatly improves his team value."[7]

Early in his career, Simmons was rarely described in the press without a reference to his stance. On June 26, sportswriter Frank Young reported on his frustration: "An interesting discussion was had in the Nats' dressing room before the fracas regarding the batting of Al Simmons, flashy Athletics flyhawk. The general opinion was that continued reference to the player as 'Foot in the Bucket Al' was getting on his nerves, and that he is changing his stance. As a result, the 'experts' claim that this season he is neither hitting as often nor as hard as he did last (season)."[8] But Simmons was hitting .330 at that point, and while he may have tinkered with his stance, he remained true to his natural form. The moniker stuck.

Simmons and his fellow A's brightened their season on July 5 when they took both games of a doubleheader against the Yankees. Later in the week, they took three out of four from the Chicago White Sox.

On July 7, Simmons hit three doubles in the first game of a doubleheader against Boston. That season the two-baggers were piling up for him — he had seven games of two doubles. Around the league, Simmons forged a reputation for hard-hit line drives. By season's end, he would smack out 53 doubles, his career high.

Hall of Fame second baseman Charlie Gehringer of Detroit recalled for writer Donald Honig how powerful Simmons was in driving a ball up the middle: "I'll tell you who hit probably the most wicked ball to second base — Al Simmons. He had that long bat, and he stood a ways back from the plate, and they tried to pitch him outside to keep him from knocking it upstairs, so then he'd hit it to the right side. And he'd slice them. You'd think you were in front of it, but you kept moving to your left and finally wound up catching it one-handed. He could blister it."[9]

Widely regarded as one of the greatest second basemen of all time, Gehringer in his career compiled a .320 average and had seven seasons with more than 200 hits. He was nicknamed "The Mechanical Man" for being so predictably excellent.

Simmons was not so mechanical that midsummer. After playing 394 consecutive games, he was wearing down a bit and losing some of his famous aggressiveness, much to the chagrin of Mack. On July 18, Mack benched the apparently exhausted outfielder in a game against Cleveland. It came on the heels of a seven-game losing streak for the A's that for all practical purposes forced them out of the pennant chase with the Yankees by early August. Tired, Simmons had failed to run out some ground balls, which greatly annoyed Mack.

No one realized at the time the significance of what Simmons had done as an "iron man" young player. He had established the American League record of 394 consecutive games to start his career (1924–1926), a record that stood until broken by Hideki Matsui, who would play 518 consecutive games for the New York Yankees from 2003 to 2006.

Talk about the glass half full—Simmons got hammered in the press for being benched. Writer Billy Evans, in a turnaround from his earlier praise, now decried the young outfielder's lack of hustle. "If there is one thing a ballplayer should do, it is run out the ball every time he is at bat.... It is regretted that manager Mack found it necessary to discipline Al Simmons. Mack is usually very reticent about taking such action, so no doubt it was deserved. Simmons is a great ballplayer, but he can wreck his own usefulness as well as a brilliant career unless he takes his baseball seriously.... Instead, we find Simmons suspended for weak batting and indifferent fielding. The moral—be serious."[10]

While Evans and other writers claimed Simmons was not producing at the plate, the facts spoke otherwise. In the 25 at-bats before his "benching," Simmons had 9 hits for a .360 average.

One sportswriter lamented how Simmons had fallen upon "evil days" in 1926. It was noted that "his disposition to fret and worry" about trying to produce in every at-bat had taken a toll, he wasn't the player he had been in 1925 and was accused of being a "bit slipshod." What were those "evil days" about? Ira Thomas, talking in 1956, the year Simmons was elected to the Hall of Fame, offered a sign of things to come in Bucketfoot Al's career. "Like most ballplayers, he slept late and had breakfast around 11:30 A.M. He went to the ballpark for the game and did his work well after the game. He would wait until 8:30 or 9 P.M. for dinner because he liked music with his meals. He enjoyed orchestra music. No doubt he drank a couple bottles of beer at dinner so when people saw him, they said, he liked the night life."[11]

Whatever the cause, a chastised Simmons found his groove by August 10. That day he smashed a two-run homer to lift the A's over Chicago, 2–1. Three days later he went 3-for-3 with two doubles in a 5–0 victory over Boston.

Simmons, in his third season, was finding his way around cities on the road. He sometimes displayed a soft touch, making friends with fans and signing baseballs when asked. In Chicago, Simmons frequented the Paprocki family drugstore on Chicago's southwest side, making friends and memories for those people. Writing in 2002, Joe Paprocki, a Catholic teacher of Polish heritage in the Chicago area, recalled childhood memories of a baseball that Simmons had apparently autographed for one of his relatives. "It was an old dirty baseball with a smudged autograph on it which, when deciphered, revealed the name of Al Simmons. The autograph, dirty and smudged from years of handling by nine kids, was not particularly valuable in a monetary sense.... So why was this ball so important in our family?"

As Paprocki explained, Simmons was a Polish ballplayer at a time when Poles found it difficult to break into the mainstream of American culture. "For a Polish family living in an era when 'Polish jokes' were still quite popular, having a hero like Al Simmons was a source of pride.... When Al Simmons stopped in Chicago, he would occasionally pay a visit to see my grandfather. Years later, this autograph remains a symbol of my family's Polish heritage, our love of a great American pastime, our old family drugstore, our grandfather, and our father."[12]

Simmons could show a tender heart for kids. In one of his early years with the A's, he received a letter from a sick child, asking for a baseball. Simmons got his teammates to sign it, and then took it to the kid's home himself. When he arrived, he discovered the boy had just died. "There were tears in his eyes as he turned away, and he was saddened for days, although he had never met the boy," according to a writer.[13]

On the field, Simmons and Philadelphia could not overcome their July floundering, and though they rebounded in August and September, they wound up finishing in third place at 83–67, eight games behind New York. It was a bit disappointing considering what they had done the year before.

Simmons' performance was solid, with a .341 average, 19 home runs, 109 RBIs, 199 hits, 53 doubles, and 10 triples. Still, it seemed a regression to some. "It has been a tough season for Al Simmons, batting sensation of last year," wrote Evans.[14]

Some scribes were harsher. Quoting an anonymous American League pitcher, one writer stated: "In his anxiety to hit, Simmons early showed the fault of being a fall guy for badly pitched balls. He would chase a high fast ball a mile, and got plenty of them ... Simmons was base hit crazy last season, which made him too anxious, with the result that he was hitting at too many bad balls."[15]

That writer blamed the A's misfortunes on Simmons' alleged lack of hitting, actually calling him the biggest handicap on the team, even though he had finished ninth in the league in batting average. Heinie Manush of Detroit won the batting title with a .378 average. But the offensive juggernaut that season was Ruth, who dished out 47 home runs with a .372 average and 146 RBIs.

In Philadelphia that offseason, Mack, seeing how his team failed to meet expectations, ruminated on what his young players needed for proper growth. In the past few years, he had been building a contender, mixing talent both young and older. But to Mack it seemed they needed some exceptional veteran influences — the kind who knew how to win championships and big games. After all, it had been a long time since the A's last World Series appearance in 1914. Though they had finally notched a second consecutive winning season in 1926, there was a lot of player polishing left to be done. Mack wanted a hard-nosed veteran. In baseball, there was a man who perfectly fit this description — Ty Cobb.

At age 39 in 1926, Cobb had hit .339 for Detroit. But he would not be returning to the Motor City's ball team. The reason is complicated, but basically Cobb was angry at baseball commissioner Kenesaw Mountain Landis for reviewing an allegation that he and Tris Speaker had been involved in fixing a game in 1919 — Detroit won the game. The Georgia Peach, as Cobb was known, sought vindication. He flatly refused the claim made by the Detroit pitcher, Dutch Leonard, who Cobb as player-manager had released. "I believe that Leonard was after what ever money he could get out of those letters. I see no possible reason why he could be sore at any other club for waiving on him ... he was considered a Bolshevik," Cobb told writers.[16]

With this affront, Cobb resigned as a player from baseball, declaring his hope to be a full-time manager. That alleviated Landis' concerns somewhat. Just when seemed as if Cobb would not play again, Mack swooped in quickly to negotiate with the deadball star, now free of the reserve clause after retiring. "I want him, Philadelphia wants him, and I think he will give us the needed punch to win the pennant," Mack said.[17]

The wily Cobb was also talking with the St. Louis Browns and considering other options. Then, on February 9, he announced his intention to wear the white elephant uniform. "I am happy to announce I will be associated with the Athletics this season," said Cobb, who traveled to Shibe Park in Philadelphia to sign the deal.[18]

Estimates of the contract ranged from $50,000 to $75,000. Mack was enthused. "I was not satisfied with the men's work during the training season last year, and although I had hoped the championship campaign would prove I was wrong, it did not.... All our players will be keyed up as never before."[19]

Mack had high hopes for a Cobb-infused A's team, and he expanded on this theme, which in many ways set a foundation for the dynasty to come —

the older players could still play and at the same time teach the younger ones until they were fully ready. That winter he also signed 40-year-old second baseman Eddie Collins, fresh off a .344 season, and 39-year-old outfielder Zack Wheat, who had batted .290—two other players like Cobb who would go on to the Hall of Fame.

On the younger side, Mack brought aboard heralded minor league shortstop Joe Boley—of Eastern European origins. Boley's original name was Bolinski.

"Think of the strength Mack has along that famous line from the plate to center field," one writer observed. "If Connie, suddenly turned spendthrift, wins a pennant at last because of his newly acquired high-priced stars, he'll deserve a medal."[20]

Many predicted that the A's would be one of the league's best gate draws in the season ahead—despite the allure of the Yankee sluggers.

Writer Jack Gallagher said of the A's, "There is youth and age, brain and brawn and balance and ability in abundance. Those points make the outfit look like the best-fortified squad of performers that ever entered a pennant race. If the youngsters waver in battle, the veterans will step in and carry on, and when they falter, youth can again be rushed to the front."

Mack could not be more happy. "I am satisfied with the team, very much so. Ty Cobb is going to help us a great deal. He may not be able to play every game, but whether he does or not he will be of much value to the club." Mack added that Cobb "still has some good baseball left."[21]

So did Al Simmons—thanks in part to Cobb.

CHAPTER SEVEN

Ty Cobb and Long Flannel Sleeves

"Baseball — with its lore and legends, its cultural power, its seasonal associations, its simple rules and transparent strategies, its longueurs and thrills, its spaciousness, its suspensefulness, its heroics, its nuances, its lingo, its characters, its peculiarly hypnotic tedium, its mythic transformation of the immediate — was the literature of my boyhood."
— *Philip Roth*[1]

"Cobb is a prick. But he sure can hit."
— *Babe Ruth*[2]

In spring training in Florida, newcomer Ty Cobb set a fighting tone for the 1927 Philadelphia A's, losing his temper and getting ejected in one of his first games, against the Boston Braves. "The ejection of Cobb from a ball game is a good sign," mused John Kieran of the *New York Times*. "It means that he is taking his training seriously."[3]

Kieran also observed that Cobb, 40, wore his uniform sleeves extremely long, well below his elbows. "Ty Cobb favored long sleeves in his uniform — so does Simmons." That wasn't Simmons' only similarity with the Georgia Peach. Ty "swaggered" across the diamond; so does Simmons, Kieran added.[4]

Beyond sleeves and swaggering, the effect of Cobb on Simmons was immediate, profound — and entirely predictable. Just 25, Simmons was a hungry pupil, and Cobb was never shy with an opinion to an eager audience. "Al pumped him with questions and Ty enjoyed having as a pupil a man who already had established himself as one of the best hitters in baseball," wrote Bob Broeg.[5]

Years later, Simmons said, "When Cobb joined our club, he taught me how to hit lefthanders. I couldn't touch them until he tipped me off. He showed me how to crowd the plate. There were two southpaws I never could touch. One of them was Sam Gibson of Detroit and another was a guy named

(Lefty) Stewart with Washington. 'Want to know why you can't hit Gibson?' Cobb said. So, he tells me why I can't hit Stewart. The next time I face Stewart, I smack one over the deepest part of the roof at Comiskey Park."[6]

Simmons flattered Cobb about his childhood ambition to emulate him, telling him how he pilfered newspapers from his south side Milwaukee neighbors to check out how Cobb had done in the box scores. "We were in such poor circumstances back then," said Simmons, "that a morning paper was a luxury we did not enjoy until long afterwards. Cobb got a tremendous kick out of my stories, and I think that was the reason he took to me." Cobb returned the flattery. According to Simmons, he said, "You are different from all these fresh bushers who are coming up now, trying to run us out of a job."[7]

Despite his adoration for the Georgia Peach, Simmons confided later on to a sportswriter how he used to "feel sorry" for Cobb. In some ways, it was a natural expression of two formidable competitors. "He couldn't run anymore. He had lost the whip in his arm. And he was a little slow on the trigger at the plate. I felt it because Ty was my idol ever since I started playing kid baseball around Milwaukee. And I never dreamed that some day he would be my roommate on the A's. The worst part is that I considered Ty a poor, old man, even though he was still pretty young."[8]

Ironically, Cobb saw it differently — to him, the brash Simmons was physically unfit. The older player claimed Simmons had shown up out of shape and overweight for spring training — clearly not in keeping with Cobb's lofty standards. "How about doing some running with the old man?" Cobb asked Simmons once in one alleged account. "Okay," Simmons replied, thinking it should not be hard to keep up with Cobb.

Ty Cobb: "I ran him until his tongue hung out. We zigzagged, trotted, walked, galloped and trotted for miles around the park. Al sweated bucketfuls, but firmed up nicely, and worked as hard on his hitting."

On the issue of Simmons' stance, Cobb followed Mack's wise lead, and did not interfere. After all, Cobb had a slightly strange deadball-era swing of his own, holding his hands far apart on the bat.

Ty Cobb: "There were some who wanted to change Simmons' odd foot-in-the-bucket stance. 'Leave him alone,' I argued. Even if he hits them standing on his ear, don't ever monkey with that swing."[9]

Sometimes Simmons' teammates toyed with him. Jimmy Dykes remembered one time when Simmons was cold at the plate, and Mack actually asked the rest of the A's to heckle him in a motivating ploy. "So every time he went up to the plate," Dykes said, "we'd holler, 'Strike out, you bum.'" It worked, according to Simmons, who broke out of his doldrums soon after the bench jockeying.[10]

Seven: Ty Cobb and Long Flannel Sleeves

Al Simmons had reason to be happy. He still holds the Philadelphia Athletics' franchise records for most career RBIs (1,178), total bases (2,998) and career batting average (.356). *National Baseball Hall of Fame*

Cobb's style of play showed the young A's what hard-charging baseball was all about. "Simmons, Lamar, Hale and Gordon (Mickey) Cochrane are playing the best ball of their careers because Ty is keeping them on their toes," *The Sporting News* noted in the latter days of spring training in Florida.[11]

Before heading north for the start of the 1927 campaign, Cobb and Simmons agreed to become roommates. It appeared to be Cobb's idea: "My ambition was to finish well up there, add what spark I could to the A's attack and lend Mr. Mack some help with his younger talent. I picked out Al Simmons as a boy who could use some advice."[12]

Through the first few weeks of the season, Cobb's competitive tutoring seemed to pay off for Simmons. On Opening Day, he smacked out two hits, including a double, although the A's lost, 8–3, to New York. The next day he went 4-for-4 in another defeat to the Yankees. By the end of April, the A's had won 9 and lost 5, with Simmons hitting .438.

Then, all hell broke loose. On May 5, both Simmons and Cobb were famously ejected from a game in Philadelphia for violently arguing an umpiring call. Simmons had come to Cobb's defense when the latter stroked what appeared to be a home run against the Boston Red Sox. The umpire, Emmett Ormsby, called it foul — and Cobb lost his legendary temper.

It happened with Boston leading 3–2 in the eighth inning. Cobb drove the first pitch over the right-field fence, perhaps inside the foul pole. Ormsby called him back, ruling the ball was foul. Simmons, who was on deck and had a good view of the drive, swore a blue streak at Ormsby, according to author William Kashatus. An enraged Cobb soon gathered his wits — then stepped back into the batter's box. He took a wide practice swing that struck the umpire on the shoulder. Stunned, Ormsby immediately ejected Cobb, and then pointed his finger at Simmons and tossed him, too. The Philadelphia crowd went nuts. Fans began throwing objects on the field toward the umpires. The police actually had to escort the umpiring crew into the locker room.[13]

Afterwards, the incident turned into a scandal of league proportions. Never a fan of Cobb, Ban Johnson, president of the American League, fined both Cobb and Simmons $200 apiece and suspended them both indefinitely. Cobb's "lack of intelligence" in bumping the umpire and Simmons' lack of "knowledge of the American League's established customs" were the reasons, said Johnson, who described Simmons merely as a "young outfielder." He deplored how the incident had provoked the crowd, resulting in a rain of "murderous pop bottles" being tossed at the umpiring crew.

Johnson defended his umpire Ormsby, who as a 20-year-old U.S. Marine soldier had fought in the "savage fighting" at Chateau-Thierry and the Argonne in World War I — which in Johnson's eyes, somehow gave him umpiring skills. "Such a man has no fear of baseball crowds, disappointed and unthinking managers and boisterous players," declared Johnson. Strangely, Johnson lifted the suspensions a week later. The fines stood, however.[14]

It is not clear why the suspensions were lifted, but it may have been because Cobb was due to be honored in a welcome home ceremony on May 10 in Detroit when the A's were to play the Tigers. He had not appeared in

Detroit since leaving the team. "The Motor City fans immediately got busy with petitions, demanding that I be reinstated," Cobb claimed. "They raised such a hubbub that Simmons and I were allowed to play in Detroit on May 10."

However, it seems doubtful that fans alone could get Johnson to end the punishment. In any event, Cobb contested the official accounting of the incident: "Whoever gave that statement is an absolute liar. It's all a mystery to me, but the story that I was kicked out because of an argument is false, as the umpire himself will admit. I never contested the decision or had any argument with the umpire."[15]

With the suspensions lifted, both Simmons and Cobb got down to business. On May 13, they both contributed to a 10–3 victory over the Tigers. With a bunt single in the third inning, Cobb stretched his hitting streak to 14 games, and Simmons slugged a homer, double and single. Back in Shibe Park two days later, Simmons homered again, but the A's lost, 8–6, to the St. Louis Browns. On May 29, he pounded out two doubles and a triple to give Philadelphia a 6–1 win over Washington.

Washington baseball was in the midst of a swan song that season. On May 30, their longtime ace, Walter Johnson, 39, tossed the last shutout and 110th of his glorious career in blanking the Red Sox, 3–0. He retired at the end of the season.

There were other luminaries around the league, some coming, some going—and plenty of them on the A's. On June 11, Philadelphia fielded a team of seven future Hall of Famers in the ninth inning of a 5–4 loss to the Detroit Tigers—Simmons, Cobb, Jimmie Foxx, Lefty Grove, Mickey Cochrane, Eddie Collins and Zack Wheat.

All the big names aside, Simmons was making one for himself. On June 15, he walloped a grand slam off Chicago's ace pitcher, Ted Lyons, for the only A's runs in a 6–4 loss. Perhaps inspired by the talent surrounding him, he was having a signature year. By June 26, he stood atop a .378 average with 10 homers and 78 RBIs.

Sounds good, but his mentor, Tyrus Raymond Cobb, was not so easily satisfied. He expected more from his star pupil, who he had invested so much time in. Cobb, a self-taught master of psychology, was watching Simmons closely and believed that he suffered from a habit of inexperienced hitters—he got discouraged and frustrated too easily.

Simmons, it appeared to Cobb, was extremely disappointed if he failed to bang out a hit his first couple at-bats—it affected him the rest of the game. "He needed a mathematics lesson," said Cobb, the eventual owner of a then-record 4,189 career hits. Cobb explained to Simmons that if he makes outs the first two times at the plate, he still has a couple more chances to get a hit — and two hits in four at-bats is a .500 average for the day. "Bear down extra hard on those remaining chances," Cobb said.[16]

Of course, Simmons understood Cobb's point in theory; it was more a matter of learning how to control his emotions — ironic, coming from Cobb. But the older player knew when to control and when to let go of his emotions; the latter for effect.

One writer described Cobb's tutelage: "First, he bore down on the value of self control, and Simmons obeyed his lectures and injunctions. He taught him a few fine points about covering centerfield, and instilled much baseball lore and stuff into his apt pupil."[17]

Cobb, certainly, let his emotions get the best of him sometimes. One time Mack sought to motivate a slumping Cobb by lifting him for a pinch-hitter. Simmons said, "It was a typical psychological move by the Old Man (Mack). Cobb had been going bad in a doubleheader, and I'd had about a half dozen hits. So Connie suggested that he be withdrawn. That Cobb was the maddest guy I ever set eyes on. 'A pinch hitter for Cobb?' he yowls. Of course, the Old Man just wanted to get him steamed up. Cobb singled on the very first pitch."[18]

Mack knew how to motivate players, whether rookies or fiery veterans. He was constantly instructing Simmons on the inside game, albeit in a more gentlemanly though equally direct fashion than Cobb.

One time Simmons came back to the bench complaining about the background behind the pitcher. "How can a guy be expected to hit against that sort of background?" he said, referring to the space behind the center-field wall where the batter first sees the ball coming from the hurler. As Simmons later put it, a "stern" Mack told him, "Al, don't ever say a thing like that as long as you live. If you're going to react that way about the background, and you're a .350 hitter, what do you think the effect is going to be on the .275 and .250 hitters?" Simmons said he "never forgot" those words from Mack. Later, as a coach, whenever a player would grumble about the background, or anything, Simmons would simply reply, "shut up." Not quite the way Mack handled it, but the same message was sent.[19]

Meanwhile, the '27 Yankees were fielding one of the greatest baseball teams ever. Known as the "Murderers Row," their lineup featured Babe Ruth, Lou Gehrig, Bob Meusel, Tony Lazzeri, and Earle Combs. By July 4, the Yankees were 53–21, just steamrolling their competition. In a series later that month, they beat Washington 21–1 in one game, prompting Senators first baseman Joe Judge to exclaim, "Those fellows not only beat you, but they tear your heart out. I wish the season was over."[20]

While New York was flattening its opponents, the season came crashing down on Simmons. In a July 24, doubleheader against Cleveland, he suffered a groin pull sliding into second base. Groins don't heal quickly. Simmons — the American League's leading hitter at .393 — was projected to be out for at least three weeks. The team physician even estimated that Simmons would be lost for the remainder of the season. Simmons was out until September 6, though he may have come back too early from the injury. He returned to the lineup that day, went hitless in three attempts, and did not see action again until September 14.[21]

Simmons continued to lead the league in hitting as Heilmann of Detroit and Gehrig, Ruth and Meusel of the Yankees chased him. Heilmann actually passed the idle Simmons briefly in August. Simmons was in danger of not qualifying for the batting title — he had only played 91 games by September.

A debate about batting title worthiness ensued. Billy Evans, again, opined that durability counted as much as the batting "rate." He cited Gehrig above all. As Evans wrote, "Should some player, who has participated in the entire schedule of 154 games, finish with a mark a few points less than that of Simmons, there would be an immediate argument as to who should be labeled champion."[22]

In a twist harkening back to 1925 and Tris Speaker, Simmons was now described as "sitting in the shade of the bench," watching the threats to his .391 average mount. When he returned to full play, he went 12-for-25 in his next six games. Throughout that season, he had notched plenty of RBIs, as Philadelphia kept winning late through the season, though never enough to overcome the dazzling Yankees.

In the last three games of the year, Simmons amassed seven hits in 12 at bats — but it was not enough. Heilmann finished strong, posting a .398 average and snatching away the batting honors from Simmons and his injury-riddled though stunning .392 — with four more hits, he would have hit .400 (he had 159 hits in 406 at-bats).

In 106 games, Simmons collected 108 RBIs, his fourth straight season with 100+ RBIs in as many years as a player. He also notched 15 homers, 11 triples and 36 doubles. Perhaps animated by Cobb, he snared 10 stolen bases. As for Cobb, he put up a highly respectable .357 average, good for fifth best in the league.

Overlooking Simmons' injury spell, the Cobb-Simmons tandem was a success for both players and the team. The A's finished with 91 wins with other solid seasons from Mickey Cochrane (.338), Jimmy Dykes (.324), Boley (.311), Sammy Hale (.313) and Walter French (.304). Overall, the team batted .304.

The heralded youngster, Jimmie Foxx, 19, saw action in only 61 games but hit .323 with a .515 slugging average — second best on the A's next to Simmons. His day would come shortly. On the mound, Lefty Grove burst forth with 20–13 record and 3.19 ERA while Rube Walberg was 16–12 with a 3.93 ERA.

While the A's had matured into a legitimate contender, 1927 was the Yankees' year. New York dominated the American League with brute offensive force and rang up a 110–44 record, a whopping 19 games ahead of Philadelphia.

Overall that year, New York batted .307, slugged .489, scored 975 runs, and outscored their opponents by a record 376 runs. Gehrig batted .373, with 218 hits, 52 doubles, 18 triples, 47 home runs, a then-record 175 RBIs. Ruth amassed a .356 batting average, 164 RBIs, slugged .772, and belted out 60 home runs, the major league mark until Roger Maris broke it in 1961.

Even New York's pitching staff excelled, leading the league in ERA at 3.20. These Yankees would eventually send six players along with manager Miller Huggins and Ed Barrow to the Baseball Hall of Fame. In the World Series, New York finished the job with an exclamation point by sweeping the Pittsburgh Pirates in four games.

Even in this glorious year, Ruth took notice of Al Simmons in a column later that year: "A man's batting form in an individual matter. A fellow like Al Simmons of the Athletics, for instance, has a batting stance that no one else in the league could use. Al stands with his foot in the bucket all the time. But he hits the ball. And that's what counts.... Pitching to a chap like that is tough ... timing and good eyes are the real secret."[23]

Ruth's home run barrage and the Yankee juggernaut were a great distraction for the country that year. But other momentous events of a life-and-death variety were unfolding throughout the world. Abroad, the German economy completely collapsed and Nazism gained a greater foothold in that country—"It is a question of power," proclaimed Adolph Hitler at a Nuremberg Rally. In Russia, Leon Trotsky was expelled from the Communist Party as Josef Stalin took control of the Soviet Union, and in China, Chiang Kai-Shek set up a separate government and turned against the Communists in a pivotal realignment.[24]

In the U.S., the zeitgeist reflected expansion outward—Charles Lindbergh made the first nonstop solo transatlantic flight, from New York to Paris, the first transatlantic telephone call was made from New York City to London, Pan American Airways was formed, and the "talking" movie, *The Jazz Singer,* took the country by storm, marking the end of the silent-film era.

It seemed anything was possible in these halcyon days of the American economy and lifestyle innovations. In the Greek myth of Alcyone, "Halcyon Days" refer to the seven days in winter when storms never occur, the seemingly endless sunny days of youth.

Endlessly sunny — major league baseball, too, was in one of its most joyful and heroic periods ever, with attendance booming and colorful stars ascending and big-city dynasties arriving and amazing records arising. Fans and baseball professionals looked ahead with bright anticipation for what would come. More than ever, it was New York's time in the sun — for awhile longer.

CHAPTER EIGHT

Nurturing the Nucleus

> "He'd roll out of bed and get dressed, exchanging small talk with this neighborhood small fry who had become a combination of alarm clock and good luck charm. A short while later, Al would saunter down the street toward the park, well before customers began arriving for the game."
> —John J. Rooney, on Al Simmons[1]

> "Every great batter works on the theory that the pitcher is more afraid of him than he is of the pitcher."
> —Ty Cobb[2]

While Al Simmons played for the white-only organization of major league baseball, he was not alone among the "bucketfoot" stars of the national pastime. Black ballplayers formed teams in the Negro Leagues, which boasted its own "bucketfoot" hitter in Turkey Stearnes, a left-handed outfielder who stood with his right foot splayed out and his toe pointed skyward. When he ran the bases, Stearnes flapped his arms like the Thanksgiving bird, hence the nickname "Turkey."

All of this was far from the mind of Simmons as he eyed the upcoming 1928 season. That winter he served as a scout for Philadelphia in scouring the Milwaukee sandlots for promising ballplayers — taking a familial and friendly approach, he signed three, including his own brother, Walter Simmons, for the Milwaukee Brewers. The others were John Shinners, nephew of his friend major league journeyman Ralph Shinners, who signed with the A's, and Joe Christie, who inked a deal with the Waterloo, Iowa, club. A dapper-looking, wide-smiling Simmons — described as "Milwaukee's most noted contribution to baseball" — was shown in a newspaper photograph of the three elated young men signing their contracts.[3]

Mack was also doing some signing of his own. He reached a deal with 40-year-old Tris Speaker, one of the game's best batsmen and defensive center fielders. The move slid Simmons over to left field, and gave the A's one of the more high-pedigree outfields of all time with Simmons, despite the ages of

Cobb (if he re-signed) and now Speaker, the latter long a "friendly enemy" of Mack's. Bing Miller, a fine outfielder himself, and the emerging Mule Haas, were slated to relieve Cobb and the others. The A's were loaded in the outfield.

As of the Speaker deal, Mack had not yet inked Cobb; bringing on Speaker may have been done to give the A's that veteran presence Mack so clearly wanted in case Cobb did not reenlist. He eventually did, but not until the first week of spring training. The excitement about Speaker brewed. "Speaker will prove helpful to the Athletics beyond question," predicted one writer. "The Texan showed youngsters how to go back on a fly ball 20 years, and he is still showing them." Speaker said the signing realized his dream of "playing alongside Cobb for one season."[4]

Even though Cobb was losing range, the aging Speaker was generally viewed as a defensive asset, and certainly Simmons benefited from possessing the youngest legs of them all. But in Fort Myers that spring, Simmons complained of a bad back. His play was erratic and it was painful for him to run. The A's coaches were concerned.

On top of this, it is reasonable to suggest Simmons, a man of great pride, was not exactly happy about the Speaker signing that shifted him over to left field. The *Los Angeles Times* ran a story headlined:

High-Salaried Speaker and Cobb May Cause Dissension in Athletic Ranks: Simmons not to relish leaving center for Tris.[5] The *New York Times* suggested giving Simmons a "bicycle" so he could chase the fly balls his 40-something fellow outfielders could not track down.[6]

A physician soon pronounced Simmons "fit" as he could "find nothing wrong." One day Simmons played a "sparkling game in left field" in an exhibition against the New York Giants.[7] However, his improving health did not last. In early April, just days before Opening Day, Simmons found himself in the hospital suffering from rheumatism in his ankles, as well as infected tonsils. Some reports indicated he had a badly sprained ankle. He missed not only the first game of the year, but did not appear in the lineup until May 22, when he came to the plate as a pinch-hitter — and coolly stroked a triple, sparking the A's to a 7–6 victory over Washington in 11 innings.

Fortunately for the A's, they had depth. With Haas and French and Miller, Mack had options for games that the injured Simmons and the elder statesmen Cobb and Speaker missed. As one newspaper put it before Simmons returned, "Simmons is perhaps the greatest outfielder in baseball, and he has been disabled all season. When he returns, Mack will have to pull out one of the veterans and there will be another star player, good enough for a regular job on any club, sitting on the bench."[8]

Also, Jimmie Foxx began to play regularly in 1928. With his talented roster, Mack devised a lineup core that proved explosive. Leadoff hitter and second baseman Max Bishop — an on-base machine with huge walk totals — was followed by Speaker, Haas or Cobb batting second with catcher Mickey Cochrane in the third spot. Al Simmons batted cleanup, followed by first baseman Foxx, and then Jimmy Dykes. The shortstop — a revolving door in those years between Joe Boley and others — batted eighth.[9]

Not often in the lineup early that season, Simmons continued to endure bouts of rheumatism that sapped his strength. He was cranky and unpleasant to be around. "He suffers such pain that at the end of a battle he can hardly stagger into the clubhouse," wrote sportswriter James Isaminger, adding that Mack nearly sent Simmons home for the season due to the flare ups. Mack had apparently set July 1 as the date in which Simmons needed to get back in the lineup — or else that was the end of the season for him. The outfielder managed to beat the deadline much earlier for one for the season's greatest match-ups.

Expectations were high in the Quaker City for a May 24 doubleheader with the rival New York Yankees. With New York in first and Philadelphia in second, the games had a pennant-deciding atmosphere for so early in the season. Fans came from far and wide for the 1:30 P.M. first pitch at Shibe Park. To accommodate the heavy interest, ticket windows opened earlier than usual, at 10:45 A.M., as thousands had been standing in line since daybreak, eyewitnesses said.

By noon, the parking lot at 21st and Lehigh was jammed to capacity with 500 cars with license plates from such places as New York, New Jersey, Maryland, Delaware, and Washington, D.C. There was an air of "feverish expectancy" around Shibe Park.

The world champion Yankees, who arrived about noon, had to muscle their way through the A's fans to get into the park. Ruth was particularly taunted. The stadium had to open the gates early, as the unruly fans were beyond police control.

Through the early afternoon, the crowd continued to swell. Ballpark reference sources put Shibe Park seating capacity in 1928 between 27,500 and 33,600. Philadelphia newspapers of the next day, according to writer Bill Brandt, indicated attendance for this day was at least 42,000. Another 15,000 or 20,000 were ticketless, milling about outside. These disappointed patrons (many holding scalped tickets) "retreated from the barricaded portals or lingered outside the concrete horseshoe to listen to the noises of the long and rapid-turning battle tide," Brandt noted.[10] It was the largest crowd to date in Philadelphia baseball history.

Inside the ballpark, spectators squeezed together and fought for the best angles. They clambered for positions in the aisles, atop the scoreboard, and perches on the steel girders. Some even risked a daunting climb to the top of the sloping left-field roof. (Two days later it was reported that several wire cutters and sledgehammers had been left in the park by people seeking "entrance" to their seating accommodations.) Remarkably, despite all lack of crowd control and restraint, no one reportedly got hurt. Writer Joe Dittmar chronicled the *Philadelphia Inquirer's* fan interest in the doubleheader:

> Over the low wall in right field, rabid rooters scaled the barbed wire walls like doughboys in France when the word was given "over the top." Despite the efforts of the police, several ladders were smuggled into the vast throng of 10,000, which banked itself on 20th Street. As if by prearranged signal, four of them were placed against the walls and the fans surged over them like Greeks over the Trojan battlements. Many, once they reached the top, were caught on the barbed wire, and their antics in extricating themselves kept the fans in riotous good humor.
>
> One rooter in jumping to the ground had his coat sleeve caught on a barb. As he slipped to earth the coat remained in the wire, much to the delight of the vast throng who followed the progress of the invasion with as much interest as they did the batting practice of the Yanks.
>
> Another less fortunate wall climber caught his trouser leg in a steel prong and dangled in the air as the thousands roared. His belt, however, did not give way and companions pulled him back to safety.
>
> Even the white pole along the right field foul line, served as a practice ground for embryonic steeplejacks, and several of them, instead of dropping to earth (from) atop the wall, "shinnied" up to the top pavilion. Each successive climb was met with a vast cheer from the crowd until so many accomplished the goal that it became monotonous.
>
> The new scoreboards did double work, serving as a parking place for a hundred or more fans as well as flashing the progress of the game.
>
> The porch and top roofs of the houses on 20th Street held five thousand more baseball bugs (fans), despite feeble efforts by the police to keep them off. On roofs two blocks away, fifty or more (fans) were sighted viewing the battle through field glasses. They must have had a good view of the tilt for in the sixth inning of the first game when a doubtful strike was called on Cobb — one threw his hat on the roof, stamped on it, shook his fist at (umpire) Van Graflan and then disappeared from sight over the sidewalk.[11]

In the first game, a major-league record 13 future Hall of Famers took the field. The impressive count does not include non-playing Hall of Famers Herb Pennock and Stan Coveleski, managers Miller Huggins and Connie Mack, nor umpires Tom Connolly and Bill McGowan. The Yankees had future Cooperstown inductees in Earle Combs, Leo Durocher, Babe Ruth, Lou Gehrig, Tony Lazzeri, and Waite Hoyt. For the Athletics, Hall of Famers included Ty Cobb, Tris Speaker, Mickey Cochrane, Al Simmons, Eddie Collins, Lefty Grove, and Jimmie Foxx.

Simmons, still healing, did not start in either game, but did get in the second game and slapped a single in a pinch-hitting appearance.

On the scoreboard, the A's and Yankees split. Led by Lazzeri's three hits and six RBIs, the Yanks edged the A's, 9–7, in the first game, handing the defeat to Lefty Grove. But Philadelphia won the second game, 5–2, behind rookie hurler Ossie Orwell.

In the standings, the Yankees were 27–7 and the A's 22–9. The Yankees kept winning, and four days later pummeled the A's, 11–4, despite a three-run homer by Simmons, who was playing again and finding his groove at the plate. On June 2, he beat the White Sox with a game-winning triple, and put together a 14-game hitting streak that month. Successive home runs by Simmons and Foxx with the score tied in the eighth inning gave the Athletics a 4–2 victory over the Tigers on June 12.

While it was well-known that Simmons "hated" pitchers, some opposing hitters also disliked him. He became quite a verbal agitator all the way from his position in left field.

Despite his reputation on the field, Simmons was getting almost as much fan mail as Babe Ruth. According to one account, he received most of his letters from female admirers, not star-stuck boys. With his dark good looks and flashy clothes, Simmons loved the nightlife and a good cigar, and some pleasant company.[12]

During the season, Simmons lived at 2745 North 20th Street, across the street from the Shibe Park right-field fence, in a second-floor bedroom in the home of Mr. and Mrs. A.C. Conwell. He was the grist of legends for the kids who played around the ballpark. He was also a notoriously late sleeper, so the polite Mrs. Conwell would ask neighborhood boys to wake him in time for batting practice. One of the kids was four-year-old John J. Rooney, whose family lived three doors away.

Writing in the *Elysian Fields Quarterly* literary magazine decades later, Rooney recalled: "Mrs. Conwell was reluctant to enter the star outfielder's bedroom to wake him up in the morning, so the job was delegated to my kid brother. Jerry waited eagerly for her signal and then scooted up to rouse him."

"Hey, Al, it's time to get up for practice," Jerry would say, wrote Rooney. "C'mon Al, you got to get your batting practice if you're gonna win the batting title." A sleepy Simmons would reply, "Oh, hi, kid. Yeah, I guess it is time for some breakfast."

John J. Rooney: "He'd roll out of bed and get dressed, exchanging small talk with this neighborhood small fry who had become a combination of alarm clock and good luck charm. A short while later, Al would saunter down the street toward the park, well before our customers began arriving for the game."

Rooney said that the year before he started school, his father took him up the ladder in the bathroom, through the skylight and onto the flat roof, where they could see the Shibe Park action. "There, Jack," he pointed down at the baseball diamond across the street, "for the rest of your life you can always say you saw Ty Cobb, Tris Speaker, and Al Simmons, three of the greatest players of all time, playing in the same outfield."

Rooney noted that all the games were played in the afternoon and that the crowds grew larger as the summer unfolded and the A's challenged for the pennant. "People would spill out of the 54 trolley that clanged along Lehigh Avenue, or would parade the six blocks from Broad Street, where the Pennsy and Reading railroads and the subway had stops," he wrote.

During batting practice and the games Rooney joined the other kids and adults looking to "snag a ball that came over the low right field fence." Rooney said if somebody got a ball hit by Al Simmons, "you could always get him to autograph it if you caught him on the street."[13]

Apparently, with help like that getting to batting practice, Simmons was finding his stroke, and now carried a .331 average that season. He smacked the ball with authority the rest of the way, piling up RBIs and extra-base hits.

On July 11, he powered three home runs as Philadelphia split a doubleheader against the White Sox. In the first game, he delivered six RBIs, and went 3-for-3 in the second contest. On July 25 against the White Sox, Simmons smashed a grand slam in the first inning against Ted Lyons. On August 9, Simmons — by now hitting a robust .388 — connected for another bases-loaded homer, this time off of Washington's Garland Braxton, in the sixth inning.

Simmons, despite missing so much time, actually thought he could win the batting title — and help the A's win the American League race. He eclipsed Washington's Goose Goslin for the lead in batting, and the A's were only two games behind the Yankees by the first day of September. Indeed, in Philadelphia, hopes were high for a pennant, with requests pouring into Shibe Park for World Series tickets that August.[14]

On September 1, the A's closed out their last home game of the season with a 14–2 beating of the Boston Red Sox. Lefty Grove won his 13th in a row, and Simmons smacked out four hits — two doubles and a pair of singles.[15] The victory capped off a 16–4 homestand, an omen of the season to come. The A's then began a long road trip through the rest of the month, and while they played well enough, it was impossible to close the gap with the Yankees. When the dust settled at the end, Philadelphia finished 98–55, a powerful testament to their rising fortunes, but still two and one half games behind New York, which went on to win a second consecutive World Series, this time against the St. Louis Cardinals.

Simmons' line for the year was 109 games, .351 average, 33 doubles, 9 triples, 15 home runs, and 107 RBIs.

Not bad, but he had missed significant time to injuries. It was a mixed year of joys and frustrations as far as Simmons and the A's rivalry with the Yankees were concerned. Though vanquished on the field, Simmons and the A's were not overlooked by Yankees like Ruth, who picked Simmons as the starting left fielder for his "All-America" team. "In previous years, Al Simmons has done his best work in center field," Ruth's ghostwriter wrote in the syndicated column. "I think he is a better center fielder than left fielder ... Simmons is a great batter and in spite of his late start this year, he deserves much of the credit for the Athletics' strong showing."[16]

Credit also went to Mickey Cochrane, who snared the league's Most Valuable Player Award with a .293 average (actually lower than his mark of .338 the year before), 10 homers and 57 RBIs. He won mostly due to his leadership skills; he also led the AL in putouts. "Black Mike" was different than most other catchers, wrote Dixon Stewart. "Cochrane is an exception to the general run of catchers in that he is a good hitter and a speedy base runner."

During these years, American League players who had won a previous MVP were ineligible to receive another one. In 1927, Ruth had hit 60 homers, but was not chosen MVP. In 1931, baseball established the MVP system that we know today.[17]

In the last days of the season, sportswriter William Duncan sat down with Simmons to write a profile of him. When the A's last game was over, it was learned, Simmons boarded a train to Milwaukee to see his "best friend"—his mother—and the rest of his fellow Milwaukeeans who look upon him as "their most famous citizen in the sports word," according to Duncan.

The article noted how much he enjoyed camping in the northern Wisconsin woods, eating ice cream, and playing golf. Under Connie Mack's rules, players weren't allowed to golf during the regular season. The manager thought the game took a player's mind off baseball and ruined his swing. Simmons evidently played, and reportedly was scoring in the low 90s around this time. He said his favorite golfer was Horton Smith, who he knew personally.

After a week or so back in Milwaukee, Simmons told Duncan he would typically head to the woods to camp with Ralph Shinners — his best friend — and a former major leaguer now playing with Toronto in the International League. Sometimes they would spend a month or two in the wilds — with "no set schedule." One gets the impression that his camping trips involved guys having fun with the usual distractions.

After his wilderness adventures, Simmons returned to Milwaukee for the holidays, spending time with his mother, brothers and sisters. He told Duncan

In the offseason, Al Simmons enjoyed hiking in the outdoors, whether in Wisconsin or near Hot Springs, Arkansas. *National Baseball Hall of Fame*

that two of his proudest moments came when St. Bonaventure College near Milwaukee dedicated their athletic field "Al Simmons Field" and when Simmons was selected by Babe Ruth as a member of the Bambino's All-American Team of 1927.

In a glimpse into what may be the origins of Simmons' looming waistline later in life, Simmons revealed that he loved "beefsteak and onions," only a few vegetables, and then "ice cream with more ice cream." As if this isn't enough, he recalled a dinner party he attended one summer in Philadelphia where he gulped down the entire meal and then ordered out for more ice cream before falling asleep on the couch. When he was awakened by the hostess, he jumped up and said he was going to drive up North Broad Street where he knew a place he could get more ice cream.[18]

Whether for ice cream or batting titles — or because of his injury-plagued campaign — Simmons was quick to sign a new contract in the offseason. Press reports stated he would receive a $15,000 annual salary; he vowed to live up to it. "My bat will speak for me from the very first day off the 1929 campaign," he declared.

Ralph Davis of the *Pittsburgh Press* claimed Simmons took only an hour to sign the contract after opening it in the mail. "He considered the treatment accorded him eminently fair.... He had rheumatism last spring, but he has no signs of it for a long time, and believes its dregs have all been driven from his system."

Fit and fiery, Simmons headed to Hot Springs, Arkansas, that February to "boil out with his teammates" before heading to spring training in Florida. Over the winter, both Ty Cobb and Tris Speaker both announced their retirements, signaling the passing era of baseball's greatest deadball hitters. The torch was passed to a new, self-assured nucleus of A's, and they would strike a powerful pose in the coming season.[19]

CHAPTER NINE

Building a Dynasty

"The thing I remember is he was such a humble person. He never argued with umpires. He'd walk away. Sometimes I thought he was too meek for his own good."

— *Nanci Foxx, on her father Jimmie Foxx*

At the start of 1929, America was feeling pretty good about itself. This was, after all, the culminating year of the Roaring Twenties, a decade of great change and opportunity. Radio, the emerging national media with about 10 million sets in use, piped in music, news and sports to an increasing number of households. On Wall Street, the stock of the Radio Corporation of America (RCA) was setting records in 1929, rising from $100 to $500 a share — a little "irrational exuberance" well before the time the term would be used to suggest a frothy market.

Behind this rise in stocks there was trouble, and not only in the markets but in the main streets of America. In Chicago, the Saint Valentine's Day massacre took place on February 14 involving the murder of seven people as part of a Prohibition Era conflict between two powerful criminal gangs.

That year the country's population reached 120 million, and entertainment choices were brimming for people hungry for new ways to spend their leisure time. The Academy Awards, popularly known as the Oscars, were started, reflecting the continued ascent of films and Hollywood in the public's consciousness. Even children had their celluloid heroes — Popeye, a muscular comic strip character created by Elzie Crisler Segar, made its debut that year.

In Philadelphia, the A's had their own version of Popeye — Jimmie Foxx, a 21-year-old strongman specimen. Yankees pitcher Lefty Gomez famously said Foxx had "muscles in his hair." After banging out 13 home runs and a .328 average in 118 games the previous season, Foxx, who had patiently waited for full-time play as he learned the game, was finally primed for a breakout season.

But it did not come easy or quickly. Foxx, trained as a catcher, third baseman and first baseman, did not have a regular position until the end of spring training when Connie Mack decided former pitcher Ossie Orwoll could not defend first base adequately. "I'll have to use Jimmy Foxx there unless Orwoll shows improvement right away," said Mack, eying Foxx for third base. Spring training did not go well for the A's as a team. Mack complained, "I can't understand what's holding us back. We have had injuries, but they haven't been serious enough to cause all the trouble."[1]

Simmons was confident, however. Over the winter, the *Los Angeles Times* noted, he had "written the boss of the Elephants (Mack) that he expects to have his biggest year in 1929 and aims to lead the league in batting, an honor he was several times within a few points of grasping."[2]

But by Opening Day in early April, the star outfielder was again suffering from that "old rheumatic trouble" that had caused him to miss playing time the last two seasons. The team told him to take a few weeks off and join the club when he felt better. It was discouraging.

Al Simmons: "I never worked so hard in my life to get in shape as I did this year, and I'm disgusted with the order of the doctor that I'll have to rest at home for a week or more and possibly be handicapped all this season as I've been for the last two years.... If I found that I couldn't come back perfectly, I'd quit baseball, as much as I would hate to. I'll come to a definite decision in a few days."[3]

Would, Simmons have even hinted he'd retire if he couldn't improve his health had Ty Cobb still been hanging around?

With all this uncertainty, some baseball writers predicted doom for the A's. One newspaper headline in the *Philadelphia Evening Ledger* read: "Macks' Pennant Hopes Struck Blow by Lack of Strong Starting Lineup." The writer, Ed Pollock, thought the A's were fatally weakened with injuries already to Simmons, pitcher George Earnshaw and shortstop Joe Boley: "The Athletics still have their eyes directed in the general direction of the pennant, but the latest blow — the incapacitation of Simmons for an indefinite period — has been the most cruel setback that Connie Mack has experienced this season ... Simmons has supplied the team's batting punch for several seasons."[4]

It was disappointing, Pollock added, for many predicted that the A's offered "a royal chance to end the monopoly of the New York Yankees."

Well, so much for early season prognostications. Within a few weeks, Simmons shed his gloomy outlook and was feeling healthy, begging Mack to write his name into the lineup. The doctors suggested waiting for warmer weather. The manager even took a rainy day off to visit Simmons. Agreeing with the doctors, Mack didn't plan to use him until the A's went on the road. Meanwhile, the A's other hard-hitting outfielder, Mule Haas, was on the bench with a leg injury.[5]

By the time Simmons appeared in the A's fifth game on April 23 as a pinch-hitter — he took a bases on balls — Philadelphia was 3–2. Things got better from that point on. On April 24, he started in left field for the first time that season. In the fourth inning, facing Washington's Firpo Marberry, he belted a two-run triple into deep center field. His return "transformed" the A's, as one newspaper described it, giving the team the same "irresistible spirit" that boosted them last year. Three days later, he walloped a grand slam against New York's George Pipgras in the eighth inning.

By May 1, the A's were in first-place at 8–4. That day they scored eight runs off Milt Gaston in the first two innings in a 24–6 shellacking of the Red Sox. Foxx blasted a pair of homers and Simmons churned out five hits, including a double and homer. Their 24 runs matched a franchise record set in 1912, and their 29 hits set a franchise mark.

On an off day in New York, Simmons wandered over to the Polo Grounds to watch the New York Giants and their budding young star, right fielder Mel Ott, who would swat 42 home runs that season. Ott had a distinctive high leg kick, something Bucketfoot Al duly noticed. "My God," Simmons said while watching Ott bat, "why don't they lay off my style? Look at Ott, he swings on only one foot and he hits them out of the park."[6]

Style in the field, though, was not a problem for Simmons. Joe Cronin, the shortstop for the Washington Senators, said, "There never was a greater leftfielder in going to the line and holding a double to a single. He'd even dare you to make the wide turn at first on a ball hit to his right."[7]

Simmons continued to stroke the ball hard, collecting five RBIs in one inning against the Boston Red Sox in a 16–4 blow-out on May 22. He tied an AL record previously set by Ty Cobb in 1909, Ray Bates in 1917, and Chick Gandil in 1919.

By the beginning of June, Philadelphia had powered its way to a stunning 30–9 record. One newspaper described the team as "The Marauding Men of Mack." At that point, Simmons was the owner of a .357 average with 11 homers and 53 RBIs.[8]

Foxx, meanwhile, was flirting with a .400 average and raising eyebrows with his moon shots. "At every park the A's visited, he seemed to be establishing new hitting records, and his power was inviting comparisons to Babe Ruth, who was having a much less successful year," wrote author Bill Kashatus, adding that Simmons was a "devastating" clutch hitter and RBI man in the cleanup spot.[9]

Ruth and the Yankees visited Shibe Park for a high-profile June 21 doubleheader. With total attendance estimated at 70,000, the Friday games marked the start of a five-game series between the defending-champion New Yorkers and the insurgent Philadelphians. In the first game, Simmons led the

Jimmie Foxx (left), Mickey Cochrane and Al Simmons led the A's juggernaut from 1929 to 1931 when the team put up an incredible 313–143 record and scored 2,710 runs or about 903 a season. *National Baseball Hall of Fame*

attack, notching five hits as the A's won, 11–1. In the second game, Ruth walloped a game-winning home run in an 8–3 New York victory.

The next day Philadelphia and New York split another doubleheader — the Marauding Mackmen won the first, 7–3, and the Murderers' Row, the second, 4–3. In the last game of the series on Sunday, Simmons clouted a home run along with Foxx and Haas as the A's prevailed, 7–4.

Pitchers and fielders, from New York or elsewhere, found Simmons especially unpredictable as a batter. He was hard to defend against because of how he chased bad balls and hit to all fields. In one at-bat, Simmons might swat a homer far over the left-field wall, and the next time scorch a liner along the right-field line for a triple. And while he might miss badly on two pitches and look terrible doing so, he could very well smack the next pitch into the seats.

Some say Simmons helped himself by "waiting" as long as possible on a pitch — thanks to his long arms and long bat. Such waiting depends on lightening-fast reflexes and eye-hand coordination. He had the gift of the great hitters — bat speed.[10]

Where Simmons was cantankerous and flashy, Foxx, the "Beast" or Double XX," was good-natured and quiet, though he frequently spoke before groups of school children. In one talk before an assembly of 2,500 students at Philadelphia's Northeast High School, Foxx emphasized the importance of education: "When I was in school, I took more interest in athletics than the books. It was a mistake. I wish I had studied more. These days, a fellow needs all the knowledge he can obtain, since knowledge is what life's all about."[11]

Life was all about hits — and redemption — for Al Simmons of the ungainly batting stance. He had a chip on his shoulder to prove himself. On July 25, writer Jack Sords penned a column accompanied by a cartoon of Simmons with a caption that read, "It looks like Al Simmons will be the big noise in leading Connie Mack to another flag." The columnist wrote, "They thought he wouldn't last, that he would be down in the minors after a short big league life, but here he is — Al Simmons, dean of Connie Mack's clique of clouters, one of the boys setting the pace for the pennant-pursuing Philadelphians.... Foot-in-the bucket Simmons is what they called him. But Al only laughed, and proceeded to show up his critics ... Al is only 26, but finds himself dean of Connie Mack's clouters."[12]

The rest of the summer, the A's continued to pile up the wins. They swept the Yankees in a series in early September, and on September 13, Simmons clubbed a home run to lead them over the White Sox, 5–2.

Fueled by a well-balanced offensive and pitching attack, the A's were at the top of the league when the dust settled. They won the pennant with a record of 104–46, 18 games ahead of the Yankees — finally, the New York stranglehold on Philadelphia was ripped off.

Simmons was making headlines everywhere — even under his own byline. Though it is unclear who helped him with the ghostwriting, he penned a newspaper column that fall about what the pennant-winning season meant to him.

"Never before in my experience with the Athletics was there such a clubhouse celebration ... Connie Mack has a real championship team this year," wrote Simmons.

There was some payback involved. Simmons noted the A's were provoked when some of the Yankee players told the press that Philadelphia would "fold up under the pressure" when playing New York early that season. "They started telling us that back in April and May," he wrote.

The hard feelings also dated back to September 1928, Simmons pointed out, when the Yankees had won three out of four in a key series with the A's. "They sure did rub it in. I'm not blaming them. It's baseball, and human nature, too, to crow over an enemy you have defeated in a fair fight," he said. However, this time around, the A's beat the Yankees in their last four games. "The boys on our team perked up when it came to the real issue."[13]

They were perking up all year. The A's led the league in on-base percentage at .365, scored 901 runs and only allowed 625 while leading the league with a 3.44 ERA.

Jimmie Foxx blasted his way to 33 home runs, 118 RBIs and a .354 average while Mickey Cochrane hit .331 with 95 RBIs. Outfielders Bing Miller (.331) and Mule Haas (.313) also supplied punch. Lefty Grove led the American League in ERA and strikeouts, on his way to a 20–6 record. George Earnshaw topped the league with 24 wins and finished second in strikeouts. Led by these two, Philadelphia allowed the fewest runs of any AL team.

Simmons lauded Mack, paying tribute to the great A's teams of yesteryear and spreading credit around the clubhouse. Clinching the pennant on September 14 was the "happiest moment of my life," he wrote. "It was not alone the personal satisfaction of having helped to win the pennant. It was the realization that at last Connie Mack, the manager and man we all so much respect and admire, had attained his ambition of winning the pennant once more ... he is no longer young, and it was being said that he would never get together another pennant winner."[14]

Though he was not there in 1910, he differentiated between the 1929 and 1910 championship A's teams. "Conditions have changed," Simmons wrote. "We have to play to suit the situations that arise this year. It seems out of order to compare Mack's 1929 team with any previous championship club. Don't think we're going to enter the World Series with any inferiority complex."

In spite of all the glory, Simmons lost the batting title by four points to Cleveland first baseman Lew Fonseca — he was still looking for his first batting title. Nevertheless, his statistics were impressive: .365 average, 212 hits, 41 doubles, 9 triples, 34 home runs, 157 RBIs (league leader), and 373 total bases (league leader). He only made three errors in his 143 games.

The Sporting News selected Simmons as the league's Most Valuable Player with 40 points, followed by the Yankees' second baseman Tony Lazzeri at 33 points and the Browns' outfielder Heinie Manush at 31. Simmons was joined in the voting by fellow A's Dykes and Foxx, the latter who had a marvelous season but received just eight votes along with Dykes. The National League honors, awarded by the league and not the writers, went to Rogers Hornsby of Chicago.

Simmons was one of the "main cogs in the Mack pennant machine through the campaign," opined *The Sporting News*. As illustrated by his penchant for RBIs, he was a "reliable man in the pinch," not at all hindered by his stance. "Bucket hitter Al was only able to make 212 hits in the official season, so ineffective was his style of clubbing," joked *The Sporting News*. "Any pitcher who thinks he can fool Simmons because he happens to step into the bucket is apt to be sorry."[15]

His seasonal pace augured well for a bright future. Through the 1929 season, Simmons had a .356 career average and was averaging 194 hits per season. And this was only at the plate — in the field, he was as sure handed as they come. "Simmons can go back for drives and he can come in towards the infield," wrote *The Sporting News*. "He has a good arm and he is a hustler, always there fighting until the last man is retired."

Writer Westbrook Pegler wrote a column on Simmons that extolled his unorthodox approach to batting. He was "like an artist who paints swell pictures with his elbows." Perhaps overstating his case, Pegler complimented Simmons by saying he was "rated above Babe Ruth in general value."[16]

Others pointed to the impact of Cobb's mentorship on Simmons. "There is no physical resemblance between the great batsman of yesteryear and his current successor," wrote Brian Bell of the Associated Press, "and their batting styles are vastly different, but in many ways the Simmons of today reminds spectators of the Cobb of yesteryear." Simmons was just a "good hitter" when the Georgia Peach joined the A's, Bell noted, but he "dropped a bat full of base hits and Simmons picked it up. The good batsman had become a great batsman."[17]

Mack, for his part was effusive about his young club, especially Simmons and Foxx. It was a product of many years of careful planning and ballplayer evaluations. Mack said, "In the spring of 1923, I thought we had the makings of another pennant winner. We needed punch in the lineup, so our scouts dug up Al Simmons, then with Milwaukee."[18]

"Connie Mack almost robbed the cradle" to sign "Foxxy" as the manager called him, wrote Bell. "He swings from the heels and is a threat almost every time he comes to the plate."[19]

Bucketfoot Al had come a long way from his Milwaukee sandlot days. Now the challenge was winning a World Series, never an easy proposition, and certainly not when confronting one of the most potent lineups to ever emerge from the National League — the 1929 Chicago Cubs.

As the first game of the World Series approached, it had all the makings of a slugfest. The Cubs had won 98 games, finishing 10 and one-half games ahead of the Pittsburgh Pirates.

MVP second baseman Rogers Hornsby, who was acquired from the Boston Braves in an offseason deal, bashed out a .380 average with 39 home runs while topping the senior circuit with a .679 slugging percentage. The 156 runs scored by Hornsby in 1929 were the most by a right-handed batter in the National League during the twentieth century.

Center fielder Hack Wilson smashed 39 home runs, driving in 159 RBIs while batting .345; right fielder Kiki Cuyler batted .360 with 102 RBIs; left fielder Riggs Stephenson notched a .362 average with 110 RBIs. All starboard swatters, these players led a robust Chicago offense that scored 982 runs and was backed by a stalwart pitching rotation featuring 22-game winner Pat Malone.

But Simmons and his fellow A's were unfazed by the Cubs' hard-throwing hurlers. He told writers, "There are some fastball pitchers in our league, too. Sometimes you can hit the best of 'em, and sometimes you can't hit any of 'em. One thing I know, I'll be up there swinging."[20]

Some sportswriters from neutral cities saw the teams as almost perfectly balanced against each other. "So evenly matched do the teams appear on paper," wrote Lou Wollen of the *Pittsburgh Press* on the eve of the opening game, "more nearly than any World Series competitors in recent years, that the swing of breaks to one side or another has been given a prominent place in naming the ultimate winner."[21]

The odds were generally on the A's to win — 7-to-5 in the week leading up to the showdown, and 6-to-5 around game time.

With the Series opening in Chicago on October 8, Windy City fans geared up for a hard-fought contest. "The full-throated roar of 50,000 fans is expected to resound in Wrigley Field," predicted one writer, adding that "so keen was the enthusiasm" that hundreds of fans waited through the night for bleacher seat tickets that went on sale at 8 A.M. the morning of the game. What fans witnessed in that opening game defied expectations.

Because seven of the eight regulars in the Cubs batting order hit right-handed, the only exception being first baseman Charlie Grimm, Connie Mack shocked everyone by naming right-hander Howard Ehmke as the Game One starter. Shrewdly, Mack had placed Ehmke in the stands at various Cubs games during the end of season to study the Cub's hitters — anonymously. The manager seemed to think the pitcher had done his homework.

But the 35-year-old Ehmke, by any stretch of the imagination, was not the best A's pitcher, or even a good one at that point. The rumored Game One starter, George Earnshaw, a right-hander too, had won 24 games with a blazing but sometimes erratic fastball. Babe Ruth once said of Earnshaw, "I used to send a taxicab to the Almanac Hotel the day he was gonna pitch. I didn't want him to get lost on the way to the stadium."22

Ehmke, by comparison, had won only seven games that season, pitched only two complete games and a total of 55 innings.

Mack had decided that he would start only right-handed pitchers against the Cubs, and keep his left-handers in the bullpen — even though two of his best starters, Lefty Grove and Rube Walberg, were southpaws.

As for Simmons, before the game, he took batting practice and signed autographs for the fans in the nearby field boxes, some of whom hailed from nearby Milwaukee. "He was under great pressure of civic pride in his own work in this close proximity to his old home town," the writer Westbrook Pegler observed.23

Mack's uncanny Ehmke strategy paid off, as the pitcher beat the Cubs' Charlie Root in a 3–1 victory — thanks to a Foxx homer — before a crowd of 50,740. He not only pitched well, but he set a then–Series record by fanning 13 Cubs.

One of the Chicago natives in attendance at the game was 9-year-old John Paul Stevens, who would grow up to become a U.S. Supreme Court Justice. A diehard Cubs fan, Stevens later said, "And that was my first game, a tragic game for a young boy to go and see in person."24

Simmons, who went hitless in the game, spun the Ehmke start adroitly in a ghostwritten newspaper column for the World Series. "What a game Ehmke pitched. I'll tell you honestly that at no time did I feel that we would lose. Howard had all the stuff he needed in the clinches," Simmons wrote. He noted that Ehmke stymied Chicago's great sluggers, Rogers Hornsby and Hack Wilson. Though Wilson would have his problems fielding later in the series, he snagged a hard drive off of Simmons' bat that left the A's outfielder in awe. "Wilson is a nifty centerfielder," Simmons wrote. "I don't want to suggest there was any luck in that catch he made off me. I know that it was a brilliant piece of fielding, but I think I can say I was collared in my first big match because Hack turned in a sensational play."25

But did Simmons really support Mack's decision to start Ehmke? No, not according to more candid statements he made years later: "Queerest thing any man ever saw on a ball field. We had a meeting in the clubhouse before we went on the field. Connie gave a little talk — just general stuff— and then asked Eddie Collins a few words ... Connie tells Grove, Earnshaw and Walberg not to do anything. That means one of them is going to start, but Connie hasn't made up his mind yet. When we all went out, (Howard) Ehmke stayed in alone with Connie, and said, 'Where do I stand?' Connie says to him, 'Howard I want you to pitch one game — just one game.'"

Simmons and others were stunned. As Simmons later recalled, he was sitting on the bench next to Mack when he saw Ehmke warming up, and said, "You don't mean that guy is going to work for us?" "What's the matter," Mack said. "Don't you like him?" "Like him?" Simmons told his manager, "I feel sick to the stomach." And then, "Well, if you like him that's enough."

Simmons recalled he said to himself, "I was pretty sure someone was crazy, and it wasn't Al Simmons," and he prepared for the worst as he took the field. "I just stared in horror when I saw he was going to pitch, and he went out there and made 'em look silly. Made me look silly, too," he said.[26]

Mack gambled, surprised everyone, and won. Mack's thinking, however, was in line with anecdotal accounts of the Cubs' devastation on southpaws. Statistics were not kept back then of platoon splits — but the writers covering the games day in and day out noticed. "There is no denying that Chicago's 'murderers row' has been death on left-handers," wrote Bert Demby, who said many of his counterparts in the press thought the Cubs would feast on Grove and Walberg. "(Chicago) has put fear into the hearts of National League portsiders."[27]

Game Two of the World Series was played in much more blustery conditions in Chicago. Earnshaw was chosen to start for Philadelphia, and Pat Malone for Chicago.

John Kieran of the *New York Times* wrote that Simmons mused if there was a rule against "wearing overcoats in the outfield." His teammate Jimmy Dykes suggested building fire in the infield to keep warm. "Chicago natives said the wind was coming in off Lake Michigan, but it felt as if it were coming out of Baffin Bay," the sea connecting the Atlantic and Arctic oceans.

In the first inning, Simmons was called out on strikes by umpire Bill Dinneen. Now hitless in five Series at-bats, he complained profusely and took his hat and drew a diagram of the plate in the dirt to show the umpire. Yet he did not get tossed out of the game.[28]

In the bottom of the first, Chicago shortstop Woody English rapped a double down the left field line after Mack had waved Simmons, who was playing left, toward center. In the bottom of the second, Simmons did some "fast fielding," Kieran wrote, in holding Chicago first baseman Charlie Grimm's knock down the left-field line to a single. "He had to go over into foul territory to retrieve it," Kieran observed. "But he ferried it back to second so fast that Grimm never even faked an advance to that station."[29]

The next inning, the A's came alive. Foxx clubbed a three-run homer in the third, and Simmons added a two-run shot in the eighth inning. Simmons wound up going 2-for-4 with four RBIs in a 9–3 victory, though the Cubs knocked out Earnshaw in the third inning; Grove came in and shut down Chicago afterwards.

It was especially satisfying to beat the ornery Malone, who had apparently been bragging to the local press about how he intended to mow down the A's. Westbrook Pegler described Malone: "He stands up there on the rise of the ground, kinks himself somewhat, unkinks and lets fly like 250 pounds of determined woman throwing a sugar bowl in an old-fashioned family disagreement."[30]

Two games up, the A's were feeling cocky. Some of them were seen leaving Wrigley Field with "wide grins" and a "jaunty manner" that spoke of "supreme confidence," according to one sportswriter. Now, they were headed home to Philadelphia in the "depressing chill of the gray October day" amid talk of a possible sweep against the powerful Cubs. This made Chicago manager Joe McCarthy upset and reluctant to expound on anything. "What is there to say?" he quipped when cornered by the press. "We lost, and that is all I can say. I'd like to talk more to you, but I'm really in a hurry."[31]

While McCarthy may have been at a loss for words, the chatter about the Series was going nationwide. Radio broadcasting of the World Series opened up the game to fans like never before. It all began back in 1921 when KDKA in Pittsburgh started covering Pittsburgh Pirate games. By 1924, WMAQ of Chicago was broadcasting home games of the Chicago Cubs and White Sox.

Fans in cities around the country followed the 1929 World Series on the radio, as the *New York Times* observed. Dramatic plays and clouts made the medium even more spellbinding. "The home run still is the biggest thrill maker in baseball, judging from the effects that Jimmy Foxx and Al Simmons's four-baggers in yesterday's game," a writer noted the reactions of fans gathered near radio stores, in Madison Square Garden in New York City and elsewhere. "The radio listeners seemed to be moved to follow the lead of the crowd at Wrigley Field," the *Times* noted, and fans expressed "cheers" and "groans" as the game unfolded.[32]

Two days later, with 29,921 fans crammed into Shibe Park, the A's looked to cement their Series lead while Chicago hoped to bounce back. That the Cubs did, winning 3–1 behind the strong pitching of Guy Bush. Simmons had been held hitless, Foxx had been shut down, and Jimmy Dykes had made a critical error. Simmons, in his syndicated newspaper column, said all the right things and took the blame. "Nobody on my club looked worse than I did. My own failure to hit with men on bases was one of the reasons for our defeat. It so happened that there were men on the sacks each of the four times I had a chance at the plate."[33]

The A's bench jockeys rode the Cubs mercilessly. Mule Haas was the "ace of the jockies," Simmons recalled years later. "He was the best and could back it all up, too. That World Series with the Cubs in '29 he roiled the Cubs relentlessly."[34]

Chicago's win put them back in the hunt, and set the stage for one of the greatest comebacks in World Series history. In Game Four, the Cubs took an early 8–0 lead on the strong arm of Charlie Root, who had held the A's to just three hits by the seventh inning.

Then it began. In the A's turn at bat in the bottom of the seventh inning, Simmons started off by walloping a monstrous home run that bounced off Shibe Park's left-field roof. That made it 8–1— but there was little anxiety in the Cubs dugout.

Jimmie Foxx followed with a single, and right fielder Bing Miller then popped what looked like a routine fly ball into center field. With the bright

Al Simmons is greeted by Jimmie Foxx (facing camera) as he crosses home plate in the seventh inning in the fourth game of the 1929 World Series against the Chicago Cubs. The A's, down 8–0 to the Cubs, went on to score a record 10 runs in the inning to win the game 10–8. They eventually won the World Series four games to one. *Philadelphia Athletics Historical Society*

sun streaming down, the Cubs' center fielder Hack Wilson positioned himself to make the catch, but suddenly lost the ball — and it fell in for a single.

Next, Dykes banged out a single, scoring Foxx. With the score 8–2 and two A's on base, the Philadelphia crowd began to stir. A's shortstop Joe Boley then delivered another run-scoring single, the fifth straight hit off Root, cutting the Cubs' lead to five runs with still no one out.

A popout to short by the next batter, George Burns only provided temporary relief for Chicago. The next batter, Max Bishop, lined a single over Root's head to drive in Dykes. Now it was 8–4. With only one out and Mule Haas strolling to the plate, McCarthy replaced the struggling Root with Art Nehf, a crafty 37-year-old left-hander who had won games for the New York Giants in four consecutive World Series earlier in the decade.

But Nehf had none of that magic left, as Haas drove one of his pitches to center field where Wilson amazingly again lost the ball in the sun. The ball shot past him and rolled to the fence, as Boley, Bishop and even Haas scored on the play. The misplay-turned-inside-the-park-home-run sent the Philadelphia crowd into a frenzy, as the A's were now trailing by just one run, 8–7.

Mickey Cochrane drew a walk and McCarthy went to the bullpen again, looking for a pitcher who could get him two outs. He called upon John "Sheriff" Blake to face Simmons, who ripped the Sheriff's first pitch down the third base line. As Chicago third baseman Norm McMillan reached for the ball, it took a bad bounce over his head for a single. Foxx drilled his club's seventh single of the inning, scoring Cochrane to tie the game, 8–8.

A perplexed McCarthy summoned Pat Malone, the Game Two starter, to replace Blake. But Malone only got the Cubs into more trouble by hitting Miller with a pitch, loading the bases. That brought up Dykes, who rammed a double to the fence in left. Two runs scored, putting the A's ahead, 10–8. Finally, Malone whiffed Boley and Burns, ending the bloodbath. Simmons, Foxx and Dykes each had two hits in the inning.

Stunned, the Cubs went down meekly the rest of the way, and the A's won their third game and stood to close out the Cubs with one more victory in Game Five.

It was one of the wildest innings ever in World Series history. The 10 runs established the record for the most runs scored in one World Series inning (Detroit in 1968 would also score 10 runs in the third inning of Game Six). The A's eight-run deficit comeback remains the largest in Series history.

A young Carmen Cangelosi of Philadelphia recalled years later sitting in Mason's Dance Hall and listening to that seventh inning of Game Four on the radio. "That inning made me a baseball fan for life," said Cangelosi, who became a graphic artist. "I was an Athletics fan for life. I still know all the players. I know where they played. I know their nicknames: Bucketfoot Al.

Double X. Old Reliable. Lefty. Mule. I know that 10-run inning and who scored and how they scored. Just like it was yesterday at Mason's. I remember when they won the World Series," Cangelosi said. "There was a buzz in the air. An energy. You felt good about yourself, about your city, about everybody around you."[35]

After the game, the A's clubhouse went crazy. Mack "shivered with emotion" and congratulated his team. "There isn't anything in baseball history to compare it to. It was the greatest display of punch and fighting ability I've ever seen on the ball field."

In the opposing clubhouse, the players sulked, none more so than Hack Wilson, as the Associated Press noted: "Hack Wilson, the gallant, chunky powerhouse of the Cubs, muttered to himself as he changed his clothing. He fought with his shoelaces, pulled his hat down over his eyes and stalked from the room.... He was heartbroken and burning with pent-up rage at the same time. Up to the final innings today, Hack was the hitting, fielding hero of the Bruins. Today he lost two crucial fly balls in the sun."[36]

McCarthy blamed it on bad luck — the worst he had ever seen. "The breaks of the game beat us today."[37]

Simmons, who went 2-for-5 with two RBIs, confidently predicted the A's would win Game Five and the championship. "When the World Series started, I had some sort of a hunch that the Athletics would win the title in five games."[38]

Sunday was an off day — the state of Pennsylvania did not allow baseball on the Sabbath. But Philadelphia was abuzz with anticipation. "It is just as well that Sunday baseball is not permitted in Philadelphia," the Associated Press reported. "If the A's and Cubs had gone out to play today, a world of conversation would have been a total loss. In hotel lobbies and on street corners, Philadelphia fairly buzzed with post-mortems of Saturday's record-breaking World Series game. Most of the spectators, too, were in a state of collapse" by the end of the seventh inning.[39]

Once Game Five got underway, the Cubs actually took control of matters, with Malone back on the mound. "Malone could throw real hard, and he was throwing very well," Cubs shortstop Woody English recalled. "All we needed was three more outs and we were back in Chicago for the last two games. It looked like we had it salted away."[40] With the Cubs up 2–0 in the bottom of the ninth inning, when the A's once again staged a comeback. Mule Haas banged out a home run with Max Bishop aboard to tie the game. Then Simmons smacked a double and scored the winning run when Bing Miller drove him in with a single. The A's won the game 3–2 — and hoisted their first World Series championship in 16 years.

Simmons, who had hit .300 for the Series (6-for-20) with two homers and five RBIs, expressed a sense of disbelief after the last game. "I don't know just what did happen in the ninth inning of that game today which made the Athletics champions of the world. I was so beside myself with joy that I guess I was in some sort of a trance ... Miller is a real timely hitter. And that is where I faded right out of the picture. I do remember dancing around down there at second base and trying to get Miller to look at me. I felt sure that my pal would come through. I wanted to offer encouragement. What happened thereafter is not very clear to me. I recall that I was in the thick of the crowd, with wild men near the home plate when I scored the winning run. But I don't know what I did or said."[41]

Crossing the plate to win the game, he added, was the "greatest thrill" he ever had. He said Haas and Miller played the best of all the Athletics. Haas hit only .238 but with two home runs and six RBIs. Miller posted a .368 average with four runs batted in, and Foxx (.350) hit two home runs with five RBIs.

Al Simmons said, "Our hitting was hard and timely, our pitching tight, our fielding excellent on the while. There were no missing cylinders in our machine."

It was a heartbreaking defeat for the Cubs. Their only World Series championships came in 1907 and 1908. But more distressing for the 1929 club was how they lost — by relinquishing comfortable leads in both of the last two games.

It was a hard-fought battle. Simmons acknowledged the rampant bench jockeying that had taken place. "Of course, there was some riding of players on both teams, but it was harmless joshing and left no ill feelings."

Mack received Simmons' most lavish compliments. "The bulk of the credit for our triumph should go to Connie Mack. He is a clever manager and a wonderful boss. I don't think we could have won without his smart and kindly handling of the team."[42]

Finally, after years of adroit team-building, the Philadelphia Athletics had risen to the top of baseball — not an easy task in the Ruth-Gehrig era.

But few may have appreciated at the time just how good the 1929 A's were.

CHAPTER TEN

Hard Times and World Champions Again

"I see nothing in the present situation that is either menacing or warrants pessimism."
— Andrew W. Mellon, U.S. Treasury Secretary, on December 31, 1929

"Baseball is a harbor, a seclusion from failure that really matters, a playful utopia in which virtuosity can be savored to the third decimal place of a batting average."
— Mark Kramer, SABR member[1]

Ten days after the Philadelphia A's won the 1929 World Series, with the city and the fans still savoring the afterglow of victory, America's economy began a rapid downward spiral that would change the country forever. On October 24, after a decade of robust growth, stock prices on the New York Stock Exchange collapsed, stunning people everywhere as the market continued to fall for a full month.

The crash created a chain of events that led to the Great Depression and economic turmoil in the decade ahead — the Philadelphia A's baseball team would feel its share of pain along with countless other endeavors and enterprises across the country. The coming storms lay just beyond the horizon — and they would be ferocious. People lost their homes and jobs in droves, and by the 1930s, shantytowns consisting of wood and cardboard began popping up throughout the United States.

The social ferment of the 1920s — dubbed the Jazz Age, the Age of Intolerance, and Decade of Decadence — was historic by any stretch. In the process, America had become the richest nation on earth, as a culture of consumerism and materialism was born.

On the eve of a new decade, all that energetic optimism and materialism was coming to an end — now, it all seemed built on a house of greedy cards, and the new decade would be one based on gritty survival and resourcefulness. But people got hurt in many ways, as did baseball, too. In Philadelphia, the A's were on top of the world, but they had the misfortune of becoming a dynasty just as the nation's worst economic crisis was settling in.

Al Simmons was spared a huge financial loss because he forgot to deposit two checks for $3,000 each that winter when banks around the country were shutting down, cutting off customers from their bank accounts. Before he could get around to making the deposits, his bank had collapsed, closing its doors to all, who lost their money in these pre–FDIC days.[2]

Over the grim winter, Simmons went back to Milwaukee as was his routine. He enjoyed a bout of rabbit hunting near Eagley, Wisconsin, with his friend Ralph Shinners.[3]

Simmons also spent time tutoring his younger brother, Walter, on how to play baseball. By spring, Walter found himself in the Cleveland Indians spring training camp. He made one headline — "Al Simmons' Kid Brother is a Star with Cleveland" — when he knocked in four runs in a 6–4 Cleveland victory over the New Orleans Regulars. But he did not make the club's roster for the season.[4]

Records are sparse, but they show that Walter played as a second baseman in 1930 and 1931 in the minor leagues — he hit .306 for Frederick in the Blue Ridge League, a Class D league, and .214 for Terra Haute in the Illinois-Indiana-Iowa Class B League.

Like his big brother, Walter employed a "bucket foot" batting style, according to writer Westbrook Pegler, who dubiously attributed it to genetics. "It seems that this family trait comes down to the boys from the time when their recent ancestors, armed only with pick handles and spades, fought off the Cossacks in the streets of Warsaw," wrote Pegler. "They had to be ready to run as they swung, which probably accounts for that foot in the bucket stance."[5]

His other brother, Anthony, also played baseball, but chose to become a firefighter instead. Decades later, after *Sports Illustrated* had published its article on the A's dynasty, this letter arrived from a reader:

> Dear Editor:
>
> Aloysius Harry Szymanski was my grandpa Anthony Szymanski's brother. I grew up hearing all about the A's and Al from grandpa. I wish grandpa were here to enjoy this, too. My grandpa used to tell me that during the Depression, he chose a year-round job with the Milwaukee fire department at $100 a month over baseball at $150 a month for six months of the year. After he died, we found press clippings he had saved saying that he would be joining his brother Al in the big leagues if he kept playing the way he was, and we found an unsigned Class D contract these days, I've been told.
>
> Steven Szymanski
> Stevens Point, Wisconsin

Hard times or not, big brother Al Simmons thought the time was right in 1930 to ask for a pay raise. He had been the best player on the A's the past five years, and had willingly submitted to the club's salary offers. This time he did not sign the contract when it arrived that January.

So he held out that spring, missing the A's entire training period in Florida. He stayed instead in Hot Springs, Arkansas, where he took baths to help his sporadic rheumatism and played some ball with the Minneapolis Millers of the American Association, which was training in Arkansas. Simmons took part in about 15 games between the Millers and another squad from neighboring Little Rock. After the spring training season ended, the A's went back to Philadelphia, still without Simmons.

Connie Mack: "When Mr. Simmons returned his contract unsigned in January, I did not think that we would have any trouble in signing him because the tone in his letters led me to believe that we would come to a satisfactory agreement.... Then when Mr. Simmons arrived in Philadelphia, after we held a conference with him pertaining to his contract, I found it impossible to come to an agreement with him."[6]

On the eve of the season opener, the press was still unsure whether Mack and Simmons would come to terms. He was reportedly asking for a $35,000 contract. "His absence leaves a big gap in the Athletics' lineup," rued one writer.[7]

Simmons had arrived in the city a few days before the date of the first game. Meanwhile, the A's split the city exhibition series with the Philadelphia Phillies, winning the first game, 13–1, and losing the second, 8–4.[8]

According to Sam Murphy, the *New York Sun* writer, the holdout was "all hokum," as Simmons was intent on playing the season opener. Indeed, on the morning of the April 15 opener against the New York Yankees, he phoned Connie Mack who suggested that his star take a taxi—at the club's expense—to Shibe Park. Once there, Simmons signed his contract—estimated at $22,500—and headed to the clubhouse to suit up for the game.[9]

The crowd roared their affection for the "familiar, long-sleeved" slugger as took left field for the first inning. One sportswriter in the press box reportedly quipped to another, "Who does he think he is? The U.S. Marines going to the rescue?"[10]

In the A's half of the first inning, Simmons clubbed the first pitch he saw for a two-run home run to help drive his team to eventual victory over the Yankees. Some said it was the "most thunderous ovation" he had received by that point in his career.[11]

Later, Simmons said, "If I had disappointed that crowd, I would never have had the nerve to face them again. I'll never forget that greeting. I thought the stands were coming down. I simply had to do something in return. When

I saw the ball in the first inning coming straight down the groove, well, I just had to hit for that crowd out there."[12]

His heroics reminded writer Will Wedge that Philadelphia fans were mercurial in their emotions toward ballplayers. Wedge cited the case of Chick Galloway, a once-heralded shortstop with the Athletics from 1919 to 1927 who batted a high of .324 in 1922.

"The fans liked Chick at first," wrote Wedge. "He went along with the A's in pretty good favor for some years. Then he got to letting grounders through him and the fans got on him. They climbed on Mr. Galloway plenty. They made his life miserable. And his value as a member of the A's deteriorated."

In 1926, Galloway made 41 errors in 133 games and followed that up the next year by making 15 errors while mostly playing part-time in 77 games. Afterwards, the A's sold him to the Milwaukee Brewers in the American Association. But before he even arrived in Milwaukee, Galloway found out he'd been traded to the Detroit Tigers. One day in batting practice Galloway was struck in the head with a pitched ball, which fractured his skull.

Over the next two years Galloway's recovery was slow at best — he suffered memory loss, dizzy spells and a speech impediment. A small piece of bone was removed from his skull during an operation. It seemed he was in no condition to play baseball ever again.

In the spring of 1930, Connie Mack invited Galloway and his family to the A's spring training in Fort Myers. "The Florida climate and the comradeship with the A's restored his spirits and it wasn't long before he was out practicing. He fielded like a flash and showed in batting practice that he was not plate shy," wrote Wedge.

Mack kept Galloway with the team as it headed north for Opening Day. Though unsigned, Galloway was seen as a possible substitute for the regular shortstop Joe Boley, who had weathered an arm injury the prior season. As it turned out, Galloway was not placed on the roster, though Mack and the A's invited him on the field for Opening Day, where he received a standing ovation from the fans early that season. "The fans are fickle in Philadelphia," Wedge observed. "If they can change quickly from cheers to boos it is consoling to think they can also change from catcalls to the clamorous cries of friendship."[13]

Aside from Galloway, the spotlight early that spring focused on Simmons and his all-around ability. "He is the best outfielder in the American League today," piped John Kieran of the *New York Times,* ranking him with Ty Cobb and Tris Speaker among the game's elite fly chasers. "He is a fine fielder. He has a strong arm. He is fast afoot."[14]

Of course, aside from Simmons, the big story that spring was the worsening economy. As Bill Kashatus notes in his book *Connie Mack's '29 Triumph*, "No other event in the 20th century had a more profound impact on Philadelphia than the Great Depression of the 1930s."

By the time the A's took the field in April to open the season, 15 percent of Philadelphia's wage earners were unemployed, and the number was rising — neighborhoods surrounding Shibe Park reportedly had unemployment rates near 30 percent. Apple sellers were a common sight on the corners of busy intersections across the city, according to A's historian Bob Warrington. He noted that Connie Mack, showing his humanitarianism, did what he could to lessen the plight of those living near Shibe Park. "Neighborhood kids were hired to be sweepers or scorecard sellers at the ballpark. Mack would also send the leftovers that were still fresh from the concession stands to St. Joseph's Home for Boys at 16th Street and Allegheny Avenue," Warrington wrote.

The economic meltdown hindered attendance at games. The diminishing gate receipts did not bode well for A's players who, like Simmons, believed they deserved raises in 1930. "Heated negotiations over dollars and cents created tension between club officials and players, especially star players," according to Warrington.

Some, like Jimmy Dykes, got no raise at all, earning $7,000 in 1930, exactly what he was paid in 1929. Jimmie Foxx got a modest increase as part of a three-year contract that would pay him $50,000 over that period. Grove and Cochrane each took home about $20,000 in 1930. "Other marquee players, by comparison, like Babe Ruth and Lou Gehrig were being paid considerably more by their clubs," Warrington said.[15]

Despite the hard times, by late April all seemed forgiven in Philadelphia about Simmons' contract disagreement, though he was not always the most fan-pleasing player. He did not generally like to sign autographs for adults — though he did so for children — and he did not speak often at baseball banquets in the offseason. Rather, he preferred hanging out with people he knew — not large crowds or strangers.[16]

Sportswriters sought to know him — but often displayed a surprising lack of knowledge about the most basic facts. One newspaper account stated that his real name was "Albert Harry Schmanski." Wrong, but they correctly listed his address as 772 American Avenue in Milwaukee.[17]

Not one to indulge writers anyways, Simmons preferred to be known by his results in the box scores. On April 19, he muscled two home runs, a double, single and four RBIs against Washington in a 9–0 victory. He was off to a good start — a week later, he average stood at .407.

If the economy was down in 1930, offense was up in baseball — to historic highs. Maybe there was an ulterior motive to make the games more exciting with more run scoring. By April 29, many people suspected that the 1930 ball was juiced somehow. On that day, a stunning 123 runs were scored in just seven major league games—more than 17 total for each game.

The offensive barrage would continue through the summer, and by the end of the season, American League hitters sported a .288 average overall while their counterparts in the National League players went even further, putting up a ridiculous .303 average. Across both leagues, the total number of home runs shot up from 1,349 in 1929 to 1,565 in 1930.

The Athletics joined in the bashing bonanza, reaching double digits in runs scored (and against) early that spring—11–6 against Washington on April 27; 19–2 against Detroit on May 1; 13–7 against Cleveland on May 12 (the A's lost 25–7 the day before); and 14–7 against Chicago on May 13.

While the A's pitchers were also taking their share of the league-wide offensive beating, the team stood 17–7 by May 13. Simmons was dishing out plenty of timely hits. On May 3, he blasted a two-run double in the ninth inning, and two days later, his leadoff homer in the bottom of the 12th won the game.

That season witnessed what he considered his greatest clutch performance. Years later, Al Simmons frequently regaled sportswriters and others about his exploits in a Memorial Day doubleheader against the Washington Senators in Philadelphia.

On that day (May 30), Philadelphia was looking up at the Senators, who were in first place by four games. Both teams seemed primed for the early season showdown. Washington sent pitchers Ad Liska and Bump Hadley into Philadelphia 48 hours ahead of the team so they could get rested for the games.

Simmons later expressed his bravado to writer John Carmichael, showing his customary disdain for the opposing pitcher, who happened to be second-year hurler Ad Liska. "Liska was one of those semi-underhanded pitchers with a little of this and that, but not much of anything," said Simmons.

But Liska had the A's off stride for most of the game. In the bottom of the ninth, Washington was ahead 6–3 when the hitless Simmons came up to bat with two men on and two outs. He had looked so bad in his previous at-bats that some A's fans were calling for a pinch-hitter. Simmons later said, "Those Philly fans could be tough."

Liska threw Simmons a pitch that he would never forget. "The ball was right in there and didn't break. I really swung." And he smoked it. The ball landed in the left-field seats; Simmons had tied the game with his mighty swat. He was not finished. In the eleventh inning, he singled again, but was left stranded. In the thirteenth inning, he doubled. When the next hitter, Jimmie Foxx, smacked a hit, Simmons rounded third base but scrambled back awkwardly on a strong throw from the outfield, severely straining his knee.

He was hurting. When Eric McNair hit a single to left, Simmons, in pain, rambled across home plate with the winning run.

In the clubhouse before the start of the second game, the A's physician — a "Dr. Carnett," according to Simmons — examined the slugger's knee and found he had ruptured a blood vessel. "It hurt," said Simmons, who was told by Mack he could not start the second game and should probably be taken to the hospital. But Carnett gave Mack some leeway, according to Simmons. The doctor had told Mack, "Maybe later, but not now. Al shouldn't play but let him sit on the bench. If the spot to pinch hit should come up, use him."

Indeed, that is what happened. In the bottom of the fourth, Mack called upon Simmons to pinch-hit for Spencer Harris with Philadelphia down 7–4. The bases were loaded. (It was not the seventh, as Simmons had told Carmichael — not quite as dramatic, in other words, as he would claim years later). To face the hobbled Simmons, Washington brought in journeyman reliever Garland Braxton.

Al Simmons: "Suddenly I saw Connie look down the line and crook that finger at me. 'Walk around the bases if you can,' Mack said. I picked out a bat, and there I was for the second time in the same day in the clutch. Hadley (actually Braxton) seemed to take a long time and finally pitched, and it was outside for a ball. He tried another in the same spot, and I let it go."

Simmons blasted the ball into the left-field stands — for a grand slam home run and second circuit clout of the day. Wincing in pain, he barely made it around the bases. When he got back to the bench, Connie's eyes "were bright like a birds," said Simmons, who would smack 10 grand slams in his 20-year career. Philadelphia went on to win the game, 15–11. After the hoopla died down in the A's clubhouse, Simmons was finally taken to the hospital for overdue treatment on his knee.[18]

The day really stuck out in Simmons' memory, and for good reason. On his self-proclaimed "greatest day," he had gone 4-for-8 with two round trippers and 7 RBIs. He was now hitting .386 and looking for his first batting title — but in a league dominated by heavy hitters in the wildest offensive year ever.

With the knee injury, he missed the next seven games, staying behind in Philadelphia as the A's went on the road. At the University of Pennsylvania's hospital, a physician punctured the knee to reduce the swelling and reopened it a few days later. "Al said Monday he was feeling fine," one report stated.

On June 7, Simmons rejoined the team in Chicago, his knee tightly bandaged. He did not want to miss the series against the White Sox because many of his Milwaukee fans were expected to make the trip to Chicago to watch him play.

In the first game against the White Sox, Simmons went hitless in a pinch-hitting appearance. The next day Mack inserted him into his familiar cleanup spot in the lineup. So many of his hometown fans were in attendance that one scribe joked it was "Al Simmons Day At Comiskey Park." Simmons lived up to expectations. "Doughty Al, sterling champion of the World Champion Athletics, showed some 200 Milwaukeeans why he deserves their admiration" by banging out an RBI-single in a 6–3 A's victory, chimed the newspaper. Then misfortune struck again.

In the final game of a series against Chicago, Simmons rushed in to cut off a single to the outfield. He had hopes of nailing the runner headed to the plate when one of his legs suddenly buckled and he fell to the grass—now his left ankle was injured.

Simmons missed the next round of games with Cleveland and Detroit. One account described his second injury that summer as a "crushing blow to the morale of the players" at a time when the A's were also missing Jimmy Dykes. Philadelphia lost five straight games in a mild June swoon.[19]

Still, the aching Simmons was at .389 on June 14, only five points behind Washington's Sam Rice in the batting title hunt. Once he got back in the lineup June 18, he exploded—12-for-24 with four home runs, a triple and three doubles—helping the A's to victory in 13 of their next 15 games.

Back in those days, the baseball press covered the batting average race almost as much as the pennant chase. "Big Six Batters" was a regularly syndicated column in the sporting pages, and each day the ups or downs of these hitters were chronicled with enthusiasm or apoplexy.

On June 23, Simmons had one of his best games of the season, walloping two homers with five hits and five RBIs in a 17–9 A's stomping of Chicago as Philadelphia swept a doubleheader. This pushed him up to .405.

With inflated batting averages like that and double-digit scores popping up all over, followers of the game were both awed and concerned. Had the game changed? "Modern day baseball," wrote Orlo Robertson of the Associated Press, "with its lively ball, home runs and two-figured scores, was exhibited to Mr. John Public in large quantities" on June 23. That day witnessed 256 hits, 159 runs and 20 home runs in 11 games played in both leagues. Chicago's Hack Wilson led the attack with his 22nd homer in a 21–8 clobbering of the Phillies. The stout slugger would go on to set an all-time RBI record of 191 and a then-NL record with 56 home runs.[20]

As for the crosstown Phillies, they could hit well enough, but their pitching was among the worst ever. Right fielder Chuck Klein received attention as one of the game's best hitters. Playing in the cozy confines of the Baker Bowl, Klein already had 24 homers with a .400-plus average by midsummer.

Sportswriter Walter Trumbull said, "You hear a lot of conversation concerning Babe Ruth, Al Simmons, Babe Herman, Bill Terry, and a lot more hitters, but you don't hear much about Chuck Klein." Trumbull said that when people do speak of Klein, who was "busting the horsehide" that season, they attributed his accomplishments to the hitter-friendly Baker Bowl. But Trumbull argued that he was more of an all-around hitter than one might assume: "Klein is just a natural clouter. For every home run he has made, he has slammed out about four other hits that were not home runs. The opposing infield plays just about the same in a small park as in a large one."[21]

As for Simmons, his legs were feeling better by July 25. That day the Athletics pulled off triple steals twice in one game against the Indians. Simmons, Bing Miller, and Dib Williams stole bases in the first inning, and Cochrane, Simmons, and Foxx stole in the fourth.

On August 4, Simmons even legged out two triples and whacked a home run as Lefty Grove notched his 17th win in the A's 13–4 victory over Boston. Not bad for a guy on the mend from ankle and knee trouble.

In those years, Simmons may have had some assistance at the plate from Eddie Collins, then a third base coach for the A's. "Sign stealing can give you a lot of help. Eddie Collins was our third base coach, and Eddie was as good as they came. He wouldn't always give the hitter the sign — only when he was sure. I hit many a long ball because he had told a fastball was coming down the alley," Simmons said.[22]

Simmons, going into a Labor Day doubleheader with the Yankees, found himself battling Lou Gehrig for the batting title — both were looking for their first batting title. The good news was that Philadelphia was in first place — New York was in third. "The White Elephants are sitting on top of the ladder, their spikes sunk deep into first place," wrote Harold Burr of the *Brooklyn Eagle*.

And so, eyes were upon the players, and for the day, at least, Gehrig outpaced Simmons. The Iron Horse had three hits in five at-bats to Simmons' one in eight at-bats, though he won the first game with that lone hit, a homer. By the end of the day, Gehrig was nine points ahead of Simmons, and his "smile spread when he read the batting figures after the doubleheader," Burr observed.

Simmons and Gehrig were quite different at the plate, Burr maintained. New York's left-handed first baseman drove the ball with "ease and horsepower" while half the time Simmons was off balance and reaching awkwardly across the plate with his strong arms, he claimed. "But Simmons gets the same results as the orthodox Gehrig," noted Burr, adding that at least the pair were alike in their "noisy, rough and kidding ways" in the dugout, which is somewhat of an eye-opening observation, as Gehrig has a latter-day reputation of a quiet ballplayer.[23]

But Gehrig was making noise that September, and by the sixth day of the month, he and Simmons were tied at .385. From there, it was neck-to-neck down to the wire.

Along the way, Simmons added to his reputation as a clutch performer. Described as the "slugger most apt to break up a ball game on short notice," opponents hated to see him at the plate in a big moment. "Rival managers and pitchers have no hesitation in saying that they would rather see any member of the A's except Simmons come up to the plate in a pinch," wrote Alan Gould.[24]

The writer Munro Elias called him the "consistently brilliant Al Simmons" who is a "tremendous hitter and a fast, dependable fielder," an "invaluable factor" in Philadelphia's attack. Despite his "bucketfoot" critics, he has "developed with rapid strides" and is "one of the most dangerous batsmen in either league."[25]

Midway into the month, the A's held a tight grip on first place. On September 18, they clinched the pennant with a 14–10 win over Chicago. Simmons had three hits, including a double and his 36th homer, his last of the year. The Sox had tied the game, 9–9, in the ninth inning when Simmons moved too slow in retrieving a line drive that went into the left-field corner. When he came back to the bench after the side was retired, third baseman Jimmie Dykes chewed him out. "If you're the left fielder, play like one. You could have throw him out if you tried," yapped Dykes. Simmons and Dykes argued until Mack, in a rare burst of profanity, said, "Dykes, shut your goddamned mouth!" Both players were stunned. "We sure got the old man riled," said Simmons. "Yea, did you hear that 'goddamn?'" said Dykes. Mack, as the players ran back on the field, turned to someone and said, "You know what those two are saying? They're gloating over getting the 'old man' mad."[26]

Simmons had a batting championship to win, and Mack agreed not to rest him during the last week of play before the World Series. Simmons nudged his average up from .379 to a final mark of .381 while Gehrig fell a tad to finish at .379. Al Simmons had won his long-sought batting crown — the first Athletic to do so since Nap Lajoie hit .426 in 1901.

Some say 1930 was Simmons' best year, despite his playing in only 138 games. Along with his 36 homers, he drove in 165 runs and scored a league-leading 152. He tied his career high of 392 total bases, slugged a career high .708, and banged out 211 hits, 41 doubles and 16 triples. He only struck out 34 times.

His feisty temperament and deadly bat were a lethal combination for opposing hurlers. "The climbing Pole was stubborn," noted writer John Kieran, adding that pitchers told him that "the most dangerous batsman in their circuit answers to the name of Al Simmons."[27]

Elsewhere on the Athletics, Foxx smashed 37 homers along with 156 RBIs while hitting .356; Cochrane batted .357; Bing Miller drove in 100 runners with a .303 average; Jimmy Dykes hit .301; and Mule Haas, .299. On the mound, the stalwarts were Grove (28–5 with a 2.54 ERA, all league highs and amazing considering the offensive context) and George Earnshaw (22–13).

In the AL, each team averaged 5.4 runs scored per game, a .351 OBP and a .421 slugging average. In the NL, it was even higher — 5.7 runs scored a game per team, a .360 OBP and a .448 slugging average. (The Phillies gave up an all-time worst 7.7 runs per game.)

When one compares the Athletics rosters in 1929 and 1930, continuity in personnel stands out. In the starting lineup, there was only one major change. Third baseman Sammy Hale, who had been with the club since 1923 but had a poor 1929, was traded to the St. Louis Browns before the season began. Dykes, who had served as a utility infielder in 1929, replaced him at third.

While the A's were ascending in the wins column, they were descending in attendance as the economy slowed. They played their home games before 118,000 fewer people in 1930 — despite their star-spangled roster.

Heading into World Series, the heavily-favored A's faced the St. Louis Cardinals, who went 92–62 under manager Gabby Street. This team could hit, too. St. Louis scored 1,002 runs on the exploits of second baseman Frankie

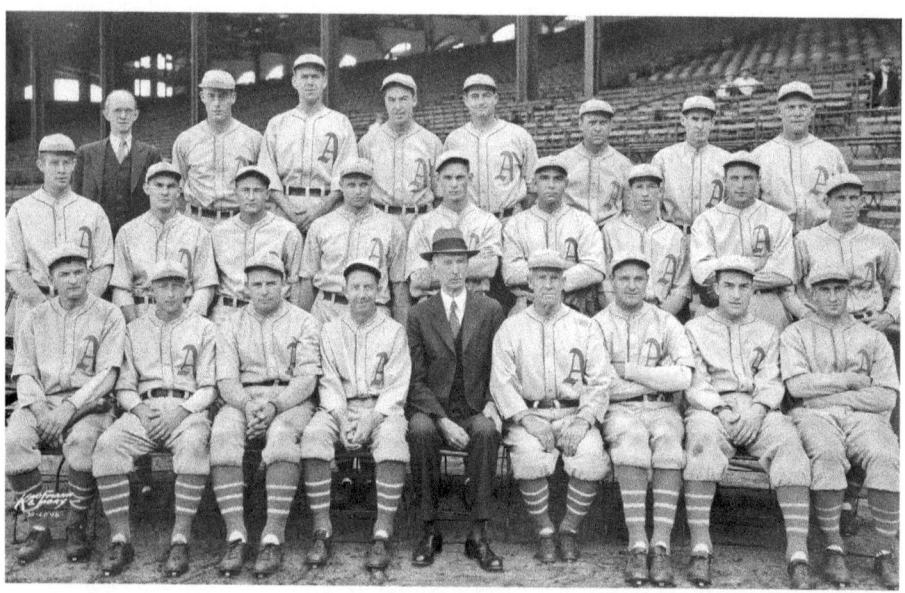

The World Champion Philadelphia A's team photograph for 1930. The A's won the series in six games, defeating the St. Louis Cardinals. Al Simmons is in the front row, second from right. *National Baseball Hall of Fame*

Ten: Hard Times and World Champions Again

Frisch, .346 and 121 runs; Chick Hafey, .336, 26 home runs and 107 RBIs; and Jim Bottomley, .304 and 97 RBIs. In fact, every starting position player had hit over .300.

When the teams held a pre–Series workout in Shibe Park, partisanship rang loud. National League president John Heydler declared, "If the Cardinals play against the A's the way they did against Brooklyn in the series that sped them to the top, I will be satisfied."

Simmons hung out after batting practice to do a "little joshing with such rivals as (Burleigh) Grimes and Bottomley."[28]

The Series opened on a chilly October 1 day in Philadelphia with 32,295 fans in attendance. Philadelphia had erected temporary seating on the tops of houses facing the park on 20th Street, though demand for tickets was down from a year ago, due to the economy. Thousands of others around the country would hear the game on CBS and NBC radio systems.

President Herbert Hoover was among the spectators, but strangely he refused to wear a heavy coat in the frigid air. The chief executive, attired in brown business suit, sat calmly throughout the game.

Before the game, the ballpark's broadcasting system spewed forth martial music, and the baseball comedy team of Nick Altrock and Al Schacht, who doubled as Washington Senator coaches, entertained the shivering crowd.

The first game went as planned for Philadelphia, with Simmons homering and Grove nailing down a 5–2 A's win over St. Louis' Grimes, renowned for his spitball pitch and cranky demeanor.

Of Simmons' clout, Grimes said, "I had that guy two balls and two strikes, so I wasted one. I threw him a bad ball wide. And what does he do? He hits it out of the park."[29]

The pitcher later said he was in bad health. It didn't help facing the A's sluggers. "My gall bladder was in awful shape. It would hurt even more when I'd look at Simmons, Foxx and some of those guys," he said.[30]

It was not all about homers and sluggers. Connie Mack called for a bold squeeze play — Joe Boley executed it perfectly, allowing Mule Haas to score. "It was a stunt that wasn't needed, but what's more important is that it had a vital psychological and technical bearing on the rest of the series," wrote one writer, who also condemned St. Louis right fielder Ray Blades as an "early goat" for letting in a run on a fly ball.[31]

In Game Two, Cochrane (home run), Simmons (double, two hits) and Foxx (double) came out swinging against Cardinals starter Flint Rehm in a 6–1 win, putting Philadelphia up two games to none.

The Series moved to St. Louis' Sportsman's Park — and momentum changed. In Game Three, the Cardinals' "Wild Bill" Hallahan shut out the A's for a 5–0 triumph. Philadelphia managed seven hits, with Simmons accounting for two of them, one of them a double, putting him at .455 for the Series.

Game Four was another low-scoring affair, as St. Louis' Jesse Haines evened the series at two games apiece with a 3–1 victory. Lefty Grove took the loss in a complete-game performance. There were just nine hits among both teams, and only two extra-base clouts (both by St. Louis). Simmons maintained his hot hitting, going 2-for-3 to reach .500.

In Game Five, A's starter George Earnshaw joined with Grove to toss a 2–0 shutout of St. Louis. It was a pitchers' duel up to the ninth inning when Cochrane squeaked out a walk in the top of the ninth. Two batters later, Foxx homered to put the A's ahead.

Simmons went hitless in four at-bats, and was "dusted off" three times in the fourth inning by Grimes, who seemingly remembered all too well the outfielder's exploits earlier in the Series. "Twice Al fell flat to avoid being hit, and one of the pitches bounced foul off his bat for an accidental strike," according to one account.

Grimes sought to intimidate the A's in other ways. "Throughout the game, Grimes engaged in a running exchange of taunts with the A's and became embroiled even with Connie Mack in one verbal tilt from the plate in the seventh inning," a writer observed.[32]

Connie Mack: "Grimes got on me when Cochrane was at bat.... The count was two and one and Mickey glanced over to the bench. I gave him the signal more openly than I usually do. Grimes, a smart fellow, caught the signal. I quickly flashed a recall. Then Grimes started shouting at me something about being a 'master mind.' The first thing I knew we were making motions at each other."[33]

Simmons factored into the dispute, as Mack noted, "It is quite possible that Grimes, who had been laughing at Simmons, did not take enough care when he threw that one across that Foxx hit into the bleachers."

Posturing aside, the A's now had a 3-to-2 Series advantage.

Mack picked Earnshaw to pitch Game Six, despite having only one day of rest. The Cardinals skipper, Gabby Street, called on the Game Three winner, Hallahan, to even the Series.

The A's struck first and hard, tagging both Hallahan and reliever Syl Johnson for two run-scoring doubles in the first, a homer by Simmons in the third and a two-run blast by Dykes in the fourth. Once again, the A's had collected a bunch of extra-base hits, and a tired Earnshaw mustered enough strength to drive the A's home to a 7–1 victory, for its second consecutive World Series championship.

Simmons was one of the key performers, hitting .364 (8-for-22), tops on the A's, with two home runs and four RBIs. Cochrane had two homers and five RBIs while Foxx had one four-base clout and a .333 average.

After the last out was made, the A's players "let out a roar that rumbled through the walls and out into the stands." Connie Mack congratulated his players, telling them "you did what I asked you to. You are really a great ball team." In the opposing clubhouse where the Cardinal players "quietly stripped away their baseball togs for another season," manager Street, said, "it was just a case of too much Earnshaw. I've got a good club, and we might of won with the breaks. We didn't get them, so the best club won this series."[34]

The win made the Philadelphia Athletics the first team in World Series history to win back-to-back championships on two different occasions. They had done so before in 1910 and 1911. Philadelphia had now won five World Series, and the franchise's final for their city until moving to Oakland where the A's have won four titles. With the 1930 championship, they were tied with the Boston Red Sox for most Series titles at that point.

Ironically, in the Year of the Hitter, the series was an extraordinarily low-scoring contest. The A's batted .197 while St. Louis hit .200. But Mack's players got the big hits, with 18 of their 35 hits going for extra bases. On the mound, Earnshaw went 2–0 with a 0.72 earned-run average in 25 innings (22 of them scoreless), and Grove won two of three decisions with a 1.42 ERA in 19 innings of work. One writer declared, "The pitching throughout the series has been by far the greatest in years."[35]

In November, Simmons went on a barnstorming trip with Jimmie Foxx and George Earnshaw. Many of the A's added to their $5,785 World Series bonus with exhibition games across the Midwest and South. They toured towns and cities in Georgia, Alabama, Mississippi, Louisiana and Texas, playing minor league and local clubs along the way. "It was a big thing in those days," said Simmons, who frequently barnstormed during off seasons.[36]

Some of the games also included contests with teams from the Negro League.[37] Author Jules Tygiel maintained in his book *Baseball's Great Experiment: Jackie Robinson and his Legacy* that Simmons did not like to play against blacks. "Several stars like Hornsby and Al Simmons refused to join barnstorming teams that played blacks," Tygiel wrote.[38] On this particular trip, it is not known if Simmons actually chose not to play against black ballplayers or not.

If Simmons was not seeing the light on the interracial issue, he saw the light on another. In what would be a preview for major league baseball four years later, he and the others played under the lights at night for an exhibition game in Peoria, Illinois. Simmons had a mixed reaction, saying that while his hitting was not affected, he had trouble seeing balls in the outfield — "the glare of the lamps"— and noted that Earnshaw had difficulty seeing Foxx's signs as the catcher.

Simmons, with a fresh batting title and another World Series championship under his belt, was in the limelight of baseball. Though writers rhapsodized about him and fans toasted him now, Simmons faced the challenge of following up success with more success — that, Connie Mack told him, is the mark of a true champion.

CHAPTER ELEVEN

"No Reason to Be Friendly"

> *"Any man who can look handsome in a dirty baseball suit is an Adonis. There is something about the baggy pants, and the Micawber-shaped collar, and the skull-fitting cap, and the foot or so of tan, or blue, or pink undershirt sleeve sticking out at the arms, that just naturally kills a man's best points."*
> — Edna Ferber, in Bush League Hero[1]

At 29, Al Simmons was one of the game's most eligible bachelors, atop the world in hitting and with championship titles in tow. Soon after the World Series ended in October, he got engaged to Dorothy Kuhn of Jenkintown, Pennsylvania, the daughter of a Philadelphia manufacturer. One of Connie Mack's daughters had apparently introduced the pair, though it is not clear when they had started dating. After the engagement, the love birds apparently flew into rocky shoals. By January, the engagement was rumored to be off. Simmons refused to comment on the press reports, other than to say, "I'll talk about anything else except my engagement."[2]

But a month later, it was official — Simmons and Dorothy were broken up. Oddly, her parents made the announcement in a way that was reflective of the cultural times — the man's reputation, not the woman's, seemed the paramount issue.

John Kuhn, the father of the would-be bride, spoke of his intense admiration for Simmons, "who I consider one of the most likable boys I have ever met ... Al will always be welcome at our home. Both my wife and myself regard him highly and nothing will ever alter our friendship for him." Kuhn said nothing about his daughter. In his rambling admiration of the would-be groom, father Kuhn almost seemed as if he would have traded Dorothy the daughter for Simmons the son-in-law. And, no reasons were given. "Dorothy and Al have decided not to marry, but to become just friends," he said.[3]

One writer wryly noted, "Al Simmons, hard-hitting outfielder of the world champion Philadelphia Athletics, is batting far below his average on the diamond" in his attempt to get married.[4]

While affection dampened in Simmons' love life, so it would as well for major league hitters in the upcoming season, thanks to some tinkering by the owners concerned about the unprecedented explosion of offense in 1930. That winter, the baseball establishment instructed the Spalding Company to change the baseballs for 1931 by using raised and long stitching and a coarser thread, all of which gave pitchers a better grip, especially in snapping out curve balls. The National League went even further, directing that Spalding thicken the horsehide covers of the balls, a move that would yield an even more precipitous drop in offense for the senior circuit.

The moves were controversial — baseball was still split on the nature of the game, though the Lively Ball era had more fans, and some unlikely ones at that. *Baseball Magazine* polled its readers and received a 957 to 451 verdict in favor of the "lively ball" game. Eddie Collins, the distinguished second baseman and now Athletics' coach, spoke up in favor of the "modern game." In the dead-ball game from about 1900 to 1920, Collins said, "you sat in the stands and admired what didn't happen and concluded that you were witnessing phenomenal pitching." Then again, Collins had a vested interest in supporting the A's powerful offense.[5]

One of the other new wrinkles involved the sacrifice fly, an oft-changed rule in major league baseball history. To that point, batters had not been charged with a time at-bat for a sacrifice hit since 1893 — but baseball has changed the sacrifice fly rule multiple times. The sacrifice fly as a statistical category was instituted in 1908, only to be discontinued in 1931. The rule was again adopted in 1939, only to be eliminated again in 1940, before being adopted for the last time in 1954. Eliminating it would affect batting averages negatively.

Simmons was disgusted by the discontinuation of the sacrifice fly rule. He complained about it loudly to writer Manning Vaughan of the *Milwaukee Journal*: "I suppose the rule makers know their business, but I think it would have been better to return to the original sacrifice fly rule rather than eliminate the rule entirely. A batter who drives in a run from third base with a long hoist to the outfield should be credited with a sacrifice."[6]

Simmons observed that Mack had instructed him numerous times to hit a fly ball long enough to score a runner from third base. He worried about falling batting averages and how the rule change would affect the record books. "Some of the boys who have a chance to better some of the old-time swat records will have a tough time," said Simmons, concerned about his own prospects of breaking hallowed records. Changing the sacrifice rule did not help.[7]

Other sacrifices of greater urgency were being made throughout the country in the winter of 1931, which witnessed the doubling of unemployment to more than 16 percent. People were beginning to realize that the stock market crash of 1929 was having profound effects. Many car manufacturers also went out of business as people did not have enough money to buy new cars.

Nature even conspired to make things worse by causing a serious drought in the Midwest, which in turn made food more expensive across America while turning some areas into gritty dust bowls.

On the other side of things, one of the year's highlights was the completion of the world's tallest building, the Empire State building, in New York City. In Las Vegas, the community there made the decision to legalize gambling. The U.S. government started making some progress on the mob, and a notable success was the conviction of Al Capone on tax fraud charges in 1931, which got him an 11-year prison sentence in Alcatraz.

With a need for national unity in these hard times, Congress adopted "The Star Spangled Banner" as the national anthem, though the custom of playing it before every baseball game began later during World War II when the installation of public address systems made it practical.

While the economy prompted tightfistedness among owners, Simmons choose to stare down the A's for a second season in a row on the subject of salary. In January, Mack sent out contracts earlier than usual to many of the players, including Simmons, Jimmie Foxx, Lefty Grove and Mickey Cochrane — Simmons did not sign his, just like the year before, though the others did.

He began his holdout by spending time in Hot Springs, Arkansas, missing most of the A's spring training in Florida. He was criticized for this by fans, writers and even other ballplayers. Simmons once explained his reasoning to the writer A.J. Schinner: "I have been accused repeatedly of being a holdout during my career when I happened to be at variance with Connie Mack over the salary question. I do not consider negotiations holding out. A man does not become a holdout until the season opens and I have found that if he has any kind of case at all and is not too exorbitant in his demands he will usually get what he wants providing he takes his contract to his manager or owner and refrains from a newspaper argument. I believe in the personal touch. It has always worked out with me, and I intend to hold to that policy."[8]

In Hot Springs, Simmons kept in shape by playing ball with minor league clubs like the Minneapolis Millers (he had three homers in a March 16 game) and some of the locals. One of them was a black youth nicknamed "Pudge." When Pudge and Simmons were tossing the medicine ball back and forth, the boy fell over his hound dog and broke the animal's leg. Simmons promised to get Pudge another hound.[9]

Simmons would not talk with reporters about his salary demands. One wrote, "No wonder every Polish kid in Milwaukee yells for a bat and ball as soon as he gets out of the romper league."[10]

Finally, Simmons signed a three-year-contract for $100,000 on April 10, making him one of the highest paid players in the game. Mack encouraged him to keep up his performance. "The challenge for a batting champion, Al, is to repeat," said Mack. "That's what Ty Cobb used to do."[11] Flushed with a big new contract, Simmons said he was "well pleased" with his talk with the "boss." Of course.[12]

The local press noticed the disparity in salary between Philadelphia's two best sluggers, Simmons and Chuck Klein, who posted awesome numbers in 1930: .386 average, 40 home runs, 170 RBIs, 59 doubles, and 250 hits. But Klein was due to receive $40,000 over three years — $60,000 less than Simmons.

"Simmons, of course, is the greatest ballplayer in the world," gushed a writer. But Klein was "very nearly as good as Al. The fates of baseball have made him a star on a tail-end team."[13]

Expectations were again high for the A's, though many insiders pointed out the difficulty of winning three titles in a row for any club. "The odds in support of the A's," wrote Alan Gould, "may not be quite as long as they were a year ago, after their 1929 stampede. Observers have detected a few creaking parts ... but there is no substantial evidence on which to dislodge the A's as favorites."[14]

But the team started slowly, losing five of their first eight games. Simmons was hitting a meek .185. The baseball press was flabbergasted — what had happened to the A's and their reigning batting champ?

The players felt "pretty glum" about their performance thus far, according to Simmons. At that point Mack called them aside and said, "We haven't done so well, but don't worry we're going to get going ... we just haven't hit yet."[15]

Laying the premature judgments aside, Simmons quickly found his groove by late April to bring his average up to .333. He continued to hit strongly and the A's started winning.

Sportswriter Edward J. Neil claimed that Simmons made some adjustments to his batting style in 1931— he may have modified his bucketfoot approach somewhat. "Now he steps forward more than he steps away, but his reputation still clings to him."[16]

Whatever adjustment he made, Simmons was getting his usual fare of big hits at the right time. On May 3, he walloped a two-run homer in the ninth inning to beat Washington, 3–1. The next day he tripled and homered as the A's beat the Senators again by the same score. Three days later, Simmons led the A's attack with five hits and two doubles in a 10–3 victory over the

Boston Red Sox. By the end of the afternoon, he had knocked out seven consecutive hits. That streak ended the next day as he (only) went 2-for-4.[17]

Around the league, Simmons drew respect. Detroit catcher Ray Hayworth said, "He had the best power to the opposite field of any hitter I saw. He used to hit the ball over the right field scoreboard like a left-handed hitter."[18]

In mid–May, Simmons boasted that the A's would once again win the pennant. "Maybe we aren't the best team in the league," he said, "but I am certain we're going to win because of Connie Mack. He has us fired up with more spirit than ever and I don't think we're going to fail him." He even compared Mack to famed Notre Dame football coach Knute Rockne for his motivational tactics. "No matter how low we feel or how tough the going is we forget about it all after our customary chats with Connie."[19]

Simmons understood that pitching was as much a reason for the A's success as their explosive lineup. In a comment that reflected how the financial shakedown had affected ballplayers, he expressed hope that lefty Rube Walberg, who posted a mediocre 13–12 record last year, would have a stellar season.

Al Simmons: "If he comes back and pitches in his real form, we ought to breeze home in front. Walberg is a great pitcher, one of the best in the game. His fastball is almost as speedy as Grove's, and when his curve is under control, it is the best left-handed hook there is in baseball. Rube is a high-strung fellow, and his financial losses affected his work last year. But he has the stuff."[20]

Walberg that season fulfilled Simmons' expectations. The 34-year-old workhorse had his best season, going 20–12 with a 3.74 ERA and league-leading 291 innings pitched.

Simmons also seemed on the brink of a career year. By May 19, he was atop the AL batting race with a .433 average, 40 points higher than anyone else. By the end of the month he had put together a 27-game hitting streak before being stymied in a 6–5 loss to Boston.

His hometown Milwaukee press was ecstatic. Manning Vaughan compared Simmons' fame with that of Babe Ruth and the boxer Jack Dempsey, the sporting world's two biggest stars. "There is a similar sensation for the baseball enthusiast when Al Simmons struts up to face the pitcher. The Polish sticker is murdering American League hurling this season, and right now is off on one of the greatest batting sprees in all major league history. His daily batting record is as closely followed as the crazy dash of the Macks up pennant pike, and in Milwaukee box scores showing what Simmons has done are devoured as eagerly as those compiled by the (Milwaukee) Brewers. Simmons' record, aside from its spectacular side, also shows the value of the big punch to any one ball club."[21]

Simmons was not the only punch on the A's, of course, who were 29–10 and in first place by June 1. Leadoff man Max Bishop was drawing tons of walks and hitting unusually well (.294 by season's end), and Mickey Cochrane was showing rare power and spraying plenty of line drives (.349 and 17 home runs that year). And Foxx, still only 23, continued to progress (30 homers, 120 RBIs).

Interestingly, the major league record for catching fly balls was set during a June 29 doubleheader between Detroit and Philadelphia. On the way to 9–1 and 5–1 victories, the Tigers' outfielders snared 24 putouts and the Athletics managed 19 of their own for a two-team total of 43 fly-outs in two games.

Another record was set that summer — by Simmons. In the second game of a July 13 doubleheader against Washington, he cranked out his 1,500th career hit — he remarkably did so in his 1,040th game played, making him the quickest player in major league history to reach 1,500 hits. At the time, no one noticed — this type of statistic was not tracked.

At the plate or elsewhere, Simmons was feeling aggressive that summer. He and Firpo Marberry, the Washington Senators pitcher, had bad blood,

During the 1931 season in the A's dugout, from left to right: Rube Walberg, Jimmie Dykes, Joe Boley, Lefty Grove, Bill Todt, Jimmie Foxx, Connie Mack, Max Bishop and George Earnshaw. *Philadelphia Athletics Historical Society*

dating back to early 1930 when Simmons accused the hefty 230-pound Marberry of trying to bean him.

The same day he collected his 1,500th career hit, the two nearly came to blows again. Marberry hurled a pitch near Simmons' head, knocking him down to the ground. After he got back in the batter's box, Simmons saw three more balls to take a walk. Instead of taking first base, Simmons swaggered out toward the mound, bat in hand, and challenged the pitcher to a fight.

But Muddy Ruel, Washington's catcher who only weighed 150 pounds, got in between the two as players rushed out from both benches. Eventually Simmons and Marberry were pulled apart, and the A's outfielder was ordered to first base, where he heckled Marberry for the rest of the half inning. Marberry then fanned Jimmie Foxx for the third out, and walked back to the Washington dugout under a chorus of Philadelphia boos. As the game continued, both players "cooled down considerably," according to a newspaper account that whimsically noted the so-called "fight is setting a long-distance punchless record."[22]

Manning Vaughan found the Simmons-Marberry feud more theatrical than dangerous—and even wished for more. "We always wish some of these brawny gentlemen of the diamond would do a little knuckle busting. They are big and strong, and a fistfight between Al and Marberry would be something worthwhile. It appears that these two gentlemen merely signed an armistice, for the feud broke out all over Shibe Park the other day. As usual the bean ball caused all the trouble. Simmons again accused Marberry of trying to hit him, and he rushed out on the field and challenged the big pitcher to come under the stands or fight it out right there. But no blood was spilled."[23]

During one offseason, the two rivals bumped into each other in Hot Springs. Simmons, who was dancing with a girl, was tapped on the shoulder by Marberry, who asked Simmons to go outside, presumably for fisticuffs. Simmons trotted outside, but found that Marberry simply wanted to make amends. They ended up drinking the night away together—and reportedly Marberry dusted off Simmons again the next time he saw him on the field of play.[24]

Simmons also found himself in hot water with the crankiest Athletic of them all, Lefty Grove. Grove, who would go 31–4 that season, had recorded a 4–2 win over the Chicago White Sox on August 19 for his 16th consecutive victory to tie an American League record originally set by Walter Johnson and Joe Wood in 1912.

As Grove sought his 17th consecutive win on August 23, he was shocked to learn before the game that Simmons was not in the starting lineup against the host St. Louis Browns. Back-up outfielder Jimmy Moore was instead in left field. Simmons was nursing an ankle injury, and had taken a train back to Milwaukee to rest and heal. In the third inning, Moore misjudged a routine fly ball by Ski Melillo, turning it into a two-out double to allow the game's lone run as the A's lost 1–0.

Grove was outraged at Simmons for not playing that game — he believed Simmons would have caught the ball. And he was mad at Connie Mack for allowing Simmons to take the day off. The pitcher had a 20-minute tirade in the clubhouse following the game, breaking chairs and other equipment and furniture in the visitors clubhouse in Sportsman's Park. "If Simmons had been here and in left field, he would have stuck that ball in his left pocket. What the devil did he have to go to Milwaukee for?" screamed Grove.

Lefty Grove was the ace of the A's pitching staff during the late 1920s and early 1930s. Grove got angry at Al Simmons for missing a game due to injury when he was going for his 17th consecutive win in 1931. *National Baseball Hall of Fame*

But Grove must have know Simmons had been sidelined all week, and would be out of the lineup a total of two weeks, according to Grove biographer Jim Kaplan who noted, "Lefty never, ever forgave Al Simmons." Grove's daughter Lynn said years later that Simmons missing the game was "an annoyance that lasted his entire life."[25]

But Grove also admired Simmons. Years later, after both players had left the A's and squared off against each other as opposing players, he called Simmons the "toughest right-hander he had ever faced."[26]

In mid-August, something happened that may well have affected the Athletics' chances later in the postseason. Hot-hitting catcher Mickey Cochrane, an adroit handler of pitchers and a great hitter himself, suffered a severe beaning in a game against the Indians — after he had hit a home run in his previous at-bat. Cochrane "dropped like a sack of cement," Cy Peterman wrote in the *Philadelphia Bulletin*. "As he lay in the dust, curled in a half circle, he never stirred and the crowd of 20,000 gasped and came to its feet like one man." In the back of everyone's mind was likely the unfortunate death of Ray Chapman from a pitched ball in 1920. But soon Cochrane got up, and with help, made it off the field. But he was never the same the rest of the season and postseason, playing sparingly.[27]

The A's continued their dominance through the late summer. On Labor Day, the team had an incredible 90 wins and only 37 losses. Simmons was batting .382, sniffing another batting title. He hoped to be the first American Leaguer to repeat since his mentor Ty Cobb did it in 1918 and 1919 — just as Mack had challenged him to do so.

Simmons spoke of his emotional-charged approach to hitting. For him, it was a grudging duel with the pitcher. "There's no reason to be friendly with a pitcher who's trying to take your bread and butter away from you. You're going to get paid off on what you hit, and those pitchers are trying to give you the works all the time. I never had any sympathy for a pitcher ... [he's] out there with a big advantage to start with. He always knows what he's going to throw, and you don't. All you have is a round bat that you're supposed to hit with. They give you that big herky-jerky motion and stall around and try to get you off stride, and play you for a chump. How are you going to feel friendly toward guys like that?"[28]

The relentless unfriendliness of Simmons and the other A's against the rest of the league resulted in their third pennant in as many years. At season's end, Philadelphia owned a stunning 107–45 record, finishing 13 and one-half games ahead of the New York Yankees. In the past three years, the A's had won a remarkable 313 games.

Simmons won his second consecutive batting crown with a .390 mark. He also knocked out 22 home runs and drove in 128 runners as the A's cleanup hitter. Posting a career high .444 OBP, he managed 200 hits (the third straight year with 200+), 37 doubles and 13 triples.

He might have hit well over .400 if the sacrifice fly rule had not been changed. In 1930, he had 17 sacrifice fly hits that did not count in his at-bat totals; in 1931, he had zero. If one were to estimate his possible 1931 sacrifice flies based on what he had done in 1930 in that regard, Simmons would have posted a .403 average.

In the field, his play continued to be near flawless — he only made four errors, showing the sure-handed consistency he had displayed the prior four years when he never made more than four errors in a season. His fielding exploits came in an era when double-digit error totals among outfielders were common.

Behind the bright celebration for Simmons and pennant-winning Philadelphia, dark clouds were gathering on the horizon. Even before the season ended, rumors had emerged that Mack intended to break up the A's due to financial losses. Attendance had fallen off sharply at Shibe Park to 627,464 from 721,663 the year before, the second consecutive year the turnstiles tumbled.

Despite a star-laden — but expensive — roster that had just won two World Series back-to-back, Mack's team was losing revenue. It was unfathomable that the year ahead would be the capstone of Al Simmons' career with the Philadelphia Athletics. But first they had a World Series to win — and Philadelphia hoped it would be the third one in a row.

For the championship, the A's again faced the St. Louis Cardinals, who were arguably better than the previous year, having tallied 101 wins to only 53 losses. The Cards featured a balanced attack of a high-average offense and strong pitching. Still, Philadelphia was the odds-on favorites as the games opened October 1 in St. Louis amid cloudy, warm skies and 38,529 fans. At the outset, the A's did not disappoint.

In Game One Lefty Grove bested Paul Derringer, scattering 12 hits in a 6–2 victory that included a two-run blast by Simmons in the seventh. "The Philadelphia Athletics unlimbered their heavy artillery on the enemy's home battleground today," wrote Alan Gould. Simmons also contributed the "most sensational defensive gesture" when he snared a line drive by catcher Jimmy Wilson against the left-field wall in the eighth. "It was a bitter blow to their rivals," Gould said.[29]

On hand to watch the game was John McGraw, the New York Giants manager that a young Simmons wanted to play for so badly. Later on, he was effusive about Simmons' spectacular play: "Al Simmons proved to me that he is a really great outfielder, especially when it comes to timing a ball. That wonderful sense of timing that makes him a great batter is plainly shown in his outfield work ... (His) catch of Jimmy Wilson's long drive in the eighth inning of the first game was one of the most brilliant bits of work in the whole series. He instinctively knew that it would be impossible, running in that direction, to make the catch with both hands. He had to make it a one-handed catch or nothing. Simmons had judged the speed and the direction of this drive so accurately that when he was within two steps of the fence he made the final leap and speared the ball with his left hand, making the perfect catch."[30]

And of course, Simmons was a menace at the plate. After the game, Derringer said, "I was in the game until Al Simmons ruined my dream. He blasted a home run with two men on. That was the end of me."[31]

But that was the first game, and things quickly changed from that point on when Cardinals outfielder John Leonard Roosevelt "Pepper" Martin unleashed himself upon the A's. Martin, after playing seven minor-league seasons and making two short appearances in the majors, had finally been given a shot at the big leagues. Now baseball's largest stage was set for Martin, who had hit .300 during the season after taking the place of center fielder Taylor Douthit, who was traded to the Cincinnati Reds. During the Series, Martin was asked how he had learned to run so fast. He replied, "I grew up in Oklahoma, and once you start runnin' out there, there ain't nothin' to stop you."[32]

In Game Two, Martin and "Wild" Bill Hallahan teamed up to even the Series with the A's. Martin got things rolling in the second, when he doubled, stole third and then scored on a long fly ball that Simmons "juggled just long enough to let the fleet youngster" cross home plate.[33] In the seventh, he singled, stole second, advanced to third on a groundout and scored on a squeeze bunt. Hallahan did his part, too, blanking the A's for a three-hit, 2–0 victory. Simmons went hitless in four at-bats.

For Game Three, the series moved back to Philadelphia where 32,295 fans packed Shibe Park on October 5. Whereas the National League's deader ball was used in St. Louis, the slightly more lively American League ball was employed in Philadelphia.

Scalpers were active, selling $5.50 tickets for as much as $10 as hundreds of Philadelphia fans waited overnight and longer for entry. The "blasé attitude" of Philadelphia fans after the opening victory had been "dissipated by the strong Cardinal opposition."[34]

President Hoover and his wife were in attendance, where they were "warmly applauded by the crowd" as the first couple took their seats in the flag-bedecked box behind the A's dugout. A phonograph amplified by a loud speaker played "Hail to the Chief."[35]

Since Prohibition was still the law of the land, the Philadelphia fans tweaked the nation's chief executive with relentless loud chants of, "We want beer!"[36]

Burleigh Grimes, the spitball pitcher, used his trick pitch to stymie the A's in a two-hit 5–2 win. Simmons belted a home run over the right field fence in the ninth to spoil Grimes' shutout bid. Now the A's were down two games to one.

At one point, Cardinals manager Gabby Street told writers he thought he'd found the hole in Al Simmons' swing. "Simmons' batting weakness was a space about a foot in diameter, waist high, through which Card pitchers tried to throw their offerings. And when they didn't find that spot, good night," said Street, though he did not say if the "weakness" was an inside or outside pitch.[37]

Their backs against the wall, the A's determined to even the score in Game Four. The 1930 Series hero, George Earnshaw (a 20-game winner in 1931), returned to the mound for a two-hit, 3–0 triumph. Simmons went 2-for-4 with a double and one RBI while Foxx whacked a solo homer off Syl Johnson in the sixth inning. For St. Louis, Pepper Martin stood out once again, getting two hits and stealing another base, his fourth of the Series.

The Series was a back-and-forth affair, and many observers thought that it would be a matter of getting the breaks — who made the big hit or mistake at the right or wrong time.

For Game Five, Mack choose Waite Hoyt, a 32-year-old veteran who he had signed on waivers from the Detroit Tigers in June, as his starter. Hoyt had a 6–3 record in previous World Series games for the New York Yankees. His opponent was "Wild" Bill Hallahan.

But the A's lost, 5–1, on more extraordinary play by Martin, who used a crowd-pleasing, unconventional belly-first slide. He had a run-scoring fly ball in the first, a bunt in the fourth, a two-run homer in the sixth and a run-scoring single in the eighth. After five games, Martin was cruising with a .667 average (12-for-18), five runs scored, four doubles, one homer, five runs batted in and five stolen bases.

Simmons had three hits in four at-bats, but that was about all the offense the A's could muster against Hallahan's stalwart pitching.

Down three games to two, the Philadelphia Athletics found themselves pinned to the back of Pepper Martin's dirt-smeared jersey. Now they had to return to enemy territory in St. Louis to stage a comeback.

The A's rebounded in Game Six on the strong arm of Lefty Grove, who hurled a 8–1 victory over Paul Derringer. Simmons had one hit and drove in two runs.

While Simmons (.333) and Foxx (.421) were hitting well at this point, the other A's were slumping. The number three hitter, Cochrane, likely still affected by his late-season beaning, posted a .190 average. Mule Haas, Max Bishop and Bing Miller all had sub–.200 averages.

In Game Seven, after a wild pitch and an error helped St. Louis to two first-inning runs, St. Louis third basemen Andy High singled in the third and right fielder George Watkins followed with a home run that staked pitcher Burleigh Grimes to a 4–0 lead. The master of the spitball was dominant through eight innings, but needed relief from Hallahan in the ninth as the A's touched him for a couple runs. Fittingly, the last out of the Cardinals' 4–2 triumph, came on a Max Bishop fly ball to Pepper Martin, who had left his mark all over the Cardinals' second World Series title.

Simmons went 1-for-3 in the last game, hitting .333 overall. It was the most competitive World Series since 1926, a seesaw battle. "The Cards played better ball than we did, and that's why we lost," said Mack. "Our boys didn't click as they did in the past."[38]

Martin, who had hit .500, led his team in runs scored, hits, doubles, runs batted in and stolen bases. Later he attributed his five steals to the A's pitchers not holding runners on well enough. "I feel sorry for Cochrane. But it wasn't his fault," Martin said.

The 1931 World Series had made Martin something of a national hero. The Midwestern Cardinals' upset of the mighty East Coast A's was especially popular throughout areas impoverished by the Depression and a worsening drought. When Commissioner Landis told Martin that he would love to trade places with him, the ballplayer famously remarked, "It's all right with me, Judge. I'll trade my $4,500 for your $50,000 (actually $65,000) any day."[39]

There was new blood rising in baseball. Though Martin would never become a Hall of Fame-caliber player, he exemplified the common man's Depression-era struggles to triumph against the establishment — in this case, the defending champions.

Wanting to put the defeat out of his mind, a chagrined Simmons joined an all-star baseball squad on a barnstorming trip to Hawaii and Japan a few days after the World Series. Led by sportswriter Fred Lieb, the team featured Lou Gehrig, Frankie Frisch, Rabbit Maranville, Willie Kamm, Lefty O'Doul, Mickey Cochrane, and Lefty Grove.

The players were decked out in uniforms with "U.S." across the front, and they were treated as dignitaries upon their arrival in Japan. Thousands greeted them, and there were many receptions as well as games.

While Lieb played chaperone, the trip to Japan in 1931 was organized by Herb Hunter, a former major leaguer for the Chicago Cubs and St. Louis Cardianls. He had been taking players to Japan since 1921. The team was nicknamed the "Hunter All-Stars," and they won all 17 of their scheduled games, drawing an impressive 50,000 crowd for a game in Tokyo.

The tour came at a controversial time in U.S.-Japanese relations. About a month earlier, Japan drew world condemnation when it attacked Manchuria in northeast China. American reaction to the aggression came in the form of the Stimson Doctrine, which stated that the U.S. would not recognize any treaty that impinged on the sovereignty of China. Tensions between the U.S. and Japan simmered throughout the 1930s.[40]

Despite the awkward timing, the tour was one of the most influential trips of its kind to Japan. Another one came in 1934 when an aging Babe Ruth visited Japan with other American all-star players. Apart from the geopolitical grievances, the two countries enjoyed a strong baseball relationship for years.

Sotaro Suzuki, a Japanese newspaper writer, said later in 1975 that the "great American team of 1931 and the later team in 1934 made such an impression on our people that it paved the way for professional baseball in Japan."[41]

Lefty Grove said of the Japanese ballplayers that they were much "better fielders than they are batters." They also seemed much more polite than their

American counterparts — they applauded good plays, and there was a discernible lack of the "razzberry" or heckling from the benches, he said. In fact, the Japanese showered them with good manners, hospitality and rabid fan interest. Grove remarked, "We had the time of our lives on that trip," noting that one game in Osaka drew 60,000 spectators.[42]

Unfortunately, Simmons — referred to as "Simmonson" by the Japanese — lost his prized bat on the tour.

It might be hard to imagine in this day and age when players go through bats almost on a daily or weekly basis, but players in Simmons' era often used the same bat for months or even years, and they frequently developed a kinship to their wood. Simmons used to make special trips to the Louisville Slugger factory in Kentucky to inspect the wood and how his bats were specifically made. He was a detail-oriented perfectionist when it came to bats. "Al is one of the crankiest players in baseball when it comes to his lumber," noted one writer.

Simmons reportedly used the longest bat — 38 inches — that Louisville Slugger ever made. It may have helped him with his unique batting approach in getting to an outside pitch. He preferred extremely heavy ones in the area of 46 ounces.

Superstitious, Simmons ordered his bats an inch too long so he could have the Shibe Park groundskeeper — a man known only as "McCalley" — shorten them to his exact preference.[43]

The details of how Simmons lost his stick were never fully explained. But he was deeply attached to this particular club, described as a "dark, sinister-looking piece of lumber." Wielding it, he had just won the 1931 American League batting championship. Years later, Simmons still longed for it, claiming he "couldn't miss with it." As if the bat were a long-lost lover, he added in uncharacteristically emotional terms: "Never could get another bat that had the right 'feel' of this one. Never felt right about any other bat."[44]

Strangely, one day they would be reunited. The more pressing question for Simmons and the A's is whether they could regain their championship ways. As the bleak winter settled in, a cruel chill fell upon the franchise.

CHAPTER TWELVE

Woe to White Elephants

"The A's were victims of the Yankee mystique. Perhaps the 1927 Yankees were the greatest team of all time. But if there was a close second, perhaps an equal, it was those A's. They are the most overlooked team in baseball."

— Shirley Povich

"The bitter truth was that we no longer had it. We no longer believed we were invincible. Our faith in ourselves was no longer there, and he (Mack) knew it too."

— Jimmy Dykes[1]

Fast forward to 1996, when *Sports Illustrated*, the nation's most popular sports magazine, published a front-cover story on the 1929–31 Philadelphia A's, raising the question whether they — and not the 1927 Yankees — were the greatest baseball club ever assembled. The publication adorned its front cover with a photo of Al Simmons, swinging away in triumphant style. The headline read: "The Team That Time Forgot."

The 11-page article by William Nack, "Lost in History," argued that from 1929 to 1931 the Philadelphia A's were the best team in baseball, with four future Hall of Famers and a lineup that manhandled Babe Ruth's legendary Yankees. In his clear-eyed prose, Nack explained that the A's were not given their due credit. When weighing the statistical record, they stood up to, or even surpassed, the Yankees of that period, he contended. "From 1929 to 1931 the A's were a juggernaut quite as formidable as the Yankees had been between 1926–1928. Both teams won three consecutive pennants and two of three World Series; both teams lost a seven-game series to the St. Louis Cardinals (the Yanks in '26 and the A's in '31). Statistically the New York and Philadelphia mini-dynasties were remarkably even: The A's had a record of 313–143 (.686) between 1929 and '31; and the Yanks, 302–160 (.654) between 1926 and '28. And while Philadelphia scored six fewer runs than the Yankees — 2,710–2,716 — the A's had 5 fewer runs scored against them. That represents a difference between the two teams, in net scoring of only one run.[2]

By that yardstick — runs for and runs against — one might argue the Yankees had a one run edge. That's an incredible minute difference over the span of three years. So the Yankees scored more, but the A's won more games. Both won two World Series in three years. Why, then, are the A's of Simmons' era not given their just desserts?

As Nack put it, "Many veteran baseball observers believe that the Yankees' far more exalted status in history is due largely to the fact that they played in New York, in media heaven, where the manufacture of myth and hype is a light industry." One of those observers, Shirley Povich, the esteemed sports editor of *The Washington Post*, is quoted as saying, "Those A's never got the credit they deserved," and that "The A's were victims of the Yankee mystique. Perhaps the 1927 Yankees were the greatest team of all time. But if there was a close second, perhaps an equal, it was those A's. They are the most overlooked team in baseball."

All good things come to an end, and the 1932 season would witness a crumbling of the champion A's. Much of it had to do with the sluggish economy. Mack, who would soon realize he could no longer afford his expensive stars, ordered his players in early spring not to discuss contract issues with the press. Perhaps that was a sign he was ready to deal and trade, all to cut expenses and help his club survive.

That year, the U.S. economy continued to deteriorate and unemployment increased to a ghastly 24 percent. There were fewer and fewer jobs, and some Americans were even forced into living in the streets or in old cars. Towards the end of the year in November, Americans jettisoned the seemingly aloof President Herbert Hoover in favor of Franklin D. Roosevelt, who vowed massive change with his optimistic-branded economic activism. Around the world changes also occurred when the British jailed Mahatma Gandhi in India, and many Russian people faced a life-and-death situation with an agricultural policy that caused mass starvation.

Despite all the economic bad news, once again Al Simmons missed the opening of the A's spring training in Fort Myers, Florida. He preferred working out in Hot Springs, Arkansas, with George Earnshaw, though he was already signed to an A's contract. Both players joined their team in time for the annual exhibition or "city series" with the Phillies in early April.

Sportswriters were more enthusiastic about the New York Yankees' chances of winning the pennant than the A's. The Yankees were the team "to beat if stars have been read all right by baseball soothsayers," suggested one scribe.[3]

Simmons, however, was robustly confident — of his own talents, at least.

This photograph adorned the front cover of *Sports Illustrated* in 1996 for an article on whether the A's were a better team than the Yankees in the late 1920s and early 1930s. *National Baseball Hall of Fame*

Into the season he carried a career .363 average, which was, at that time, two points higher than Rogers Hornsby, 14 points higher than Babe Ruth and 21 points higher than Lou Gehrig. He also had 173 home runs by this time.[4]

In an interview, Simmons talked about his penchant for disliking pitchers, the ups and downs of a hitter's life, the law of averages, and how to succeed in the majors. "I have no cousins nor jinxes among the American League pitchers. One of them may fool me in one game and he will be unable to get me out the next time he pitches to me. On the other hand, I'll fatten my batting average off a pitcher today and next week he will not let me get to first base.... To stick in the big leagues, a player must have plenty of confidence. He must fight to get in the game. He must never be content to sit on the bench."[5]

Those words likely haunted him later. When his career was winding down, and he tried in vain to reach the 3,000-hit milestone, he publicly lamented the days off he took, injuries or no injuries.

Both Simmons and the A's started cold that April. By the end of the month, he was hitting .281, far below his usual output, and Philadelphia was struggling at 4–10. On the other hand, the Yankees, riding the broad shoulders of the Ruth-Gehrig duo, were 10–3.

Through May, both Simmons and the A's picked it up a bit. He began hitting for more power and average (.312), but the real story was the frequent clouts of first baseman Jimmie Foxx, who that season would challenge Ruth's then-record 60 home runs.

With Foxx having a spectacular season, rumors were spreading that he and Simmons were having some difficulties. Perhaps Simmons felt Foxx was usurping his star status. It became such a story that Simmons went to lengths to downplay any "feud" when asked about it in 1933 by writer John P. Carmichael, who described the Simmons-Foxx relationship as "courteous but unfriendly" based on accounts he heard in "sporting circles." Simmons always dispelled the claims: "There was never any trouble between Jimmy Foxx and myself at any time. The fact that he had a big year while I didn't do so well as fans might have expected means nothing. I hope he has many years like it."

Foxx and Simmons had roomed together for four years, and no one knew more about the legendary strength of the ballplayer nicknamed "Double X" and the "Beast" as Simmons. Simmons said, "He can tie me in bowknots. They wonder where he gets all his power from. He isn't as big as some of the rest of us. But he's a bundle of muscle right off the farm. When we start rough-housing in the room, he can just reach out and grab me and I can't swing."[6]

Simmons compared Foxx to Ruth, giving him an edge. "Jimmy Foxx today hits the ball harder than Ruth ever did, whether it's a home run or a single. I have never seen anybody put quite so much into a swing." Simmons even claimed that American League pitchers tried to protect Ruth's record from Foxx. "He came within two of tying Babe's mark last year, with every pitcher in the league bearing down against him, every inning. He had no soft spots. They all wanted Ruth's record to stand."[7]

Simmons displayed an occasional soft spot at times. One Sunday when the A's did not have a game, some of the players made plans to go fishing. Fellow outfielder Bing Miller usually organized the affair, and Simmons would always go. But this time he begged off, showing Miller a telegram he had received from a sick kid in Gettysburg, who had asked Simmons to visit him that Sunday. "I don't want you fellows to think I don't want to join you," Simmons said, "but this kid probably lives a drab life and if I can put some pleasure in it, I'm going to."[8]

While he enjoyed kids at times, Simmons always disapproved with fraternizing with opponents, simply content with mere "hellos." But he made some lifelong friends while in the game.[9]

Meanwhile, 1932 seemed like the Yankees' year.

On June 3, Lou Gehrig and the New York Yankees played the A's in Philadelphia. This was the day when Gehrig became the first AL player to hit four home runs in a game. And he might have hit another one if it had not been for Simmons. When Gehrig came to the plate in the ninth inning, he smashed a screaming high line drive toward left field. Simmons made a leaping, twisting catch near the top of the fence for an out. Years later someone asked Simmons if he felt badly about spoiling Gehrig's great day. "Why should I be sorry?" he retorted. "Why should he have a triple and four home runs?"[10]

Any other day, Gehrig's feat would have been the top baseball headline. But this day, John McGraw, the celebrated manager of the New York Giants, announced his retirement and thereby grabbed the biggest headlines.

You never know what will happen in a given baseball game. On July 10, the Athletics and Cleveland Indians battled for 18 innings before Philadelphia won, 18–17, one of the highest scoring major league games ever. A's starter Lew Krausse was removed in the first inning after giving up three runs. Reliever Eddie Rommel then went the distance — all 17 and one-third innings — allowing 14 runs and 29 base hits. In all, the A's stroked 25 hits while the Indians hit safely 33 times. Simmons went 5-for-9. Indians second baseman Johnny Burnett set a record that still stands today — 9 hits in 11 at-bats in a single game.[11]

Not to be overshadowed by Gehrig's performance a month earlier, Simmons powered three home runs on July 15, marking a career high. He went 4-for-4 that day and drove in six runs. After that amazing performance, Simmons suddenly slowed down, and things got really bad when Mack publicly questioned his dedication.

In an August 5 game with Cleveland, with Simmons ailing from a minor injury suffered the day before, Mack took him out of the game in the fourth inning and replaced him with Mickey Cochrane in left field. "We were getting nowhere in the game (down by five runs) and with Simmons acting so languidly at the plate I thought I would rest him for the remainder of the day," said Mack after the 8–7 loss to the Indians. Cochrane biographer Charlie Bevis said Mack used the incident to send a message to Simmons, who he wanted to motivate back to his batting title form of 1930 and 1931.[12]

Afterwards, Simmons struggled, going 1-for-13 in the next three games, and performed barely better after that. At the time he was benched, Simmons was hitting .312, and 12 days later he had fallen to .307 before snapping out of it with a 5-for-5 performance in a 9–7 victory over Cleveland.

On August 23, it was reported that Philadelphia fans heavily booed Simmons. That day he went 3-for-6, and the day before had managed one hit in five at-bats. His average stood at .307. Some speculated the booing was a combination of his underachieving play and the surge of Foxx in the home run chase. The turn of events bothered Simmons, who fought to raise his average and regain his popularity.

"It seems to be the idea of Philadelphia fans," wrote William Braucher, "that since Foxx has become so successful, Simmons is sulking in his tent. But umpire Will McGowan tells me that never did a man try harder to regain his greatness than Al Simmons tried this year." Braucher said the Simmons' saga was a warning for young ballplayers to not let their "heads swell" after a few good years. "The downfall of Simmons this year is about the swiftest plunge a star of his brilliance ever has taken, and the most unexpected," McGowan observed.[13]

As the second-place A's entered September trailing the Yankees by 11 and one-half games, rumors sprouted about which A's might be wearing different uniforms next year. The name of Al Simmons was repeatedly mentioned. Now 30, an age when some players begin to decline, Simmons also faced the twin problems of a disappointing Philadelphia season and the club's growing financial losses. Other names cited were George Earnshaw, Jimmy Dykes, Bing Miller, Mule Haas and Max Bishop — basically, any of the veteran regulars.

Some writers found the idea of trading Simmons unthinkable, notably Chuck Voorhis. "Rumors to the contrary," Voorhis wrote, "Al Simmons will undoubtedly wear a Philadelphia uniform next season and patrol left field for the men of Mack." Voorhis observed that Simmons had "regained a lot of his old fire and dash" and argued that the fans had been both supportive and dismissive of him that season—"they were largely responsible for making the Milwaukee Mauler want to get away from Philadelphia. When Al failed to come up to his brilliant play of last season, the fans went to work on him." But the fickle fans changed their tune as Simmons and the A's gathered some steam down the stretch drive. "Al gets a hand every time he steps to the plate and when he walks out to his post in left field, the bleach rites give him another hand."[14]

But it was soon reported that Simmons was interested in an offseason trade to the Chicago White Sox, where he would play closer to his Milwaukee hometown. He was supposedly "sick and tired of hearing Shibe Park fans boo him."[15] Bent on reclaiming his reputation—and poking his critics in the eyes—Simmons finished on a strong note.

On the first day of September, he launched his 29th home and then followed it up the next day with more two home runs in a three-hit performance. On September 14, he went 5-for-6 with two doubles to begin a 10-game hitting streak that included three doubles, two triples and three home runs. He also showed some gusto on the basepaths, stealing two bases in that span. He raised his average six points in the month and blasted 7 home runs with 21 RBIs.

By season's end, Simmons had notched a .322 average (low by his standards, but good for most other players) with 216 hits. He also plastered 35 home runs and amassed 151 RBIs (his ninth consecutive 100-plus RBI season). This was a good power year for Simmons.

While Simmons had played in a career-high 154 games and posted a league-leading 670 at-bats, he also struck out the most he ever had, 76 times. The latter may have been frustrating for fans, as possibly were his lower-than-usual doubles (28) and triples (9).

While the A's still mounted a good offensive club, they lacked the quality pitching of their two prior championship seasons. At the end, they sported a 94–60 record, winding up 13 games behind the 107-win Yankees with Ruth's 41 homers and Gehrig's .349 average and 41 circuit clouts.

But in Philadelphia, a new star was ascending, as 24-year-old Foxx had a breakthrough season—he hammered 58 home runs, two shy of Ruth's record, to go along with a .364 average and 169 RBIs.

Foxx retired after the 1945 season with 534 home runs, 1,921 RBIs and a lifetime batting average of .325, but statistics hardly express the hair-raising drama he brought to the plate. He often cut-off the sleeves of his uniform to show off his muscular arms, and he could drive balls 500 feet with a whip of his powerful wrists. Stories of his most titanic clouts have become myth, along with well-documented accounts of his gentle, somewhat naive persona.

On the other hand, the tempestuous Simmons was in a spiteful mood at the end of the season. Taking aim at Ruth, he disparaged the Yankees' chances in the World Series against the Chicago Cubs (New York would win).

Al Simmons: "Babe Ruth is not in the pink. That's why I believe the World Series is a toss-up. Babe did not seem to be physically fit when we played our last series against the Yanks recently."[16]

Later, Simmons reversed himself and picked the Yankees to win the series. "I think they'll win, but it won't be so easy."[17]

The A's dynasty was ending with a whimper, not a bang. Despite the home runs and RBIs, many insiders thought Simmons had a sub-par season. For the first time in many years, *The Sporting News* left him off its All-Star team.

The bang came on September 29, before the World Series even started, when the Philadelphia A's announced they had sold Al Simmons, Mule Haas and Jimmy Dykes to the Chicago White Sox for a reported $150,000. While some expected such a move, it was stunning news.

Despite all the rumors — and his apparent tacit approval — Simmons expressed shock. Years later, he bitterly recounted how he had learned of the trade from reporters — not from Mack or the A's — while barnstorming in Sheboygan, Wisconsin, with Mickey Cochrane and Jimmie Foxx. "A man met us at the hotel, and his first words were, 'Did you hear it?' 'Hear what?' said Cochrane, 'Why, Al, he answered, turning to me, 'You were sold to the White Sox with Mule Haas and Jimmy Dykes.'"[18]

In another account, Simmons said he heard of the trade on the radio while driving with Foxx and Cochrane. "After my first surprise, I looked at Jimmy and Mickey. They were staring at the dashboard, mouths wide open."[19]

It was hard to fathom, but the reign of the White Elephants had come to an end. In the war between Philadelphia and New York for baseball ascendancy, a death blow had been dealt to the legion of A's fans. The Gotham City would go on to win many World Series titles in the decades ahead while Philadelphia would scrape by with more lackluster than stellar teams.

It was a seismic change for A's baseball, and an unfair one in the eyes of their fans, who had a hard time understanding how such a complete team could be so quickly dissembled.

Simmons was wide-eyed with both trepidation and possibilities. He had just completed his ninth season with the A's, and figured he had more productive years ahead. But he was leaving a comfortable environment, and would have to regain his focus in a new and different environment.

Al Simmons: "I looked first at Foxx, who is one of my closest friends and had been my roommate for four seasons, and then at Mickey, who is also one of my best pals. I just couldn't speak."[20]

According to Simmons, Foxx said, "There go the Three Musketeers (as

A's infielder Jimmy Dykes with a prized possession, a new automobile. Dukes was traded with Al Simmons and Mule Haas to the Chicago White Sox after the 1932 season. *Philadelphia Athletics Historical Society*

the trio were known) all to hell." After they heard the news, Simmons said, it was an eerily quiet drive into Sheboygan.[21]

Though well-documented he had more than an inkling this would happen, Simmons claimed Mack had assured him he would not be traded, "and that's another reason the deal came as such a shock," he said.[22]

Simmons likely knew the trade was a possibility, and was probably consulted on it. Years later in his 1967 biography, Jimmy Dykes aired his candid feelings. "The bitter truth was that we no longer had it. We no longer believed we were invincible. Our faith in ourselves was no longer there, and he (Mack) knew it too."[23]

In Chicago, the reaction was joyous. Even at 30, Simmons seemed destined for more years of greatness, and now he would have the possible psychological advantage of playing closer to home. One news account described him as baseball's "best all-around" player at that time.[24]

The ebullient Chicago press speculated that the 1933 White Sox with Simmons' big bat could be the franchise's best team since the infamous Black Sox of 1919. "Very bright," gushed writer Bob Ray, adding that finally other American League teams were willing to trade worthy players to the White Sox.[25]

Later on, Simmons sounded more positive and even lauded Mack. He told one writer he welcomed the chance to play closer to home and looked ahead one day to managing a ballclub. "My sale to the Sox is a good break," he said. "My long association with Connie Mack has given me a wonderful baseball education."[26]

Realizing the challenges ahead, Simmons began his winter workout routine early. In November, at 20 pounds over his playing weight, he left for Hot Springs. He said, "It will be an easy matter to get rid of the excess weight in the baths, hiking over the mountains and playing golf and tennis. This is what I'm going to do for the next three weeks. By the time the regular training season begins I'll be in first class condition. My one ambition is to give the White Sox my best efforts and regain batting honors in the American League."[27]

Meanwhile, the financially plagued Mack's dismantling of his championship squad had begun in earnest, and it was likened to what happened 18 years before when he sold off his top ballplayers after the Boston "Miracle" Braves upset of the A's in the 1914 World Series.

In his defense, Mack complained about Pennsylvania's blue laws that forbid baseball on Sundays. According to author Bruce Kuklick, Mack blamed the trade of Simmons, Dykes and Haas on the legal restrictions. "We cannot meet our payrolls" on 77 home games, said Mack, adding that Sunday baseball would not hurt religion, but would be good for the "morale of cities."[28]

Before the stock market crash in 1929, Mack had borrowed $750,000 to revitalize Shibe Park. Now that the renovations were complete, he had to repay the loan — likely a major factor in his dissembling of the A's. On top of this, his payroll was among the highest in baseball, with every player making at least $10,000.[29]

As the seasons turned that winter, so did the franchise that had achieved so much so recently. In a way, maybe few then appreciated what they had just witnessed in the Philadelphia Athletics juggernaut of 1929 to 1931. As William Nack wrote decades later, "according to most old-timers who played in that era, the 1927 and '28 Yankees and the 1929 and '30 Athletics matched up so closely that they were nearly equal, with the A's given the nod in fielding and pitching and the Yankees in hitting."[30] He added, those A's "left a generation of Philadelphians with memories of what it was like to have a team that ate the great Yankees for dinner."

The team that time forgot was no more. In the years ahead, the great A's players moved on to different cities. For Al Simmons, it was a bittersweet transition. He got to play close to his Milwaukee home—but he seemed streaky and casually productive, never quite what he was in Philadelphia.

CHAPTER THIRTEEN

New Socks for the Sox

"Hail to Al Simmons, new monarch of major league baseball."
— Arch Ward

"Chicago — a pompous Milwaukee."
— Leonard Levinson, radio writer[1]

As the Great Depression sunk in, the gap between the haves and have-nots in major league baseball widened. League-leading clubs like the Yankees played before mostly packed parks, but the losing or small market teams could not fill the stands. Bank closings left many Americans short of cash, and baseball attendance plummeted 40 percent from 1930 to 1933, not returning to pre–Depression levels until after World War II, when millions of soldiers returned. As a result, players' salaries fell by 25 percent on average. In a nod to the widespread hard times, Commissioner Landis started the year by taking a 40 percent pay cut.

Echoing the widespread hardship, writer Ray Robinson, a lifelong resident of Manhattan, recalled his childhood experience of visiting the Polo Grounds to watch the New York Giants. "Like many other recreational activities, people did go to the ballpark to get away from the economic horrors of empty wallets and ice boxes. I was very aware of the guys selling apples on street corners for a nickel. Along the Hudson River, you had some of these guys living in ramshackle huts in rags. So going to the ballpark was a big thing," he said.[2]

Many teams kept costs down by reducing the number of coaches, or by eliminating them and employing player-managers. The club owners reduced rosters to 23 players, down from 25, saving money in salary costs.

In the headlines in 1933, the federal National Recovery program was launched in an attempt to boost the economy; Prohibition was finally repealed to the delight of many; the movie *King Kong* starring actress Fay Wray and a mechanical ape hit the movie screens; and spam was invented, ushering in a processed-food era.

In November, Pennsylvania voters approved a measure to make Sunday baseball legal — but it was too late for Al Simmons, who had found himself in an unfamiliar Chicago White Sox uniform earlier that spring.

Despite the initial euphoria about Simmons, some in the Windy City had their doubts. Sportswriter Ed Bang observed, "A lot of the wiseacres made up their individual and collective minds that Simmons had been well press-agented and would fall down on the job with a dull, sickening thud."[3]

Others wondered if Chicago's acquisition of Simmons, Dykes and Haas spelled the doom for White Sox manager Lew Fonseca. Dykes was considered managerial material — and therefore a threat to Fonseca — and Simmons was his ally. Simmons attempted to reassure the press: "Dykes is a mighty fine man. But I don't know any reason why I shouldn't get along with Fonseca or anybody else for that matter. I know how to play ball." He added, "There is no good reason we shouldn't feel right at home."[4]

For the White Sox, acquiring Simmons was a shift in player development strategy, said Harry Grabiner, White Sox secretary. No longer were they content to merely cultivate young players and wait to see if they would blossom. "We're going out and getting our players," said Grabiner, adding in hyperbolic language that the move was "probably the biggest in American League history."[5]

Baseball is a business, and over the winter Simmons took out a $100,000 insurance policy to protect himself in case of injury.[6]

In January, White Sox President Lou Comiskey organized a press conference and had Simmons try on his new uniform — which was also a new color scheme for Chicago. In a photograph in *The Sporting News*, a grinning Simmons looks at himself in a tall mirror under the headline, "New Socks for the Sox," and was described as a "new member who is expected to give the Pale Hose bigger and better socks," with his bat.[7]

The season before, Chicago had switched to socks with a single blue stripe. They also wore dark blue uniforms for road games. This season, the team returned to the more conservative all-white outfits — except for the "Sox" logo across the jersey front.

In January, Simmons unwisely told writers he picked the Yankees as the favorites to win the pennant. In a comment sure to have displeased the Chicago owners who took on his considerable salary, he ruled out the White Sox in the race before the season even started. "Those Yankees should be 25 games in front of the field by the last of July. Who's going to stop them? Certainly not the Red Sox, nor the Browns, nor Detroit, nor the White Sox. I don't think the Indians can muster enough strength to keep a steady pace and Connie Mack is depending on youngsters to stay up there. Washington won't do it either."[8]

He also took a few shots at his old team. "It's a lot to ask three kids (Doc Cramer, Finney and Pinky Higgins) to take over veterans jobs and make good right off the bat. Cramer, naturally, will be all right, and that pitching staff will do better this year," Simmons said.[9]

The White Sox faithful hoped the additions of Simmons, Haas and Dykes would improve the team offensively and defensively. Some even expected them to finish in the first division in the American League, among the top four teams in the eight-team league. "That is just what we're going to do," owner Comiskey declared, despite the fact that since the Black Sox scandal erupted in 1920, the White Sox had never finished in the first division.[10]

In 1932, the White Sox had lost 102 games, winning just 49. They surely needed the bat and glove of Al Simmons, but all was not well with the ballplayer. That winter press reports leaked out about his lingering injuries. Writer Edward Neil, in an article bedecked with the startling headline, "Practically Everything Wrong with Al Simmons," the slugger's numerous nagging injuries were described, doubtlessly rattling Chicago's front office that had just invested heavily in him.

Quoting a "variety of sources," including Simmons himself, the writer noted that the player recently had five abscessed teeth removed in Hot Springs, suffered from rheumatism in his right arm and hand, as well as weak ankles. But the most worrisome ailment was a severe hand injury he received off the field the previous November after his trade to the White Sox.

"The understanding is that Al was hurt when the shaft of a golf club broke and penetrated his right hand," Neil wrote. "Simmons, himself, in a letter to friends here, wrote that he had suffered a strained ligament. He made light of the entire matter, expressing confidence that he was due for a big season." Simmons apparently went to Hot Springs with his hand in a cast. Still, it proved a fly in the ointment of Sox expectations. "Banked upon as the slugging wheel of a White Sox recovery from the slump of the past few years, Simmons received permission to remain at Hot Springs until March 12, instead of reporting early to Pasadena," Neil observed.[11]

Hearing this, the White Sox called Simmons and urged him to report to camp as soon as possible. But Simmons said he needed a couple days rest after the extraction of five teeth, so in five days he would show up at training camp. He chose not to have the teeth replaced with false ones in Hot Springs.

When he did arrive in the White Sox training camp in Pasadena, Simmons exhibited a grumpy aloofness, according to Arch Ward of the *Chicago Daily Tribune*. "Al Simmons roomed alone last year, which gave voice to high hat charges, but snobbishness wasn't the reason," said Ward, implying that Simmons was simply difficult to live with. Naively, the White Sox hoped to inspire rookies by letting them room with Simmons in the exhibition season.

The problem was, Simmons wanted none of it, and quashed the idea by simply being a boor. "The turnover in recruits was so tremendous that Al nearly had a roomie every night. It got so that when he walked in on a fellow in his room he wouldn't know whether he was a teammate or burglar," Ward said. Simmons demanded to room alone during the regular season, and the White Sox finally agreed.[12]

On Opening Day, April 12, however, Simmons live up to his hype, smacking a home run and another hit in 4–2 victory over the host St. Louis Browns. Only 4,500 fans turned out for the game in Sportsman's Park. The next day Simmons again led the White Sox attack, punching out three hits in an 11–7 triumph over the Browns. By the end of the ninth game of the season, he was hitting .400 and Chicago stood 6–3.

Then the hits quit falling, and Simmons fell to .297 by the end of the month, though he made a spectacular unassisted double play in an April 20 game against St. Louis. At the end of that day, Chicago found itself in second place, buoyed by good hitting and solid pitching.

On May 4, Simmons' bat warmed up and he got the first hit in what would become an 18-game hitting streak. He was stopped May 28 by his old teammate, Philadelphia's George Earnshaw, in the second game of a doubleheader.

Washington and New York were the dominant teams in the American League that season. Simmons' former teammate Jimmie Foxx was powering the A's into mild contention with another monster year, though Philadelphia had difficulty forming a well-balanced attack with the loss of Simmons, Jimmie Dykes and Mule Haas.

Writer Alan Gould spoke of Connie Mack's post–Simmons future for the A's after Philadelphia suffered a bad road trip, and suspected Mack might trade or sell more of his players. "It is bound to become increasingly apparent, as the season develops, that the man Mack will miss most is Al Simmons. Connie admitted as much himself, with a tear in his voice, and the reverberations from the middle West, indicating that Al is already up to his familiar clubbing tricks, confirming our suspicions."[13]

Chicago, though teasing fans with a fast start, looked unlikely to break out of the second division as the season progressed.

Simmons was hitting for average, but not as much power as he usually did. On pitchers, Simmons recalled years later how he had trouble with the Yankees' Red Ruffing, a soft-spoken right-hander who pitched his way to a career 273 wins and the Hall of Fame, despite missing four toes on his left foot from a mining accident before his baseball career. "The big redhead always had me in trouble," said Simmons. "Ruffing pitched me in on the fists, just a little below the letters. He'd let me see a pitch to swing at, then come inside where I had to swing."[14]

Ironically, Ruffing found pitching to Simmons equally difficult. "With men on base," he once said, "Foxx can be a pain, but Simmons is a plague."[15] In his career, Simmons banged out six home runs off of Ruffing. His most prolific targets were George Blaeholder, Hank Johnson, Earl Whitehill and General Crowder — eight homers against each.

That season, he walloped a bunch of homers in a three-game period from June 9 to 11 — four to be exact, along with 10 RBIs against Detroit. He was heating up as midsummer approached; as for the White Sox, their 30–27 record was good for a slight toehold in the first division. But then Chicago started losing games at an alarming rate, and by June 28 the team was below .500. The fresh hope of the early season and a Simmons-infused march toward October had suddenly faded.

Good news for Chicago came in the form of major league baseball's first All-Star Game on July 6. Held in Comiskey Park, the contest was initiated by Arch Ward, sports editor for the *Chicago Tribune*, to coincide with the concurring celebration of Chicago's Century of Progress Exposition.

It was a boon for Chicago and the hometown faithful. Managers and fans around the league cities were allowed to vote on the players to play in the game — ballots were printed in 55 newspapers across the country. Few may realize this, but Al Simmons received the most votes of any player in the first All-Star Game, even though Babe Ruth was on the ballot. Simmons amassed 346,291 votes to Chuck Klein's 342,283 and Ruth's 320,518.[16]

And why not — Simmons was having a great year so far, batting .368 with 10 home runs and 73 RBIs. Ruth was on the decline, and Klein played for the perennially-losing Phillies.

In many ways, Simmons was positioned by 1933 to be the game's biggest star. While he had lost the prestige of playing for the Philadelphia A's, the 31-year-old Simmons seemed to have many more hard knocks under his belt.

"Hail to Al Simmons, new monarch of major league baseball," came the florid prose from Arch Ward. "The fans of America have voted him the crown in the greatest test of public sentiment the sport has known." But Ward was quick to point out the vote did not equate to a loss in "popularity" to an American legend like Babe Ruth, who he expected would receive the most applause when the players took the field at Comiskey Park. "This was not a popularity contest," wrote Ward, calming his pen. "It was an effort to choose the strongest teams that could be recruited in the major leagues."[17]

With the All-Star Game, baseball had established itself as America's favorite pastime, and Chicago's national exposition provided the perfect stage to introduce the national pastime's finest players to the rest of the country. The idea of pitting the top talent in the rival American and National Leagues against each other was both innovative and unprecedented. There was no interleague play back then; the World Series provided a unique setting for such battles.

"We wanted to see the Babe," said "Wild" Bill Hallahan, the National League starting pitcher. "Sure, he was old and had a big waistline, but that didn't make any difference. We were on the same field as Babe Ruth."

Fittingly, John McGraw came out of retirement to manage the National League team, and Connie Mack was assigned to head up the American League squad.

Here is what the American League lineup looked like in that first All-Star Game:

1. Ben Chapman, OF
2. Charlie Gehringer, 2B
3. Babe Ruth, OF
4. Lou Gehrig, 1B
5. Al Simmons, OF
6. Jimmie Dykes, 3B
7. Joe Cronin, SS
8. Rick Ferrell, C
9. Lefty Gomez, P

The National League lineup:

1. Pepper Martin, 3B
2. Frankie Frisch, 2B
3. Chuck Klein, OF
4. Chick Hafey, OF
5. Bill Terry, 1B
6. Wally Berger, OF
7. Dick Bartell, SS
8. Jimmie Wilson, C
9. Bill Hallahan, P

The specter of Simmons, Ruth and Gehrig on the same team made a monstrous impression. "Mack had the mightiest murderer's row of all time in his lineup," wrote George Kirksey, adding that McGraw would need to bank on the "classy pitching" of Carl Hubbell, Hallahan and Lon Warneke.

After all the hoopla died down and the game got under way, the American League struck first in the second inning when Hallahan gave up one-out walks to Ferrell and Cronin, and two batters later, pitcher Gomez singled home Ferrell for the AL's first run.

In the bottom of the third, after a walk to Gehringer, Ruth slugged the first home run in All-Star Game history, putting the AL up 3–0. Hallahan was yanked after walking Gehrig, and replaced by Warneke. The NL staged a comeback bid in the sixth — Warneke, the pitcher, hit a one-out triple and scored on a Pepper Martin groundout. Frisch smacked a home run to bring the NL to within a run, but after a Chuck Klein single, Crowder got out of the inning safely.

Cronin started the bottom of the sixth with a single. He scored on an Earl Averill single to give the AL the lead at 4–2. The NL threatened again in the top of the eighth. With Frisch on first with two outs, Hafey drilled a shot to right field that looked like it could be home run, but Ruth reached over the wall to snare it, shutting the door on the NL's chance to tie the game.

When the senior circuit could not score in the ninth, the AL won the game, 4–2. Simmons had one hit in four at-bats, a single to left field in the fifth inning. But it was Ruth's heroics — his home run and brilliant catch of Hafey's would-be home run — that highlighted and headlined the first All-Star Game.

When the season's second half got under way, Chicago peaked briefly at 42–41 on July 14. Afterwards, the losses outnumbered the wins, and the White Sox fell into the second division.

Simmons maintained his spot among the top-ranked batters though July, though his home runs were rare. Playing in Comiskey Park did not help his power numbers — nor his nerves. Just like he did with the A's, Simmons occasionally let loose with verbal barrages toward the opposition. Again, he reminded some of the ornery Ty Cobb.

"Simmons is a throwback to the good old days when the ballplayers would rather have the friendly enmity of the bleacherites than the dinner patronage of the ultra-fashionable in the grandstand," wrote John Drohan. Unafraid of most anything on a ball field, Simmons spoke his mind and did not shy away from engaging the rudest of fans, Drohan wrote. "The moment Al takes up his position in the field he's usually greeted with a flock of pithy questions," he said. "They don't bother Al. He snaps back the answers as neatly as he does a ball hit into left field." He noted that Simmons, like most ballplayers, was a bit superstitious. When he would return to the bench after playing the outfield, he stepped over the white chalk line that ran down third base or the first base side.[18]

Fitting his brash demeanor, Simmons on July 18 publicly declared — again — that the Yankees would win the pennant, dismissing the Senators and the A's. He picked the White Sox to finish third. In doing so, he could not have made Chicago's ownership all that happy, nor possibly his old Philadelphia buddies.

"The Yankees have the best team in the league. If they don't repeat, they will only have themselves to blame. They dislike the Senators so heartily that they have been pressing themselves out of a lot of games with them," Simmons said. Of Philadelphia, he said, "If George Earnshaw were pitching in his old form, the A's would be right up there. He's given me more trouble than any other pitcher this year. He struck me out three times in one afternoon." On Foxx, who Simmons trailed for the league lead in batting average by nine points, he observed, "Nobody respects his ability more than I do, but I'm in there swinging," perhaps alluding to Foxx's penchant for walks.[19]

Swinging away, by the end of July Simmons was briefly on top in the batting title chase, passing Foxx with a .361 average. That was, however, as good as it got. By August 26, Heinie Manush of Washington at .343 surged passed Simmons, whose bat had cooled off to a .341 tune.

Manush's club also took the league lead away from New York, causing Washington coach and baseball funny man Nick Altrock to say Simmons was a "total loss as a prophet" for so brazenly predicting a first-place finish for the Yankees. "Do you remember six weeks ago Al Simmons awarded the pennant to the Yanks? ... At that time I gave Al the bird. Well, now I am now shipping him a carload of eagles and a crate of 'razzberries.'"[20]

The failed-prophet Simmons continued to lose ground in his batting average. Increasingly unhappy on all fronts, he vented in an apparently ghost-written September 7 column for the *Chicago Daily News*. Simmons talked about his first season as a White Sox player, his offseason trade to Chicago, the Windy City fans, and a sore point—Comiskey Park. "I believe I had failed to hit in sixteen times at bat. Yet every time I stepped up to the plate I was cheered lustily. You would have thought I was in a hitting streak instead of a slump.... As for my batting slump, well, I hate to alibi, but I'll have to say without a question that Comiskey Park is the toughest park in the league because of its bigness.... The wind, too, is something that's tough to combat. When it blows from the south or west, it's OK, but most of the time it blows from the northeast directly in toward the plate, it slows up a lot of drives and makes it possible for an outfielder to get under them."[21]

The not-so humble Simmons declared that, though he typically hits a ball "unusually hard," the fly balls that used to "bounce off the walls" back in Philadelphia were now easy fly balls in Chicago.

Rumors were starting to fly. One had Simmons being offered the White Sox manager's job, and another had him going to New York in a trade whereby Babe Ruth would be sent to Chicago to play first base. Simmons poured cold water on the gossip. "No, I like to play baseball in the day time, and not replay it at night, as all managers do," he said. About his manager, the outfielder said, "Lew Fonseca is a good leader, a grand fellow and deserves a chance to prove that he is capable of finishing higher than the Sox are at present. Comiskey and Lew know our weaknesses and I'm sure they'll do their best to find new men to remedy them."[22]

Simmons' conditional support of Fonseca was clearly predicated on whether the team won. But that did not seem to matter to White Sox ownership. Two weeks later, Fonseca signed a contract to pilot the club for the 1934 season, thereby squashing speculation Simmons might head the club if it stumbled.

But stumble the rest of the way in 1933 the White Sox did — they finished in sixth place at 67–83 while Washington won the pennant over New York. With Chicago out of contention, Simmons sat out the next-to-the-last game and appeared in the season finale as a pinch-hitter.

His line for the year: .331 average, 14 home runs, 119 RBIs, 29 doubles and 10 triples. He had played in 146 games, and his 119 RBIs marked his tenth consecutive season over the century mark. He also notched 200 hits for the fifth year in a row. But his home run numbers were down — the lowest since his rookie season.

Elsewhere, Jimmie Foxx brilliantly won the American League triple crown with a .356 average, 48 homers and 163 RBIs. In the National League, Chuck Klein of the Phillies pulled off the same feat —.368, 28 homers, 120 RBIs.

That season, Foxx and Gehrig (.334, 32, 139) stood out as the league's top hitters — which likely riled the ultra-competitive Simmons. Foxx, 25, and Gehrig, 30, were younger than Simmons, 31, and in the midst of their best years and performing for attentive clubs. For the time being, Simmons was destined to play in massive Comiskey Park. After the season ended, a frustrated Simmons told owner Louis Comiskey that "catches of his long hits got on his nerves."

Comiskey quickly found himself between a rock and a hard-edged star. The shy and benevolent Louis Comiskey lived in the shadows of his far more famous father, Charles Comiskey, a nineteenth century baseball player, manager, team owner and a key figure in the formation of the American League. Charles owned the White Sox until his death in 1931 when Louis, who had worked for the team since 1910, took the reins of the club from 1931 to 1939.

In 1912, Louis had contracted scarlet fever and, for the rest of his life, had to maintain a hospital suite at St. Luke's in Chicago. He reportedly weighed more than 300 pounds. But he was competitive in a different way than his father. When Louis took over the moribund White Sox, he pushed toward building a better franchise, first pulling off the Simmons-Haas-Dykes purchase and then starting the first White Sox farm system, which began yielding results by 1939. Louis was not as tightfisted as his notoriously cheap father, as shown in Chicago's $150,000 acquisition the previous winter of the three A's players.

To appease Simmons, Lou Comiskey decided to do something about the layout of the ballpark. In November, the White Sox moved home plate 14 feet out into the field. This reduced the distances to the fences in left, right and center. The change quickly became controversial: "Comiskey Park, home of the White Sox, is being made over to the specifications of Al Simmons," noted the *Chicago Daily Tribune*.[23]

Interestingly, the revamping had other effects — some potentially negative for the hitter. It increased the amount of foul ground behind the catcher and along the first and third base lines. More foul balls are caught for outs in parks where the foul ground is expansive. Still, the fence adjustment was plugged as a victory for hitters. "Pitchers will have to alter their techniques," wrote Edward Burns.

It looked to many like the White Sox were catering to a grumbling Simmons. So extensive became the media coverage that Simmons actually began denying that he had asked for the adjustment when it was clear he had. Part of the problem may have been the press' disappointment in the once-promising White Sox that year.

A "scowling" and "bitter" Simmons "snorted" and told reporters in a rambling diatribe that moving the fences in was not his idea — but that the park was a problem. To critics, his statement was a classic "having it both ways" approach.

Al Simmons: "I'll you what's wrong out there. It's those damn breezes from Lake Michigan that whip across the playing field and give outfielders plenty of time to camp under long drives that would go for homers in the average park. See, I'll hit them in any park. The fielders will be playing closer in and will catch many of my drives that fall for base hits. I really believe I was cheated out of 15 or 20 homers because of that nasty wind from the lake. But I have never asked for any favors from anyone.[24]

Simmons lamented that the changes had "put me on the spot" and that now fans would expect 35 or 40 home runs from him. Speaking like a lawyer, he said, "I deeply regret the implication that I requested the change."[25]

The writers would not let the issue die quickly — the word was out. "Comiskey has loosed surveyors, architects, excavators and landscape gardeners on his magnificent baseball acreage with instructions to make Al happy," observed one scribe.[26]

Taking Simmons' defense at face value, Edward Burns snidely noted, makes it appear that Simmons, "who certainly is one of the greatest ballplayers who ever lived, though not so good on interviews, really wanted Comiskey Park made larger, instead of smaller, as his obliging boss, Lou Comiskey, had supposed.... But what in the hell can even Mr. Comiskey do about heading off the lake breeze?"[27]

Laying aside his tweaks—aimed at Simmons and his perceived overreaction—Burns deemed the change a "fair one" to hitters. In this view, it was not a "deceptive" revision to the field like the Boston Braves had committed a few years ago when they installed a "fake" grandstand that did not hold people in an attempt to bring in the fences.[28]

Simmons maintained his awkward position, saying the old dimensions hurt him but that he had nothing to do with the adjustment. "I really believe I was cheated out of 15 or 20 home runs because of that nasty wind. I deeply resent the implication I requested this change," he said.[29]

The proud Simmons was not about to let his image take a beating. But he was at a crossroads—hostage to an unfriendly hitters' environment, a franchise that was far from contention, and arguably still at the peak of his batting powers. What kind of player would he become?

Chicago, for Simmons, was not the best place to be. He would have to muddle through it all, but not without plenty of low points to go along with a few high ones. Maybe some complacency began to set in—meanwhile, the clock kept ticking on his body, his talent and his determination.

CHAPTER FOURTEEN

Changes in Chicago

"Late hours, careless dieting and dissipation have ruined many a young athlete."
—Al Simmons

"Men marry because they are tired; women because they are curious. Both are disappointed."
—Oscar Wilde, *in his play* A Woman of No Importance

In early 1934, there was a brief glimmer of hope that the Great Depression was coming to an end—it was not—but the unemployment rate did begin to drop and things looked a little rosier for awhile. Other serious threats emerged, as the Dust Bowl in the Midwest that caused major ecological and agricultural damage. At times the clouds blackened the sky reaching all the way to cities such as New York and Washington, D.C.

The outlook grew darker in baseball, where Connie Mack continued his dissembling of the great A's dynasty. Early that winter, he sent famed catcher Mickey Cochrane to the Detroit Tigers for $100,000 and a journeyman player. Cochrane's competitive nature would drive the Tigers, who had been picked to finish around .500, to the 1934 American League championship—their first pennant in 25 years. Mack also sent ace hurler Lefty Grove, pitcher Rube Walberg and on-base machine Max Bishop to the Boston Red Sox for two second-tier players and $125,000 in cash. All the A's had left in star power was Jimmie Foxx.

That January, Al Simmons not surprisingly headed to his customary off-season training locale, Hot Springs—once there, the popular player soon found himself in the headlines.

Working out in Whittington Park, Simmons joined a baseball game with kids aged 8 to 15, according to a newspaper. He wound up breaking two bats and losing three balls on hits that apparently did some property damage. But the "owners of the property were repaid handsomely by the slugger" and the "youngsters were pleased, for the had played baseball with the mighty Al." In fact, two of the boys, Joe Sweat and Freddy Young, were given special bats with their names engraved on them. Simmons had King Wade, a friend of his only described as a "local sportsman," check on the addresses of the youngsters so he could personally present them with the bats.[1]

Despite the hard times, Simmons had plenty to feel magnanimous about. After signing a two-year contract worth $27,500 a season, he arrived in Pasadena in early February a full two weeks ahead of the White Sox training camp—a direct contrast to his star days with the A's as well as the prior year, when he was the last to arrive in camp. While his new salary was a drop from the $33,000 he had received the year before, Simmons understood he was lucky to be earning such a tidy sum in the midst of the Great Depression when so many were out of work.

More than ever, he sought redemption in the season ahead—especially on the home run front in the newly-shrunk Comiskey Park.

But Simmons came into camp with an aching thumb. Mysteriously, he had suffered a "gash" to it while traveling through New Mexico on the way to California—the facts behind the injury have never been disclosed. Oddly, one newspaper account stated that Simmons received treatment for his thumb from a "medicine chief" before seeking out a physician once he go to Pasadena.[2]

"It's just a cut," Simmons told the writers. "Got it on the way out here, but it'll be healed up by the (February) 25th. I'm going to have a new bandage put on it now. I don't have any chance of infection." Thumbs up or down, Simmons wouldn't make any predictions about the season, as he had been so outspoken the year before. "It's a little early in the year." This time around, he preferred to witness the entire spring training period to see how his teammates and other clubs performed.[3]

He seemed a bit less bold. Leaving the perennially contending Athletics for the woeful White Sox was hard on Simmons, a stubborn and prideful soul. Was the prospect of playing another two years for Chicago causing him to lose his famous intensity? Some thought it was.

Bob Broeg said, "After Al had come out early one morning, asking extra men to pitch batting practice to him, another Chicago regular came over and asked, 'How come you're out here trying to show us up?'"[4]

The Cobb-influenced Simmons of yesteryear would have decked someone for a comment like that, Broeg maintained. But Simmons did not retort—perhaps it just wasn't worth it, the writer surmised. As Broeg revealingly observed, "Simmons had apparently accepted the Sox' second-division syndrome."

And so it went in 1934. Simmons that April was a chilly as the weather—but something historical happened along the way.

Four games into the season on April 22, Simmons collected his 2,000th career hit in a 6–5 loss to the St. Louis Browns. It came in only his 1,390th game — to this day Al Simmons stands as the quickest player to 2,000 hits. Next is Ichiro Suzuki, who made it in 1,402 games. The accomplishment speaks for itself.

No one realized the significance at the time, and by the end of April — 10 games into the season — Simmons had a .244 average with three homers and six RBIs.

He was the victim of some bad luck, too. On May 6 in a game against Washington, Senators shortstop Joe Cronin threw a ball that smacked Simmons in the head while he was about to slide into second. Down for the count, Simmons was taken off the field and rushed to Garfield Hospital — X-rays revealed no skull fractures, but he was hurt.

At the hospital, Simmons' door was marked with a "No Visitors" sign. Once the X-rays came in good, his teammates and some writers were allowed to visit. They found him a bit cranky, holding an ice pack to his head and reading the sports pages. "If I sit up I get dizzy," he told everyone, "but as long as I lie down it's a breeze." There were five large baskets of flowers in the room. The cards had been removed and were placed under Simmons' pillow.[5]

Al Simmons: "I don't remember. I was running into the bag, bent on breaking up the double play, of course, and then, blooie! I thought it was an explosion. I thought somebody had thrown a bomb. I was out 10 minutes. It felt like 10 years. A fellow was taking pictures of the play and he showed me one. I'm diving right into the ground on my nose ... I swung across in front of Cronin and must have instinctively turned my head as he turned loose his throw. Joe was all right. It was my fault."[6]

Still, Simmons suffered so badly from nausea and headaches, he stayed behind one day to rest and then joined the team in New York. Back in the lineup on May 18, he went 2-for-5 with a double.[7]

He was also playing for a new White Sox manager — his friend, Jimmy Dykes, also the team's third baseman. Lew Fonseca had been ousted. Comiskey, even though he had signed Fonseca to a two-year contract the previous fall, jettisoned the not-wildly-popular manager in favor of the combative Dykes after the Sox got off to a disappointing 4–11 start.

Dykes had little to say about it, except that he promised "plenty of fight."[8]

Simmons, perhaps buoyed by Dykes managerial presence — and despite his aches and pains — walloped the ball once he got back on the field. By May 23, his average had skyrocketed to .341, and he was finally busting out some extra-base hits, too.

One change he made around this time was switching his bat to a shorter and lighter one — from 37 to 35 inches — in an attempt to gain more speed.[9]

Still, he seemed to have cold moments at the plate. On June 2, sportswriter Edward Burns wrote that Simmons had "developed a certain timidity with runners on." In that 3–1 loss that day to the White Sox, he left the tying runs on as he "struck out with his bat on his shoulder."[10]

Such ups and downs for Simmons were commonplace during the 1934 season. One high note came June 27 when he heroically blasted a grand slam against Lefty Gomez of the Yankees in an 8–7 loss.

By the All-Star break on July 9, he had a .348 average with 10 homers. The latter was above his pace from the prior season, arguably helped by the shortening of the fences in his home ballpark. Still, some expected more home runs from Simmons, who truly was a line-drive hitter rather than flyball power guy. "That change in the White Sox Park seems to have done everyone good, except for Al Simmons, for whom the fences were moved in," lamented one scribe.[11] To be sure, the changes in Comiskey Park did not help the White Sox. They stumbled into the All-Star Game break with a 25–51 record.

The midsummer classic was played July 10 in the Polo Grounds, home

Al Simmons (left) on the tennis court with A's pitcher George Earnshaw, who joined Simmons as a member of the Chicago White Sox for the 1934 season. *National Baseball Hall of Fame*

of the New York Giants. Fittingly, a Giant—Carl Hubbell—put on one of the All-Star Game's most memorable performances—and Simmons was involved.

Off to a shaky start with two on base in the first inning, Hubbell used his famous screwball to strikeout Ruth, Gehrig, and Foxx. He then whiffed Simmons and Joe Cronin to start the second inning before Bill Dickey cracked a single to break up the strikeout streak consisting of five future Hall of Famers in a row.

After three scoreless innings, Hubbell left with the NL ahead, 4–0. But the American League rallied, scoring nine runs, as pitcher Mel Harder sealed the win with five shutout innings in relief for a 9–7 triumph.

Far less known than Hubbell's feat is the fact Simmons was the offensive star of this second All-Star match-up. He dished out three hits, two of them doubles, and scored three times while driving in one run. His performance was tops among the American League hitters—Gehrig and Ruth were held hitless while Jimmie Foxx notched two hits, including a double.

The 1934 installment of the midsummer classic featured some of baseball's all-time stars—17 of the 18 starters eventually were elected to the Hall of Fame. The AL Hall of Famers were Simmons, Foxx, Charlie Gehringer, Heinie Manush, Ruth, Gehrig, Joe Cronin, Bill Dickey and Lefty Gomez. The NL Hall of Famers were Frankie Frisch, Pie Traynor, Joe Medwick, Kiki Cuyler, Bill Terry, Travis Jackson, Gabby Hartnett and Carl Hubbell. The odd man out was Wally Berger, no slouch himself—in an 11-year-career, he batted .300 with 242 homers.

Three days after the All-Star Game, trade rumors started popping up about Simmons, who seemed discontent, despite the change of pilots on the White Sox ship.

Press reports quoted player-manager Jimmie Dykes as saying he would swap Simmons for younger talent—the 32-year-old outfielder seemed a perfect addition to a contending club like Detroit or Cleveland, he said. The White Sox, it appeared, wanted to clean house now that the Simmons-Dykes-Haas infusion had not produced a winning club barely a season and a half later. Down in the farm system, there were slim pickings talent-wise. So, the White Sox once again thought trades would improve the ballclub.

Perhaps Dykes was trying to do his friend, Simmons, a favor by sending him to a better organization; it is only speculation, but certainly Simmons would have been vocal in his unhappiness, and probably would have talked to Dykes about an escape plan.

"Prohibitive prices asked by the minor league clubs for untried players," Dykes declared, "is the biggest difficulty in rebuilding a major league club." The option, according to Dykes, was shipping out studs like Simmons for multiple younger players. Pressure was also coming down from above. Louis Comiskey had accompanied the team on its two eastern road trips, the first time in memory that a Sox owner had done so. And, he had fired manager Fonseca after the first couple of weeks in the season. With the losses rapidly piling up, the situation was embarrassing for the front office.[12]

While his name was bandied about in trade rumors, Simmons did some major league hitching up of his own. On August 6, Al Simmons married Dores Lynn Reader of Chicago in a discreet wedding ceremony out of the public's eye. It helped matters that the White Sox had an off day. From a wealthy family and extremely beautiful, Reader was registered as living at 1063 North Shore Avenue in Chicago. Dores was only 19, and Simmons was 32. They may have been dating for as many as three years.

The wedding was held at the Church of St. Thomas the Apostle at 55th Street and Kimbark Avenue in Chicago. Monsignor Thomas Shannon performed the ceremony. When Simmons filled out the marriage license paperwork, he gave a Chicago hotel as his address.

Simmons told writers that he and his wife honeymooned at Middle Lake, near Lauderdale, Wisconsin. He returned the next day for the scheduled White Sox game — so the honeymoon was very brief, if at all. With the distances involved, it is hard to imagine how he could have made it back in time for the game; there is little reason to believe the honeymoon was anything but an overnight stay and close to Chicago.

One account has Simmons meeting Reader three years before — when she would have been 16 — at an exhibition game in her hometown of Racine, Wisconsin. Another report claimed they met in Pasadena, in 1934 when Dores was visiting with her parents, and began dating steadily thereafter. "They were seen together about town on many occasions, and friends predicted marriage would be the outcome," the *Chicago Daily Tribune* noted.[13]

The pair did not announce the wedding in advance. On August 10 — after Simmons had already played in a couple White Sox games — Dores' parents eventually confirmed the marriage to members of the press. Confusing the matter, Chicago sportswriter Arch Ward on August 1 had speculated that the two would marry after the World Series — not in August. So the wedding came as a surprise to a lot of people. "She does not deny they are engaged," wrote an unaware Ward just five days before the wedding took place, "but Simmons says there is nothing to it."[14]

In explaining the secrecy, Ward noted Simmons' failed engagement back in his A's heyday. It seemed that Simmons wanted to take no chances in case things went askew. "The romance (in Philadelphia) ended before they reached the altar," the writer said.

Why get married in the middle of the season? Rather implausibly, the

Chicago Daily Tribune observed that Simmons had "suffered an injury to a finger on his right hand in a game in St. Louis last week and decided to turn his enforced vacation into a honeymoon" with his new wife, "an attractive brunette." It is true that he missed four games on July 31, August 1, 2 and 3. Injured finger or not, it all seemed like a rush. Dores, by the way, was not pregnant.[15]

Simmons could be intensely private, and felt perhaps that a secret wedding with his much younger bride when no one was expecting it was a good way to handle what would have been a blizzard of media interest.

Once back on the field, Simmons bashed the ball with intensity through the end of August, raising his average from .345 to .355 with seven triples, two homers and 24 RBIs.

The newly married Simmons freely gave advice that season to younger ballplayers. His Hall of Fame file contains a clipping under his byline from 1934, and though it is unclear where it was published, the article is a deep study in his high standards and how to succeed in tough times: "More young men should be playing baseball, not only as a pastime but if they have ambitions to become professional players. Baseball is overcoming the Depression and there are going to be more chances for the young amateur or semi-pro player to land in the ranks of organized baseball. There are more minor leagues this year than there were in 1933 and there will still be more in 1935 for the reason that several sections were merely marking time to see how the new leagues came out this year. The amateur who seeks to go up the ladder of baseball success should diagnose himself."

Simmons advised kids to decide whether they are best suited to be a pitcher, catcher, infielder or outfielder. "As a rule, you find the larger men in the outfield, on first base or in the box. Yet I know of many comparatively small men who have made good in the outfield and at bat. I know of several crack catchers who never weighed more than 160 pounds. Few players, however, who weigh less than 170 pounds, have made good as pitchers. So much for size and weight," he said.

While he seemed focused on size, pure talent and Spartan-like conditioning mattered as well.

Al Simmons: "To be an outfielder, the player should have speed and a strong throwing arm in addition to ability to hit the ball. Size and weight will not keep an outfielder in the major leagues if he has a dead arm or cannot move off a dime. The infielder need not be as large but he must have a good pair of hands, speed and ability to do some quick thinking. The first sacker should have the size to provide a good target at which his teammates can throw and also be shifty on his feet and have the ability to reach out and take a throw."[16]

The trade rumors kept swirling around Simmons as the 1934 season wound down. One placed him in Boston for the next season, and another again in Detroit. Meanwhile, White Sox officials denied any such moves.

Simmons cared little for conjecture, and kept up his handiwork. On September 17, he knocked in his 100th RBI for the 11th straight year since entering the big leagues. A stunning achievement, it marked, however, his last consecutive season doing so.

Al Simmons remains today the only major league ballplayer who started his first 11 seasons with 100-plus RBIs — though Albert Pujols has already done it 10 straight seasons through 2010 and could eventually top Simmons' mark.

When the 1934 season ended, Simmons had fared better than his team, which finished 53–99, last in the American League. In 138 games, he posted a .344 average with 18 home runs, 104 RBIs, 102 runs scored, 36 doubles and seven triples.

As for the trade rumors, Simmons stirred them up with an offseason vacation trip to Hawaii with old friend and current Tigers manager, Mickey Cochrane. A West Coast writer wrote that Cochrane wanted Simmons on the Tigers in 1935 — and that Simmons wished to go there. If Cochrane had made such a statement, he would have found himself in violation of baseball's "tampering" rules. The baseball establishment frowned upon making the obvious too obvious.

In an effort to clear Cochrane and repair any damage with the White Sox, Simmons took the highly unusual step of writing a letter to the *Chicago Daily Tribune* staff. He blamed the writer for being "anxious to put Mickey on the spot," and said that Cochrane was "far too smart" to "make silly cracks" like that. "Can't a couple of pals make a trip together anymore? I have never indicated that I do not like to play in Chicago," Simmons wrote. He then applauded Chicago as "the best baseball town in the country."[17]

Chicago might be a town, or a city, but either way he would be playing ball there the next season.

Only 33, life was changing in 1935 for Al Simmons. Some writers thought getting married would help the irrepressible ballplayer in his future outlook — or so claimed Edward Burns in flowery prose reflective of that era's chauvinism. "He naturally will want to appear as the world's best in his chosen field in the eyes of his bride, who is a dozen years his junior, young enough to look up to Al as her great big hero," Burns said. Bedazzled by her great, big hero, the "cheerful Mrs. Simmons" strived to not let her husband fall into "slumps" made worse by his tendency for "melancholia," Burns speculated.

After all, Burns had high hopes for Simmons in 1935, though he readily called him a "moody cuss." In a column featuring pictures of both Simmons and his wife, the scribe predicted the ballplayer would win the batting title with a mark in the .360s. He was, after all, a "torrid second half hitter," Burns noted. "Al didn't really start hitting until the last two months of the season," and he could broach .400 in the best of circumstances. Also, Simmons was in the last year of a two-year contract, and "to stay in the real big money, he will have to bat out some handsome sales points," the writer maintained.[18]

As it turned out, Burns was far off the mark. Simmons would struggle like he never had to that point in the 1935 campaign. Around the country, other trends seemed off the mark, too—1935 was the sinkhole year of the Great Depression, one of doubt, uncertainty and rash ugliness.

That year the U.S. Supreme Court ruled that the key New Deal legislation—the National Industrial Recovery Act—was unconstitutional. This infuriated the labor movement, which at the time was suffering a backlash and was branded as being un–American, Bolshevik, communistic and socialistic. Down in the South, an upsurge of lynchings worried those in favor of civil rights, and around the country the Daughters of the American Revolution urged loyalty oaths for teachers. Meanwhile, President Roosevelt signed into law the Social Security Act, and the populist though corrupt Senator Huey Long from Louisiana was assassinated.

In this strange, eventful year, Babe Ruth, now with the Boston Braves, would exit from the playing field. In one of his last games that May before retiring, he unleashed a power show—as if to prove he was still the Babe, though old and fat—with a three-home-run performance against the Pittsburgh Pirates in Forbes Field. One of his moon shots cleared the right-field grandstand, the longest ball reportedly ever hit there.

With that and more, 1935 seemed like the end of the era of 1920s baseball stars, and the start of another chapter. New blood was rising—Cleveland signed a 16-year-old pitcher named Bob Feller, and in San Francisco, an elegant young outfielder named Joe DiMaggio tore up the Pacific Coast League in the season before his Yankees' debut. At the same time, a prodigious San Diego high schooler, Ted Williams, was bashing the opposition. Along with Ruth, this year the game witnessed the retirements of Rabbit Maranville, Dazzy Vance and Earle Combs.

Despite all the talk—and there was much—Chicago did not trade Simmons that offseason. In fact, he seemed primed for the possibilities ahead, changing his usual offseason routine of returning home to Milwaukee to feast upon his mother's opulent meals. Instead, he had been "in training since the close of last season," and had spent time swimming off Honolulu (with Cochrane), "eating daintily in tropical hotels," and three weeks in Hot Springs.[19]

Good thing he ate daintily in Hawaii, as the Chicago front office deliberated on switching him from left to center field where he could expect to run a lot more.

Chicago wanted to try a good-hit, no-field outfielder from the minor leagues named George Washington in left field. But the move appeared to worry the 33-year-old Simmons, who pleaded with Lou Comiskey that he was not a natural center fielder and not as fleet-footed as before. Besides, he said, Connie Mack had tried him there and had given up. But Comiskey's reaction was a "series of loud laughs" and a reply along the line of "that's too bad." So, the team earmarked center field for Simmons, despite his pleas against it. It doubtlessly made him angry that his opinion was dismissed.[20]

While Washington did play for Chicago that year—.283 but with just eight homers and 47 RBIs—he was marginal, and would not stick in the big leagues.

Over in Philadelphia, the aging Mack reminisced about Simmons. His decimated A's, filled with young players, lost 91 games during the 1935 season. "Simmons has a natural baseball instinct, and during his nine years with me, made only one bad play," Mack told *The Sporting News*, though did not elaborate on what that one bad play was.[21]

Things got off well enough for Simmons and his team. On Opening Day, he got one hit in four at-bats in a 7–6 White Sox victory over Detroit. By the end of April, he was at .302, and hitting a season high of .324 on May 8.

Word came in April that Simmons was such a hero in Milwaukee that a 15-cent cigar was named after him. "Al smokes 'em himself," the newspaper claimed.[22] Also smoking were the White Sox, who enjoyed a 21–14 record by June 1. It seemed Dykes' hard-boiled style was turning around the team.

Maybe playing center field was taking a toll on Simmons. His average began to drop precipitously that spring, all the way down to .250 by June 9—and he was dropped from third spot in the lineup to fifth.

Two days later, he belted a grand slam off Washington's Bobby Burke in the first game of a doubleheader, but his five RBIs were not enough as Washington won, 9–8. The Sox took the nightcap, 9–3. Still in the groove, Simmons three days later whacked another grand slam, this time off Washington's Belva Bean.

It was a strange season, and Simmons was not as feared as before—on or off the field. Even the writers were needling him.

In July, Arch Ward of the *Chicago Daily Tribune* wrote, "Carl Hubbell wears his baseball pants like Al Simmons because he can't stand the elastic around his knees. Simmons wears them low because he is sensitive about his cowpuncher legs."[23]

In the *Dictionary of Slang and Colloquial English,* "cowpuncher" is defined as a cowboy or herdsman. It is not clear what cowpuncher legs expressed, but slang in the first half of the twentieth century often had a different flavor.

Fourteen: Changes in Chicago

Simmons, sometimes unwisely, many times confided in Ward. In August, mired in the midst of a slump, he told Ward that he "abandoned his habit of drinking a few bottles of beer in his room before turning in for the night."[24]

Not for that reason, but just for a cold bat, Dykes benched Simmons for a July 2 game against St. Louis. Chicago won, 4–1. Around the league, Al Simmons was not the only perennial star sagging at the plate. "Big guns on the batting range a year ago — Al Simmons, Heinie Manush and Hal Trosky — are not booming so impressively this season," noted the Associated Press, adding that Simmons was almost 100 points below his 1934 average at .250.[25]

Oddly, Simmons attributed his performance to too much swimming in Honolulu during the offseason. He thought it affected his "batting muscles."[26]

Fred Clarke, the former Pirate manager and Hall of Fame outfielder, said Simmons' trouble is that "he cannot get his body behind his swing and as a result does not swat with any of his former power." Simmons had only eight homers to that point in the 1935 season.

Bucketfoot Al still had his backers. One scribe recalled that Simmons was recently considered a "much better hitter than Babe Ruth" and "just about the perfect hitter."[27]

Amazingly, Al Simmons was picked for the July 8 All-Star Game in Cleveland, where he cracked out two hits in a 4–1 American League victory. His safeties gave him a then-All-Star leading .462 average in the first three midsummer classics. Jimmie Foxx, once again playing third in deference to Lou Gehrig, belted a two-run homer in the bottom of the first.

With the All-Star Game in the rear view mirror, Simmons had a 4-for-5 game in a July 19 victory over Washington. Just as it seemed he was finding the sweet spot on his bat, he suffered a groin injury and missed about a week's worth of games toward the end of the month.

In some ways, he felt caught between two eras in baseball — or two chapters of his life. However, when he showed up in Cleveland for a series, he admitted not being much of a factor in the surprisingly strong showing by the White Sox, and even said he did not merit his All-Star selection. "The Sox wouldn't be very far out of first place today but for Al Simmons," he said. "Jimmy Dykes' pitchers have done their share to keep the club out in front. So have the infielders. Everyone has done a lot for the club except for me." He blamed Comiskey Park again for his offensive woes. "Before I was sold to the Sox by Connie Mack, I never was a good hitter on the Chicago south side. Why? Because I'm a long fly ball hitter, and outfielders play way back when I come to bat," he said, also citing the wind from the lake that "pulls my long drives in for easy outs."[28]

On August 14, the Chicago fans booed Simmons for the first time in his tenure with the team. Over the course of two games, he went hitless in five run-scoring possibilities before banging out a triple in a 9–5 loss to Boston. The White Sox had lost six games in a row, and were down to 52–48.

By the end of the month, rumors percolated on a Simmons' trade to Detroit in the upcoming offseason. George Kirksey of the United Press International wrote that the Chicago outfielder was "definitely slated" to go to the Motor City.

Simmons was beginning to hit for more power as the season neared its end. He smacked three hits and collected four RBIs in a 9–6 win over Cleveland on September 1. He soon lost momentum. The whole month of September he managed just one home run, and his average fell to .267 by the last game of the season. His line otherwise: 16 home runs, 79 RBIs, 140 hits, 22 doubles and seven triples. He saw action in just 128 games. It was the worst year of his storied career. Not only did he fail to hit .300 for the first time in his career, but his record-setting streak of 11 consecutive seasons with 100-plus RBIs had come to an end.

After the season, the White Sox told Simmons he would have to take a $17,500 pay cut, offering him a $10,000 salary. Simmons was outraged. He tore up the contract offer in front of Dykes, who in turn said he was "thoroughly disgusted with Simmons' play."

Losing Dykes as an ally did not help matters. Shirley Povich of the *Washington Post* captured the melodrama of a ballplayer on the downside of his career. "Knowing that his munificent contract expired at the end of the 1935 season and that he would have to produce with his bat to earn such salary in 1936, Simmons had every incentive to play the game to the hilt. Instead, he encountered his worst season, and the league's managers now have definite suspicions that the guy is by no means the Simmons of old."[29]

It was an unpleasant situation. That winter the White Sox sought takers for Simmons—Detroit was tops on the list, though not the only team. And, the price was steep.

Chicago apparently wanted between $75,000 to $100,000 for Simmons. One day Dykes called Simmons to say the team had two cash offers for him—one from the New York Yankees and the other from the Detroit Tigers. New York was about to bring aboard rookie phenomenon Joe DiMaggio, and Detroit had just won two straight pennants under manager Mickey Cochrane, Simmons' old teammate. Either franchise was a promising destination.

Dykes asked Simmons which team he preferred playing for, according to writer Bob Broeg. "I'll take Detroit," said Simmons. But years later, he called it one of the worst decisions he ever made. "If I'd gone with the Yankees, I'd been on four pennant winners."[30]

And so, the Simmons deal was consummated along with another important one involving his former team in Philadelphia. The A's sold Jimmie Foxx and pitcher Johnny Marcum to the Red Sox for $150,000, getting in return the nondescript Gordon Rhodes and minor league catcher George Savino. Mack had finally jettisoned his last star of the 1929–31 champion Philadelphia A's.

The trades were linked, wrote Edward Burns. "If the Red Sox had not given Mickey Cochrane and the Detroit Tigers a chill by closing for Foxx, Cochrane would probably would have refused to meet the White Sox's $75,000 demand for Simmons." The 28-year-old Foxx, who had averaged 41 homers over the past seven seasons, uttered a brief comment—"my dream has come true"—while Philadelphia fans once again mourned the loss of a favorite gate attraction.[31] Foxx would enjoy several highly productive years in Boston. On the flip side, Simmons would spend but one productive—though contentious—year in Detroit.

In a twist of gamesmanship, Cochrane offered a bet with Dykes for "the best hat in New York" that Simmons would hit better than .325 for the Tigers the next season. Dykes refused, and Cochrane retorted, "I wanted to be sure that Simmons wasn't through."[32]

After the trade, rumors continued to circulate that Lou Comiskey traded Simmons because the player had rejected a $12,500 contract—higher than previously reported. Simmons, always protective of his image, tried to dispel the press reports. When he reached Hot Springs in January, he wrote to Edward Burns to deny the contract rejection story. Only a year ago Burns had gone out on the prognostication limb to pick Simmons as the likely favorite to win the American League batting title.

Al Simmons: "That tearing up the contract story started in Philadelphia. I never tore up any contract. Some fellows in Philadelphia have been trying to get me ever since I left Philadelphia to play in Chicago. I sat down and told Mr. Comiskey it was all a lousy lie. I thought I was even lucky to get a contract from him after the year I had. No one has to tell me how bad I was last season. I know, and it made me sick ... I would have given my right arm to help Lou and please the Chicago fans, but damn, I just couldn't do a thing. I'm sorry. I was a flop and my confidence is gone."[33]

Simmons sounded edgy, if not a little conspiratorial, in his defense of the matter. Besides, he was just unhappy in Chicago. He ended his letter to Burns advising him not to make any more predictions about him winning batting titles. Perhaps those expectations were too heavy to bear.

Burns, who alternated from being an unabashed ally to harsh critic of Simmons, described the outfielder as a "temperamental cuss" and in a "constant fret" about the spacious Comiskey Park, despite the fact the White Sox front office even shortened the distances to the fences. The left fielder got in such a "rut" that he began having trouble hitting in the "smaller" ballparks, he added.[34]

While his baseball world seemed frayed and uncertain, the Duke of Milwaukee opened a new chapter on the domestic front. On November 25, 1935, his wife Dores gave birth to John Allen Simmons, a five-pound baby. Two weeks later a newspaper photo appeared of the smiling slugger with his infant son, who would be nicknamed, appropriately, "Duke." There was more to life than just baseball — or was there?

CHAPTER FIFTEEN

Tail of the Tiger

"You know, I've got a reputation for being coarse and a little bit ornery, but believe me, enough things have happened to me in my lifetime to account for that."
—Al Simmons

"He turned out to be, under that gruff exterior, a very kindly and thoughtful man."
— George Case[1]

In 1936, major league baseball took a step toward recognizing its all-time greats — the first five men selected for the National Baseball Hall of Fame and Museum were Ty Cobb, Babe Ruth, Honus Wagner, Christy Mathewson and Walter Johnson. Three years later, it would open in Cooperstown, New York, honoring these players and many more in the years to come.

In lean times, the nation was hungry for heroes. In the year ahead President Roosevelt won reelection, the gigantic Hoover Dam opened on the Arizona-Nevada border, auguring more development in the Far West, and overseas, the Spanish Civil War began as the Rome-Berlin axis was formed.

In Detroit, Al Simmons had finally escaped the doldrums of the Chicago White Sox to a world-champion team eager to repeat. The Tigers were loaded — they had won the 1935 World Series against the Chicago Cubs, and had won the American League pennant in 1934. "With Al Simmons in our lineup," said Gehringer, "I can't see how we could miss repeating."[2]

The Tigers were Simmons' kind of team, built around the offense and featuring Hank Greenberg, Charlie Gehringer and Goose Goslin, among others. However, how Simmons would fit into Detroit's equation would prove interesting.

Simmons was still viewed as among the game's top players. During spring training, *The Sporting News* columnist Dick Farrington eschewed the player's plunge in 1935. "The Duke of Milwaukee is not so old," the columnist wrote. "There is spring in his legs, he can throw and there is nothing wrong with his eyesight. So it is possible he may make a remarkable comeback in his new surroundings." Simmons' troubles in Chicago were "more mental than physical," Farrington wrote. It all unraveled there for Simmons when it "got it into his head" that Comiskey Park was bad for hitters. Now, Farrington chirped, "Al is on the spot" to prove himself worthy of the excellent Detroit Tigers ball club.[3]

Unlike previous seasons, the humbler Simmons did not seek to drive a hard deal on his salary. He realized that he had little leverage, due to the twin effects of the economic conditions and his poor statistics from the year before. "Pay me what you think I'm worth," he told the Detroit front office.[4]

In March, Simmons bumped into Ira Thomas, his old minor league manager and mentor, in Durham, North Carolina. The new Detroit outfielder was walking through the hotel lobby after Detroit's exhibition game with Cincinnati had been rained out when he stumbled upon Thomas, who was there to scout some prospects at nearby Duke University. For some reason, the encounter impressed witnesses, and in the florid prose of one newspaper account, "the meeting was reminiscent of overseas days when French officers gave the doughboys a few pointers on how old friends should be treated," whatever that meant.[5]

In the beginning, Simmons was excited to be with Detroit. "Al is frisking around like a colt at his first training trip," wrote one scribe. "He wears four sweat suits." His life, however, was bigger than just baseball. With his newborn son, Simmons talked about giving young John Allen daily baths and "bouncing his boy in a tub." His habit of rising late in the morning was altered by parenthood, too. It was only a few years ago on a trip to Japan that he and his roommate Ralph Shinners would stay in bed for a day and a half, according to a news account. With a baby in the house, that routine was no longer possible, of course.[6]

Al Simmons spent the 1936 season in Detroit, following three seasons with the Chicago White Sox; for the Tigers he hit .327 and drove in 112 runs. *National Baseball Hall of Fame*

Out on the playing field, it was becoming clear that the 34-year-old Simmons had lost a few steps. At the close of spring training that season, manager Mickey Cochrane acknowledged the difficulty of replacing the speedy Jo-Jo White of 1935 with Simmons in center field.

The problem was that Detroit's lineup also featured the 35-year-old Goose Goslin in left field alongside Simmons, who is "no gazelle," as one scribe put it. Several times in exhibition games opponents were able to get extra-base hits because of the slowness of Simmons and Goslin.

Goslin was not exactly an admirer of Al Simmons. Years later, he said of him, "He was at his best when a game was at stake," but had taken too many days off and left too many games early to visit his "old Milwaukee haunts."[7]

With Hank Greenberg briefly holding out that spring, Cochrane toyed with the idea of using Simmons as his cleanup hitter. One writer noted that Simmons' spring training work had convinced "observers that he is likely to have a good year, perhaps even a great year." Not only was he hitting well, but he seemed to have a better attitude, it was noted.[8]

Some of the other Tigers appreciated Simmons' intensity, and applauded ownership for acquiring a player of Simmons' caliber. "We haven't lost a thing this winter, and we added Al Simmons to the outfield," said pitcher Schoolboy Rowe. "You can watch out for Al this summer. He's going to have one of his best seasons."[9]

At Detroit's spring training complex in Lakeland, Florida, Simmons got off to a good start—one reason may have been that he was using a lighter bat, around 33 ounces. Cochrane had recommended the change. After Simmons slugged a homer into the left-field stands, the manager quipped, "You see, the guy's hitting like old times. I thought the lighter bat would help."[10]

Cochrane's expectations for his old A's buddy were high. "We've got the same ball club that won the flag two years in a row, plus Al Simmons." Simmons was hitting as well as ever, the player-manager said, and had his confidence back. "I'm predicting we will win."[11]

Detroit opened the season in Cleveland with a lineup of Billy Rogell at shortstop, Cochrane at catcher, Charlie Gehringer at second base, Hank Greenberg at first base, Simmons in center field, Goslin in left field, Pete Fox in right field, Marv Owen at third base, and Rowe on the mound.

Rowe twirled Detroit to a 3–0 victory, and Simmons whacked a double in four trips to the plate. He continued hitting through the month, collecting at least one hit in all thirteen games he played. "A change of scenery has acted as a tonic to Al Simmons," observed one writer.[12]

Back in Chicago, manager and old friend Jimmy Dykes gave him a backhanded compliment: "Al's got some hitting left in him. He didn't hit much for us, but he ought to do better for Detroit."[13] Dykes replaced Simmons in the White Sox lineup with Mike Kreevich, a small but fast outfielder who would hit .283 with little power over a 12-year career. At the outset, Dykes too boldly suggested Kreevich would make Chicago fans forget about Simmons.

In Detroit on April 29, bad news hit when the team lost Hank Greenberg for the season after he broke his left wrist in a baseline collision with Washington's Jake Powell. It was suggested that Powell, who was openly anti–Semitic, intentionally caused the collision. This was the same wrist that Greenberg had broken in the second game of the 1935 World Series. The stunned Tigers lost the game, 7–3, as they collected just two hits, including a ninth-inning home run by Simmons.

Losing Greenberg put a bit more pressure on Simmons in the middle of the batting order. He put together a 15-game hitting streak, but it ended on May 3 against Boston. He cooled down the rest of the month, falling to .269 with four home runs by June 1. Detroit, at 23–21, had not exactly clicked.

The big sensation that spring in baseball was the appearance of rookie Joe DiMaggio of the New York Yankees. He made his major league debut on May 3, batting ahead of Lou Gehrig in Ruth's old number three hole. The Ruth-less Yankees had not been to the World Series since 1932, but they would win the next four Fall Classics, as DiMaggio would lead the Yankees to nine titles in his 13 years.

Simmons seemed to be heading in the opposite direction. In June, he was benched twice. Now 34, he began to hear catcalls from the Detroit faithful. In response, he claimed he was trying too hard to live up to his big contract. Then he turned his season around. He hopped his batting average by 30 points by the end of June, and the Detroit fans that were so recently booing him at Navin Field were now cheering.

Simmons reached 50 RBIs before the All-Star break and was frequently delivering timely, run-producing hits. His Tiger teammates, who had noticed that Simmons was pressing too hard before — his "muscles tightened to destroy the rhythm of his swing"— now witnessed the return of his fierce swing.[14]

On June 23, he crushed two homers and belted out a single — good for five RBIs — off his old Philadelphia teammate, Lefty Grove, who still won the game for the Boston Red Sox. Four days later he walloped another home and drove in three runners, pushing his average to .302.

The stage had seemed perfectly set for Detroit, and now Simmons had returned to form. But cruel fate continued to strike the club, which had already lost Greenberg.

Sixty-seven games into the season, the hard-driving Cochrane suffered a nervous breakdown after being elevated to general manager duties, which he undertook along with his player-manager role. Perhaps he had too much responsibility. Cochrane's collapse came soon after he smacked an inside-the-park grand slam against his former team, the A's, in a wild 18–9 win on June 4.

Cochrane would be away from the team for six weeks. One likely cause of stress for Cochrane was player relationships. For example, benching Simmons twice in June surely elicited an angry response from the player. The fact this happened a few weeks before Cochrane melted down is interesting.

It is true that later, during the upcoming offseason, the press claimed Simmons was not exactly a positive clubhouse influence in his lone season with the Detroit club. In any event, handling tempestuous players was not the easiest part of his job — Cochrane stressed himself out over much of it.

"When I was a player, I worried only about myself. Good money and easy work," Cochrane once said, according to a 1960 profile in *Sport* magazine. "Now I have to worry about everybody. I have to see that they're in shape and stay in shape. If one of them eats something that makes them sick, I get sick too."[15]

On June 9, Cochrane entered the Henry Ford Hospital, where he would spend the next 10 days under careful scrutiny. There, physicians treated him for what was discretely described in the newspapers as an "over secretion of the thyroid gland." Afterwards he spent several weeks at a Wyoming ranch — hunting, fishing and horseback riding.

Tigers coach Delmar Baker took over managing the Tigers. He tried to rally the shocked troops. "We've won four straight games," he said before opening a June 30 series in Chicago, "but more than that is the fact our pitching is steadily improving and Al Simmons is hitting — and I think will continue to hit."[16]

The Tigers won 13 of 16 games under Baker. On July 15, Cochrane returned to the Tigers, but was soon back at the Ford Hospital, as Baker guided the Tigers the rest of the way.[17]

Though enjoying a midsummer resurgence, Simmons, for the first time in three years, was not chosen for the All-Star Game. The National League won, 4–3, in Braves Field in Boston.

Later, in mid–July, Simmons suffered a stomach ailment. Some thought he might have an appendicitis, but he began feeling better and soon got back in the lineup.

Of his hitting, Simmons did not have much to say. "Every time I talk I seem to fall into a slump. So I'm not to say anything for a spell. I'm going to be a wise, old owl," he said, holding steady with a .302 average on July 31.[18]

Simmons hit with authority throughout August and September. He cracked two home runs and five RBIs among four hits in a 13–4 walloping of the Senators, and put together a flurry of three-hit and four-hit games in the next week. On August 18, he had a four-hit performance in a 15–3 win against St. Louis. Toward the end of the season, he notched a 16-game hitting streak before having it snapped in the last game of the season.

When the season ended, the New York Yankees were on top with 102 wins, 19 and one-half games ahead of the second-place and disappointing Tigers. The Yankees beat the crosstown New York Giants in the World Series.

Simmons, in 143 games, had a solid year as the Tigers' center fielder (he even played one game at first base, the only time in his career): .327 average, 13 home runs, 112 RBIs, 186 hits, 96 runs scored, 38 doubles, and a .986 fielding average (tops in the AL).

Despite the solid showing, Simmons learned in December that he was again on the trading block. The Detroit front office and Cochrane were worried that he had lost range and gained too much weight. It's also likely they found him a bit too obstreperous.[19]

No trade deal was struck over the winter. In March, Simmons showed up early at the Detroit's spring training site in Florida, about 19 pounds lighter and feeling vulnerable that his job was at stake. "Just thought I'd come a week early," he said, "and get the jump on the other fellows," referring to outfielders Goose Goslin, Jo-Jo White, Gee Walker and rookie Chester Laabs. He added, "If this is going to be a battle, you can bet that I'll be right in the middle of it."[20]

Now 35, it appeared to onlookers that Simmons had aged considerably in his legs. It was clear he could not play center field like he did last season, and now he faced competition for the left field spot.

"Simmons is much slower than he was last year," wrote H.G. Salsinger of the *Detroit News*. "He is probably the slowest man among Detroit's infielders and outfielders.... He runs with an awkward and laborious step, much like a man trying to pull his feet out of a bog." Realizing this, Salsinger said, manager Mickey Cochrane gave Simmons "extensive opportunities" to play more innings to work himself into shape. On the other hand, Goslin, who was almost two years older than Simmons, looked faster and perhaps even quicker than a year ago, according to the *Detroit News* writer.[21]

Detroit had to make a decision before the 1937 season started. On April 5, the Tigers sold Simmons for a reported $15,000 to the Washington Senators. The transaction was finalized after Detroit had played an exhibition game with Washington in Orlando.

Aside from his decreasing speed, Simmons had not worked out in Detroit in the clubhouse chemistry area, especially with his old friend, Cochrane. Detroit had paid $75,000 for him. Yet the ripple effects of acquiring Simmons in the first place—the benching of Jo-Jo White so Simmons could play—

Fifteen: Tail of the Tiger

and the inability of the Tigers to win the pennant last season created unhappiness among some players.

Speaking to the media, Cochrane was cagey, but one can easily enough read between the lines. "There is no need to make the price public. It would

One of Al Simmons' best friends in baseball was Milwaukee native Chet Laabs (right), shown here during spring training in 1937 before Simmons was sold to Washington. *Milwaukee Public Library*

add fuel to a fire and I'd like to forget the whole thing. You might say that both sides are satisfied and that's all that's necessary," he said. A writer noted that "sending Simmons away improved the team morale."[22]

Another claimed that his "presence and salary irked some of the Tiger men who believed Al was crowding some of the younger, better players out of a job."[23]

As he turned in his Detroit uniform, Simmons described the sale as "a great break for me" and spoke candidly about his tenure in the Motor City. It was the second team he had left unhappily in two years now. He risked getting labeled as a bad influence in the small fraternity of major league baseball.

Al Simmons: "I never had had things easy in Detroit and was under pressure all the time. It was no fault of mine; I tried hard enough, but fate had thrown me into a tough spot. Over in Washington things will be different."[24]

As Cochrane biographer Charles Bevis points out, Simmons and Cochrane mixed better as A's teammates than as manager and player with the Tigers. "Bringing in old friend Simmons was a big mistake on Cochrane's part. Simmons disliked Cochrane's authoritarian airs as Detroit (vice president) as well as catcher. Cochrane was annoyed with Simmons for assuming he was entitled to special treatment based on their friendship. And many Tigers resented the way Cochrane just handed right field to Simmons and benched (Pete) Fox."[25]

Over in Washington, manager Bucky Harris welcomed his new outfielder with a direct challenge. "We'll give him every chance to prove he still has some good baseball left in his system," Harris said.[26]

Simmons made other headlines off the field that spring. On April 19, he testified before the Securities and Exchange Commission on how he had lost $1,100 in a company named Atlas Tack back in 1936. The commission was investigating an alleged stock manipulation by W.E. Hutton and Company. Simmons told how he had bought 200 shares of Atlas stock after receiving a letter from Mickey Cochrane — ironically enough — who had been advised to buy the stock by a Hutton broker. "Mickey and I had been teammates for years," he explained to the commission. "Whenever he had a tip that might make us a few dollars, he passed it on to me, and I did the same."[27]

But his job in Washington wasn't about testifying before the SEC — it was about hitting baseballs hard, of course. Right away, he got some good news. That spring, Simmons received a package in the mail from Tokyo, Japan. Unwrapping it, he found the bat he had lost in Japan during the post–1931-season tour. Herbert Hunter, a "promoter" who routinely organized Japanese baseball tours for major leaguers, had sent it to the ballplayer.

Al Simmons: "No matter how many sticks I ordered from the factory, they couldn't duplicate it, somehow. They needed the original, they said. Well, they're gonna get it. I'm shipping this stick to Louisville tonight and getting myself two dozen made up just like it."[28]

One scribe quipped, "Everybody thought it was the old eye that Simmons had lost."[29]

As teams gathered to launch the 1937 campaign, the news from around the world was mostly grim with a few bright spots.

The *Hindenburg* airship, the pride of a rising Germany, exploded in flames above New Jersey, killing 37; Japanese military forces captured the Chinese city of Nanking, massacring more than 200,000 people; Italy joined an anti-communist pact already in force between the Japanese and the Germans. The pact established the Triple Alliance that became known as "The Axis."

In other news, Amelia Mary Earhart mysteriously disappeared over the Pacific Ocean during a circumnavigation flight; after a number of strikes in the auto industry, General Motors were forced to recognize the United Auto Workers Union; and the Golden Gate Bridge opened in the San Francisco Bay Area.

On the cultural front, artist Pablo Picasso painted his anti-war masterpiece, "Guernica"; architect Frank Lloyd Wright completed "Falling Water"; and writer J.R.R. Tolkien published *The Hobbit*.

One might feel like a hobbit playing in spacious Griffith Stadium, Simmons' new home ballpark, one of the most expansive fields ever. The outfield fences were set way back, which did not bode well for a power hitter like Simmons, who at this point needed any help he could get. It seemed as if he had returned to his Comiskey Park troubles. But this time he had no choice if he wanted to keep playing ball.

When the season opened April 19 in Washington, Simmons found himself in familiar surroundings — in the cleanup spot, in left field, and facing his old team, the Philadelphia A's. However, he went hitless in four at-bats as the A's won, 4–3. The next day, he banged out a home run and two other hits to lift the Senators to a 3–2 triumph over the Yankees.

Simmons was on a mission that early spring. The Tigers' handling of his last-minute trade to Washington had angered him, and he was hell-bent on regaining his reputation, wrote Joe Williams of the *New York World-Telegram*. "This [trade] has done something to Simmons. It has made him a grim, determined young man. He is going to show the baseball world that he is still a star. His vanity has been hurt."[30]

He added that Simmons was the "most hated" baseball player by Washington fans when he used to visit the city as a member of the A's, White Sox or Tigers. Now the fans who once booed him had to get used to the idea of cheering him.[31]

Simmons tried to put the best spin on it all. "I always liked to play here when I was on the Detroit team. You can get a lot of extra base hits in this park."[32]

Clark Griffith, owner of the Senators, thought he had pulled off a nifty trade in acquiring Simmons. The year before, Washington had posted an 82–71 record, good for third place. This season, Griffith expected to finish in at least second place with the help of Simmons. He wanted big hits off the bat of Bucketfoot Al.

But the talent was just not there on the 1937 Senators. Iron-gloved but strong-hitting Cecil Travis at shortstop and swatting second baseman Buddy Lewis were the best position players, but were hardly dominant league-wise and represented about all Washington offered in the way of offense. Wes Ferrell was the best pitcher they had. To plug all the gaps, Washington would use an astounding total of 41 players that season as the team tried to shake out a regular lineup from the marginal talent.

Perhaps Simmons was affected by the mediocrity. After his homer in the second game, he floundered, and by May 2 was hitting only .114. That day he found himself benched — in favor of Freddie Sington, a big, strapping Alabama-born outfielder of little talent and who had played in just 54 games in the past three seasons. It must have felt like a huge slap across the face for Simmons.

Sington bumbled his chance. He went hitless, striking out once with runners in scoring position and hitting into a double play. With the whole lineup stumbling, manager Bucky Harris, in the next game, put Simmons back in the lineup, though he dropped him in the batting order to the fifth spot, moving Johnny Stone up.[33]

Simmons regained some of his touch at the plate, climbing to .274 — but with only three homers — by the end of May. Then bad luck struck on June 18. That day St. Louis Browns pitcher Oral Hildebrand threw a pitch that smacked Simmons in the hand. Apparently, there was bad blood between the two, for Hildebrand walked in toward Simmons and "made some comment that Simmons resented," according to news reports. The two came at each other, but teammates and the umpires quickly pulled them away, and Simmons took first base on the hit batsmen.

The next Washington batter, Cecil Travis, grounded to Hildebrand, who then turned and threw to second baseman Bill Knickerbocker for the force out on Simmons, who came in with a "high slide" and collided with Knickerbocker, who lost his cap and fell to the ground. Seconds later, fists were flying between Simmons and Knickerbocker. "They banged away with both fists until players of both teams rushed out and separated them," wrote the Associated Press. Afterwards, both Simmons and Knickerbocker were ejected from the game.[34]

X-rays after the game showed Simmons had a broken bone in his hand — whether it was due to the pitch or the fisticuffs, is not clear. He would be out of the lineup for two weeks.[35]

Simmons was always a tough customer and never shied way from altercations, but at this late stage of his career he was more prone to fights and shouting matches. He had fallen far from his star days with the A's, often landing on teams in the grip of frustration.

The 35-year-old Simmons' resentment literally bellowed forth onto the field in the form of physical and verbal aggression. He would not get arrested or spend time in jail, like other ballplayers who had truly crossed the line, but he was increasingly confrontational.

On the flip side, Simmons showed an inner humanity sometimes when he was not feeling threatened. George Case told author Donald Honig that Simmons was mostly oblivious to rookies and young players. But when he opened up, especially after a few libations, his life story and a touch of generosity came pouring out.

A fleet-footed outfielder, Case joined the Washington Senators in the fall of 1937 and went south with the team the next spring. A year later, Simmons didn't remember him from the previous fall, he told Honig. "I had to reintroduce myself to him," said Case, at that point not expecting much from the gruff Simmons. Then something happened.

"One evening in Boston I was sitting in the lobby of the Copley Plaza after the ball game," Case retold the night's event. "Simmons came in at about 9:30 P.M. with a newspaper under his arm. He stopped, looked around, then looked at me. He was never particularly friendly to me, but I was the only ballplayer sitting there, so he came up to me."

Simmons said, "Young fellow, come on and have a drink with me."

Case recalled, "He's the great Al Simmons asking me to have a drink with him, and all I could get out was, 'Al, I don't drink.'"

"Hell you drink ginger ale, don't you?"

"Sure," Case said, who then sat in the bar until 2:30 A.M. drinking ginger ale with Simmons. "It was coming out of my ears," he said. "For some reason, he told me the story of his life, practically from the day he was born.... "One of the things he said was, 'You know, I've got a reputation for being coarse and a little bit ornery, but believe me, enough things have happened to me in my lifetime to account for that.'"

Simmons told Case about growing up in Milwaukee — "a rough time," he described it — and how poor his family was. He had to work long and hard hours as a boy to help his family pay the bills. "It was all very interesting and sad," said Case, "and I got to know Al Simmons that night. After that, he was my closest friend on the ball club."

Simmons gave Case advice on hitting, and encouraged his development as a ballplayer. "He turned out to be, under that gruff exterior, a very kindly and thoughtful man," Case told Honig. He was also a very proud — and sensitive — man. Simmons' blustery persona was a defense mechanism to shield his deeper feelings and need for acceptance and respect.

Case described what happened one day when manager Bucky Harris took Simmons out of a game for a pinch-hitter: "Al was having some difficulty making contact and we were in the late innings of a game. We had a couple of men on base and Al's turn was coming up. All of a sudden Harris called him back. Frankly, I was stunned, and not because I thought Harris was making the wrong move, but because it was happening. We all looked at one another on the bench, but nobody said anything. Those few seconds were highly charged; the moment Bucky called out to him we knew what it was, and when Al turned around there was a look of puzzlement on his face; he couldn't believe it ... [he] then took that bat and threw it up into the air about 15 feet, let it drop, and walked back to the bench, right on through the dugout and into the clubhouse without saying a word."[36]

Instead of a fight, Simmons chose flight.

Off the field, Simmons had domestic concerns. Frequently on his mind was his 17-month old son John, or "Dukie," who was back home with his mother Dores in Racine, Wisconsin. A cute newspaper photo of Dukie with the headline "Rooter" appeared in May. Dukie, it was claimed tongue-in-cheek, followed his dad's games by radio. He is shown in the photo with a wide-open mouth and wide eyes, holding a baseball in his right hand.

After his hand healed from the June 18 Hildebrand-Knickerbocker incident, Simmons got back into the lineup on July 14. He hoped to raise his average from .271 and lift Washington out of its funk. A few days earlier he had been seen at the All-Star Game in Griffith Park. Not selected, Simmons was in the stands "perched on a camp chair and taking movies of the game" while admonishing his old teammate Charlie Gehringer to "git holta one!" as portrayed in the fanciful vernacular of the sporting press.[37] In fact, Gehringer got a hold of more than one — he had three base hits — leading the American League to an 8–3 victory over the National League in the midsummer classic.

After the break, Simmons struggled to get above the .270s, and then reinjured his hand in early September, missing two weeks. His numbers at the end of the 1937 season were disappointing: 103 games, .279 average, 8 home runs, 84 RBIs, and 117 hits.

Many surmised Simmons would have to take a big pay cut to stay with Washington. Trade talk again surfaced in Washington, which had fallen to sixth place with a 73–80 record — well short of owner Clark Griffith's goal. Meanwhile, New York won the pennant and the World Series for a second year in a row.

On top of all this, Lou Gehrig broke a tie with Simmons that year by notching his 12th consecutive season of 100 or more RBIs — but not from the start of his career, like Simmons (Gehrig had his first 100-plus RBI season in his fourth year of play.)

The future of Al Simmons looked uncertain. In the end, he remained with the Senators — there were no big takers for him over the winter. But as the year ahead would prove, maybe both the player and team should have parted ways sooner.

CHAPTER SIXTEEN

Mr. Simmons Leaves Washington

> *"I haven't saved a dime for four or five years, but that's all right. I've been living a full life. In the offseason I go where I please when I please. Nothing is too good for the Simmons family."*
>
> —Al Simmons

In 1938, the world inched closer to all-out war. Nazi Germany began an occupation of Austria and started a crisis in Czechoslovakia when Adolph Hitler promised "protection" for German minorities living outside the Third Reich. In a vain attempt to dodge war, the leaders of Great Britain and France met with Hitler in Munich at the end of September. During the meeting, they acceded to Hitler's demands to cede the Sudetenland to Germany, and others as well.

In Germany itself, Nazis burned synagogues, destroyed Jewish shops and killed Jews at random in a one-night spree. The night became known as "Kristallnacht," the night of the broken glass, and it signaled the coming Holocaust.

Back in America, part of baseball's charm is that it does not involve important life and death matters. Still, the clash of personalities can be ugly and unforgiving. Early that year, Al Simmons and Washington owner Clark Griffith got off on the wrong side of things, foreshadowing more headaches to follow.

Simmons, who had received $15,000 in 1937, flatly turned down Washington's first offer of $10,000 for 1938. After negotiating with the front office for a couple of months, Simmons demanded a sit-down conference with Griffith. The owner agreed, thinking his player was a bit high-maintenance. The two wrangled and finally reached a compromise at $12,000.[1]

In the midst of the Great Depression, few ballplayers were getting paid well. Only a few years ago, Simmons was making $30,000. Now he was lucky to make a decent buck on the downside of his career, and reportedly was "beaming" after he emerged from negotiations in Griffith's hotel room. He even vowed to report to spring training two weeks early.

Simmons, 36, realized his good fortune and talked about how he protected his financial future by buying $140,000 in annuities that would begin to pay off in 1941. He liked to spend his yearly income, he said, and that was one reason he kept playing ball. "I haven't saved a dime for four or five years, but that's all right. I've been living a full life. In the offseason, I go where I please when I please. Nothing is too good for the Simmons family."

He lived with flair, at least that was the image. Shirley Povich, the writer, said Simmons cast a strong veteran shadow on the Senators. "On a team comprised mainly of country kids whose idea of a high old time is a double-feature movie, Simmons was a standout, a picturesque bon vivant."[2]

When the season opened in April, Simmons was in left field. He started slowly — and was frequently benched against right-handers — but gradually picked it up. On May 14, he hit a grand slam off of Boston's Fritz Ostermueller in the third inning and another homer later for a total of six RBIs and four hits.

Twelve days later, he struck again. He sat on the bench for the first game of a doubleheader in St. Louis, and then played in the second game, where he was shown little respect. With the scored tied in the ninth inning with a runner on second base and two out, Browns pitcher Jim Walkup walked Buddy Lewis to bring Simmons to the plate, thinking him an easier out. But Simmons swung at the first pitch, blasting it against the wall for a double and scoring the winning run. He had found his swing again.[3]

June was a prolific month for Simmons, as he walloped seven home runs and drove in 27 runners. His average stood at .307 on June 3, and remained around that the rest of the way. On June 26, he went deep again with the bases loaded against St. Louis' Bobo Newsom.

The writers were chattering of the "comeback" by the "pounding Pole." Simmons wasn't "any more washed up than the week's laundry at 4 A.M.," and Griffith's acquisition of him looked like a "bargain." Last season must have been a "mistake."[4]

The Senators were playing better ball, too. On July 1, they were 34–34, thanks to Simmons and strong seasons by first baseman Zeke Bonura, shortstop Cecil Travis, second baseman Buddy Myer, third baseman Buddy Lewis, outfielder George Case, and catcher Rick Ferrell. The pitchers were another story, as starter Dutch Leonard was the only one having a decent campaign.

In a mostly left-handed lineup, the right-handed Simmons was a counterbalance against left-handed pitching. For his career, he hit .365 in games begun by left-handed starters as opposed to .326 for right-handed starters.

"The Washington Senators are hailing Al Simmons as the man who delivered them from a monotonous diet of left-handed pitching," observed a writer.[5]

It was an "Indian Summer" for the Milwaukee native, exclaimed Jack Cuddy of the *Pittsburgh Press*. Simmons was wandering around with an "expansive grin" and "confident smile that stretches his broad mouth and looks like a lover's hammock." Cuddy continued, "Big Al, who impresses one now as a gray-haired, gray-faced, gray-uniformed man, is laughing off the years ... I'm only 36 now, and I'm improving every day."

The writer said of Simmons: "Admire his confidence and eagerness and the doggedness" after three "questionable seasons" and lingering doubts about his unorthodox stance. Bucketfoot or no bucketfoot, Simmons had a .342 career average at this point. Simmons said playing every day helped him. If manager Bucky Harris kept him in the lineup, he vowed, he would "show the boys something."[6]

Still, it was not all roses. The Washington club was not quite convinced he was a full-time player.

On July 19, Harris removed Simmons late in the game for a pinch-hitter after he went hitless three times. He would have come up to the plate in the ninth inning with the winning run on base. But instead, rookie Taft Wright stood in for him at the dish — and he struck out.

"He plainly showed his dejection as, with head down and measured step, he returned to the bench," wrote Shirley Povich. "Al Simmons is not a philosophical sort of fellow. He is still confident he can hit big league pitching." For a cocky ballplayer like Simmons, watching his skills slowly erode was difficult. Povich described him as a "fellow who delights in hitting that ball, in making his hits and strutting, in acting just a bit high and mighty."

Realizing that time was not his ally Simmons tried to improve his diet. One press account reported that he attributed the July hitting spree to his new food choices — "raw fruits only for breakfast, starches only for lunch and no bread at any time." He claimed he had lost 10 pounds since the start of the season.[7]

Simmons reached a milestone on September 5 when he played in his 2,000th game, collecting two hits and a double in the first match of a doubleheader that Washington lost, 14–4, to Boston.

In the last few weeks, his batting average hovered close to .300. Broaching the magical mark once again, as he had done so often when younger, meant a lot to Simmons — both in terms of pride and money. His contract stipulated that if he finished the year above .300, he would receive $800 in extra pay. Plus, it would be the 13th time in 15 years he had hit higher than .300.

Washington played its second-to-the-last-game on September 29 against the Red Sox. In that contest, Boston prevailed, 13–5, as Simmons managed just one hit in four at bats to put his average at .298. In the long view, it may have been better if the season had ended then for Simmons, without the .300 average. But that would not be as good a story.

The last two games were scheduled for October 2, when the Senators were set to host the A's in a doubleheader. In the first game, Simmons bashed out three hits, a double and two singles, putting him at a .302 average. He did not start the second game, thereby ensuring he would remain above .300. Sammy West took his post in the outfield instead. In the seventh inning of the second game, manager Bucky Harris called on Simmons to pinch-hit for Rene Monteagudo. He took a base on balls — interesting, for he did not usually take many — which had the effect of protecting his .302 average.

A few minutes later, as he was rounding third base, a fan behind home plate swore a blue streak at Simmons, who became enraged. According to witnesses, the "leather-lunged" fan had been "riding" Simmons throughout the first game, and continued his "biting remarks" when Simmons entered the second game. So Simmons challenged the heckler. "Tell that so-and-so to meet me under the stands," was the sanitized newspaper version of Simmons' retort, which surely was more harsh.

James Kenney, a recently retired Washington D.C. police detective, was in the stands that day. He later told the *Washington Herald* that the fan had made a "disparaging reference to (Simmons') race in calling him 'yellow'" and "pop-out Simmons," among other rude insults — probably Polish slurs. Simmons, turning around, called out to the abusive fan to "meet me under the stands."

One female fan sitting close to the drama came to the player's defense, saying, "Al would have been justified in giving that man a good smash in his mouth, and I wish he had."[8]

The fight never happened, but it was a loud spectacle nonetheless, apparently embarrassing the Washington front office.

After the incident, owner Clark Griffith reacted strongly — against his player, though, not the fan. In an extraordinarily candid session with the media, Griffith told writers that Simmons' days with the Senators had come to an end — either Simmons would be traded during the winter or he would receive an unconditional release. He then fined Simmons $200. "Simmons' exhibition on Sunday when he cursed Washington fans was disgraceful," Griffith was quoted as saying. "I won't tolerate that kind of player on my ball club."[9]

Simmons angered the owner by claiming that the $200 fine was an attempt to recoup some of the extra pay he had just earned for hitting .300. Simmons was unapologetic, and with the season over, he lashed out publicly at Griffith. "I don't suppose I'll ever talk contract with Griffith again. I think he's going to try to get even," he said.[10]

The issue continued to escalate, unnecessarily so.

"That is absurd," countered Griffith. "Simmons should be ashamed to make such a statement. He should have been ashamed, too, to beg off from playing that second game of the doubleheader because he would risk his .300 average."[11]

Griffith's hard-line stance was unpopular among some Washington fans. Elizabeth and Peter Huidekoper of 2934 Edgevale Terrace in Washington, D.C. wrote a letter to the Senators decrying the treatment of Simmons. It is not clear if they had a connection to Simmons or anyone else on the club.

According to the Huidekopers, the man in the stands had "made himself very objectionable throughout the first game and seven innings of the second game by heckling Al Simmons every time he came out of the dugout." "It is a good thing we cannot be fined for our thoughts on the heckler," they stated. The loudmouth didn't have the "courage to meet Al Simmons 'under the stands,'" they wrote.[12]

Under pressure, Griffith dashed off a terse letter to the American League offices and Commissioner Landis:

"It is my opinion that the American League and the Commissioner should take drastic measures in this case ... Simmons also let out a tirade of curse words at Yankee Stadium last week against umpire Basil when called out on a strike.... To show you the caliber of Simmons, he had a bonus coming to him if he batted .300 this year. He kept such close tabs on his batting average that he asked to be taken out of the second game so he could collect said bonus. He didn't even have the guts enough to go through with his part of the program,"[13] Griffith wrote.

It got even more complicated. The umpiring crew, led by Bill McGowan, also sent their report to the American League offices. In particular, McGowan was upset by an article that appeared in the *Washington Star* in which Simmons was quoted as saying he "had the umpires on my side." McGowan said, "I did not know what was going on except I saw Simmons at bat, step out of the batter's box, and turn to the stands. Later as he rounded third base I saw him point to a spectator. I was umpiring at second base. The game was not held up one second. There was no commotion. I was concentrating on my job. Mr. Griffith mentioned the Simmons incident to me after the game. I explained I did not know anything about it.... It is absolutely untrue that I even indicated I was on his side or anybody else's side."[14]

In hindsight, the apparent lack of awareness on McGowan's part implies that Griffith overreacted. After all, if the umps on the field hardly noticed it — and it did not stall the game — why the fuss? Home plate umpire John Quinn also sent a letter saying it was no big deal — Griffith noted this, claiming that if had Quinn "been on the job," he would have acted.

Simmons then sent Commissioner Landis a Western Union missive on his version of the story: "I was fined by the Washington baseball club yesterday and I understand Griffith is referring the case to you. Wish you would hear my part before making decision. Will be in Chicago for (World) Series," he wrote.

On October 4, Landis summoned Simmons, Griffith and Arch McDonald, the radio broadcaster for the Senators, to his offices in Chicago. They were all in the Windy City for the 1938 World Series between the Chicago Cubs and the New York Yankees, which the Yanks won for an unprecedented third straight time.

The meeting opened on the point of whether Simmons had called the heckler a "son of a bitch."

Landis asked McDonald, "Did you hear any of the ballplayers on the Washington team say anything in the way of language that included the word, 'son of a bitch?'"

Replied McDonald, "Well, yes. I have heard that expression on the ball field a number of times. I heard Al."

Though McDonald said he did not "like to be put on the spot"—and Simmons tried to interrupt to ask a question—Landis kept pressing the point. "I want to find out."

Then it was the player's turn. "You have been in the stands and everywhere else," Simmons told the commissioner. "Haven't you heard a fellow come back to the bench after he pops out and says, 'Why, you son of a bitch.' How can I miss hitting a guy like that? How many times have I heard fellows in your ballpark, Mr. Griffith, yell to people? You hear them day after day."

Griffith disagreed. "I don't say that is so." Landis said that swearing after making an out was one thing, but cursing a spectator was far more heinous.

At this point, Simmons denied addressing anyone in the stands. Questioned again by Landis about this particular incident, McDonald pleaded not to be drawn into the matter. All he admitted was that someone else told him Simmons had called the fan a "son of a bitch."

In fact, McDonald said he had come that day to the commissioner's office on another matter and was suddenly injected into this affair. "You put me on the spot."

Replied the commissioner, "that is one of the penalties of being a bystander."

Simmons declared the entire affair hypocritical. He recalled that only a few weeks ago teammate Zeke Bonura had grabbed a fellow in the stands at Griffith Stadium and almost yanked him out onto the playing field. Everyone knew there was plenty of cussing all the time on the diamond.

After more bickering, Landis ended the meeting with the agreement that Simmons could send him witnesses on his behalf.[15]

A few days later, a letter was published from Naomi Craver of 801 Mt. Vernon Ave. in Alexandria, Virginia. In it, she vouched she "did not hear one word that Al said nor did my companions." As for the rude fan, Craver was appalled — "I am embarrassed by some of the deeds of some fans of Washington, such as throwing pop bottles and booing the players." As for the Senators, the fine against Simmons was "the worst yet" in a series of front office moves that has deeply angered the fan base, she added.[16]

Not surprisingly, Landis upheld Griffith's fine on Simmons. The commissioner relished his stern disciplinarian image. Besides, fans could not be fined — but players could be.

On October 28, Landis sent Simmons a note explaining his decision: "There is no escape from the conclusion that, in the game at Washington on October 2, you used the language as reported (with which you are entirely familiar) and that you used that language with sufficient force to project it into and pretty much through the stands."[17]

As stated above, bad language in baseball is commonplace and as old as the game itself. Simmons just happened to get on the wrong side of an owner who may have wanted some of his money back from a player he disliked.

Finally, it was over, and so was the 1938 season.

Simmons had finished at .302 with 21 homers and 95 RBIs — strong numbers for playing in one of the most difficult hitting parks in the majors. In the field, he again registered a near flawless game with only four errors. But time was taking a toll on the aging outfielder. He had only played in 125 games.

Years later, Simmons would regret missing games when otherwise healthy, realizing the lost opportunities cost him the glory of 3,000 hits. But for now, he vented at the Washington front office. His relationship with the Senators had ended on bad terms. "The Washington baseball team and I are through," said Simmons, expressing his desire for an unconditional release so he could find his own team. "I don't expect to be back after what happened ... I hope I am not."

It didn't work out that way quickly. Initially, Griffith wanted him to twist in uncertainty, and refused to give Simmons his freedom.

Finally, on December 29, Washington sold him to the National League club in Boston — the "Bees," formerly known as the Braves — for $5,000. Washington had given Simmons permission to negotiate the deal for himself. Boston had apparently refused to pay the waiver price of $7,500, and so Simmons had lowered his demand by $2,500.

Even after the deal was consummated, Griffith continued his public blasts at Simmons. "I want no dissatisfied ballplayers on my team," he said. "Simmons didn't fit in with our plans for next season. We are rebuilding and we want a young team." Hard-hitting rookie Bobby Estallela, Cuban-born and one of the game's Hispanic pioneers, was slotted to fill Simmons' position.[18]

Long an established American League star, Simmons would now play in the National League for the first time. He did so needing 323 more notches on his bat to reach another milestone that few players ever achieved — 3,000 hits.

CHAPTER SEVENTEEN

Chasing Three Thousand

"To Al, baseball was so close to war it affected him as war affects some men — he didn't scare, but it filled him with a cold, bloodless fury that literally turned him pale."
— *Red Smith*[1]

Poet Mark Schraf wrote once wrote a poem about Al Simmons, titled "2927." The work is found in Schraf's *Cooperstown Verses: Poems About Each Hall of Famer*, a book of baseball poetry.

>   2927
> Conlon photocloseups
> 19 with freckles and an
> unlined confidence I can
> hit anybody with or without
> a bat
> 37 going on ancient
> freckles dissolved
> into late night creases
> white temples the ignored omen
> that 3000 should have but would never
> come.[2]

Poetic license was what Al Simmons was looking for at the outset of the 1939 season. Now 37 years old, he attempted to ease expectations in Boston.

"The National League is going to be as new and mysterious to me as the majors are to a rookie coming into the major leagues for the first time," he said. Still, his new team environment was "an incentive to my playing. I'll certainly give my best." In an overstatement, he described Boston president Bob Quinn as "the Connie Mack of the National League."[3]

When Simmons arrived early at Boston's spring training camp in Bradenton, Florida, he worked out at the Bees' complex with pitcher Danny Macfayden.

Over in the American League, a young Boston Red Sox rookie, Ted Williams, was making headlines. The Splendid Splinter, as Williams would become known, smacked 31 home runs, drove in 145 runners and posted a .327 average in his rookie campaign.

Simmons, even from a distance, understood right away that Williams was in a class by himself. He made hitting look so easy, so smooth — totally unlike Simmons and his ungainly stance. "Only a fellow with wrists like Williams could hit like he does. He doesn't ever seem ready. He's fidgeting at the plate, moving his arms. Most of us have to get set to hit. He can swing at the last moment and get his full power into the swing. You can't fool a batter with a pair of fast, powerful wrists like Williams. I have seen him pull pitches into right field that were actually past him before he swung. I didn't see how he could do it."[4]

But Simmons, apparently forgetting one Joe DiMaggio, claimed Williams did not have the hitting competition he had faced from the likes of Ruth, Gehrig, Cobb, Speaker and Foxx. "There's nobody around to crowd him for the spotlight expect Mickey Vernon, and Vernon isn't in the slugger class ... (Williams) would just be another guy."

Al Simmons: "I hit .387 in my second year up, and didn't come close to winning the batting championship. I was just another guy trying to beat out Ruth and Heilmann and Speaker and Cobb. Williams doesn't have anybody like that to compete with. And then Foxx and Gehrig and Goslin and Manush and Cronin came along. The fellow who won the batting title in those years had to be a super hitter."[5]

In a wide-ranging interview during the exhibition season, Simmons ruminated on his comeback with sportswriters, who noted his graying temples. The player boasted that he would have one more solid year before hanging up his cleats. "I feel good," said Simmons, "except for a pulled muscle in my leg. That'll be all right soon, and I believe I'll have a good year."[6]

But in the exhibition game that followed, he showed his age. He let a pop fly fall right in front of him in left field. He would have caught it only a few years earlier. "It's just about Al's last stand, and he knows it," wrote George Kirksey of the United Press International.

Shirley Povich wrote about an encounter with Simmons and his son, John Allen Simmons, now just about three. As the writer described it, John was a reflection of his father — in his father's eyes. Simmons always called him 'Little Duke.'" "The Duke hasn't changed much. Al Simmons has taken on a few sprays of gray about the temples and he's playing in the National League these days, but he hasn't lost an ounce of his strut and swagger."[7]

Povich speculated that Simmons might have an easier time in the "curveball throwing" National League. American League pitchers, he said, had been "blowing fastballs by him" the last few seasons.

"The years had taken something from his reflexes and he wasn't breaking his wrists with that hair-trigger action every great hitter has," Povich explained, noting that the Washington Senators were "not losing much of a ballplayer" when Simmons moved to the Bees. "Pitches that he would have murdered in his heyday were getting him out."[8]

Compared to the rest of the Bees, Simmons packed as much offensive punch as anyone. Boston, a low-scoring but good pitching team, posted a 77–75 record for the 1938 season. Outfielder Vince DiMaggio, Joe's brother, had led the club in homers with the low total of 14.

Second-year pilot Casey Stengel managed the Bees, who played in one of the major's largest parks. Simmons suffered the misfortune of playing in three of baseball's most cavernous ballparks — Comiskey Park, Griffith Stadium and now Braves Field.

That spring, Simmons appreciated the chance to just play ball. With a tone of melancholy, he said he looked forward to a new club and his 16th season in the big leagues. He was no longer taking anything for granted.

Al Simmons: "This is the funniest club I've ever been with. Never seen anything like it. It's crazy about defense. Casey Stengel says it's his only hope. He doesn't have the hitting power up and down the lineup and doesn't see much chance to get it, so he's gone overboard on defense.... We may not get many runs for ourselves, but the opposition isn't going to get many either."[9]

In such a lineup, Simmons figured, he mattered. On Opening Day, he cracked out three hits in a 12-inning, 7–6, win over the Philadelphia Phillies. He batted in the team's cleanup spot, behind right fielder Buddy Hassett and ahead of second baseman Tony Cuccinello.

On May 5, he reached a major milestone — his 300th home run — in a 5–4 loss to Cincinnati. He slugged it off Lee Grissom in the bottom of the third inning with a runner on.

There was little if anything written about that achievement in the newspapers — the Associated Press game account did not even note it. But one interesting tidbit did pop up that week about Simmons, written by Jim Isaminger of the *Philadelphia Inquirer*, who was apparently not on good terms with the player back in his Philadelphia days.

Jim Isaminger: "One of the most changed players in the majors is Al Simmons. To tell the blunt truth, there was a time when the Milwaukee native was anything but companionable. He had a 'stiffish' attitude with teammates, fans and writers. But starting a National League career with the Bees, Al is different. He goes out of his way to be friendly. Manager Casey Stengel is

Opposite: Al Simmons hit .282 for the Boston Bees in 1939, his only year in the National League. ***Philadelphia Athletics Historical Society***

delighted with him and thinks he will be a big help to the Bees in the race this season."[10]

He was ready for playing as well. Simmons played in 30 of Boston's first 31 games through the end of May. The hot months of summer would prove another matter, as Simmons took more games off in June and July.

That season he bumped into Eddie Collins, general manager of the crosstown Boston Red Sox. The former second baseman and A's teammate pointed out to Simmons the grandeur of the 3,000-hit plateau, then just gaining notice among fans and insiders. Collins had finished his 25-year career with 3,312 hits.

This may have been the moment Simmons realized the significance that 3,000 hits would bring to his legacy. There is no other record of him first reacting to the possibility. "I learned too late about the 3,000-hit record," Simmons said in later years. "I never heard of the mark before. Had I known it earlier, there were days I could have played instead of resting."[11]

On July 16, Simmons was given a rude reminder of his place in the baseball food chain. On that date, he collided with Bees' All-Star shortstop Eddie Miller while going after a fly ball. Miller fractured a bone in his ankle, and wound up out of the lineup for the season. It was a devastating loss for the Bees, who had invested heavily in the bright, young ballplayer.

But what about Simmons? Few seemed to care, according to Boston catcher Al Lopez who later told author Donald Honig about the incident. Lopez said, "One day there was a fly ball hit into short left, and Miller and Simmons went for it. It was one of those situations where you just want to close your eyes because you can see the collision coming, and there's not a thing you can do about it. They ran into each other with a smack and went tumbling to the grass. Everybody went running out there to see how Miller was. Hardly anybody paid any attention to Simmons.... One day he came into the clubhouse and sat down next to me. He had a wistful little smile. 'You know something, Al?' he said. 'Ten years ago, when I was playing for Mr. Mack, if that collision had happened, they would have sent a goddamned kid shortstop nine hundred miles from Philadelphia for running into me.'"[12]

Simmons suffered another close call on August 24 in a 4–1 Boston victory over Brooklyn. A sidearm curveball from Brooklyn's Van Lingle Mungo struck him on the back of the head. He dropped instantly to the ground, knocked unconscious. A few minutes later, with his Boston teammates gathered around him, he regained consciousness enough to wave off a stretcher that had just been brought onto the field for him. He walked instead, helped by some of the players.

Later the Bees announced that he had suffered a "slight concussion" and would be out of the lineup for a few days. "We're letting him stay in the hospital overnight," said Boston road secretary George Lewis. "But there's nothing much wrong with him. He even asked for a steak, so you can see just how badly he's hurt."[13]

By the late days of summer, Simmons' performance had fallen —.281, but only 42 RBIs in 93 games. Boston waived him on August 29.

The Cincinnati Reds, in danger of losing their lead atop the National League to the Cardinals, needed a veteran stick for possible postseason play. So they bought Simmons from the Bees for the bare minimum waiver price of $6,000. With the deal done before the August 30 deadline for acquisitions, Bucketfoot Al was eligible for the postseason.[14]

The Reds would be the first truly good team that Simmons would play on since his old Philadelphia A's days, now seven years ago. It probably felt like much longer to Simmons after his erratic journey through the second-division clubs of Chicago, Washington and Boston.

The Reds had plans for him. Manager Bill McKechnie earmarked Simmons for left field and a possible October match against the New York Yankees, who were dominating the American League again that season.

The Reds speculated that Yankees manager Joe McCarthy had nightmare visions of Simmons from the 1929 World Series when the McCarthy-led Cubs gave up 10 runs to the Philadelphia A's in one inning and went on to lose the Series. So Cincinnati acquired the fading star "just to wield that 1929 whammy," wrote one scribe.[15]

Simmons got into nine Reds games that September, but hit only .143 with no extra-base hits.

Cincinnati did make it to the World Series to face the three-time defending-champion Yankees, who swept them in four games. Simmons sat on the bench for the first three contests, then replaced center fielder Harry Craft in the sixth inning, shifting to left field, in what would be his final World Series game ever.

Simmons made a fly ball out in his first at-bat, then doubled to deep center field in his next plate appearance in the bottom of the seventh, moving Frank McCormick to third base. He scored on a single by Willard Hershberger. An inning later, he grounded out. In his final at-bat, Simmons, with one out in the tenth, lined out to right field.

In that 10th inning, a famous play at the plate occurred. New York's Charlie Keller scored when he and the ball both collided with catcher Ernie Lombardi, and then Joe DiMaggio also scored while Lombardi, rolling on the ground, tried in vain to retrieve the ball.

Lombardi had been smacked in the groin area, but the puritanical press reported it as if Lombardi was "swooning" or "snoozing" at the plate. The Yankees had jumped on top, 7–4—thanks to the infamous "Lombardi snooze."

After the Series ended, Cincinnati released Simmons. It was not a particularly emotional event, as both player and team had understood the temporary nature of the signing.

Afterwards, rumors involving minor league assignments, trades and even managing swirled around Simmons, who meanwhile was toasted for what many thought was the final chapter of his career.

"The release of Al Simmons by the Cincinnati Reds," wrote one scribe, "provides another strong candidate for baseball's Hall of Fame. Simmons hung on in the big leagues for a few years longer than he should have, and he was no galloping gazelle toward the last." His "fat years" gave him the qualifications for baseball's hallowed pantheon.[16]

While Shirley Povich thought that Simmons was finished, "apparently at the end of his tether in the majors," he was premature in his judgment.[17] Simmons had become fixated on reaching 3,000 hits, and now was only 134 away. He could rack up that total in a season of full-time play, he speculated. So, in December, he signed with the Philadelphia A's, returning home to the club where he had his best years.

Sportswriter Vincent X. Flaherty made a late October sojourn to Simmons' home in Milwaukee near the shores of Lake Michigan. In the flamboyant prose of the day, the writer described a scene of apparent tranquility.

"Here was a picture of domestic bliss," Flaherty puffed. "A crackling log fire fought with its grating, spat infinitesimal bombshells upon the hearth and sent shafts of light and warmth to the far corners of the room. Pretty Mrs. Simmons, intriguingly brunette and youthful, lost herself in the billowy middle of a big easy chair, and fingered through a glossy magazine. Off to the side in his kingdom of toys, 4-year-old 'Dukey' Simmons made siren sounds as he rushed his fierce little red fire engine around imaginary corners."

Simmons, though, punctured the tranquility with his usual candor. "I'm a washed up ballplayer," he said. "I felt this thing coming a couple years ago." Before signing with the A's, he told Flaherty he had considered managing in the minors, perhaps the Pacific Coast League or his old American Association. He also claimed he turned down a baseball broadcasting job.

"This radio thing is just a crazy cycle," he said. "They're hiring ballplayers to broadcast songs, but that won't last long. I've never heard a former ballplayer, except Harry Heilmann in Detroit, who was worth a darn on the radio. Playing ball is one thing and broadcasting is another."[18]

To get ready for 1940, he left Milwaukee for Hot Springs and three weeks of "winter conditioning."[19]

In March, Connie Mack announced that he was bringing Simmons back so he could get 3,000 hits in an A's uniform. The team planned to use Simmons in right field if outfielder Sam Chapman failed to hit. Despite the youth

Connie Mack takes a few swings in batting practice during spring training. Mack brought Al Simmons back to the A's in 1940 to try for 3,000 hits in his career. *Philadelphia Athletics Historical Society*

movement on the A's, Mark had a perceived need for a veteran like Simmons. Some writers found the reasoning dubious.

"Quite a shock to baseball experts was Connie's bland statement that Al probably would be in the A's outfield when the season opens," wrote Bill M'Adams, "because Simmons, nearing 39, was thought to be through as a major league regular ... maybe Mack is mixing business with sentiment." Still, Mack thought Simmons had something left. "I don't think he is washed up by any means. Al is a great hitter, seems to be getting around in the outfield and on the bases pretty fast already. We expect to get a lot of baseball from him."[20]

Mack also penciled Simmons in as a coach, hoping his intensity would rub off on the younger A's.

But winning a lot of games was a long shot anyhow. The A's had lost 97 games in 1939, and with Simmons in 1940 would lose even more—100—for a last-place finish.

One bright spot was a powerful outfielder named Bob Johnson. Part

Cherokee, "Indian Bob" Johnson was a seven-time All-Star in the 1930s and 1940s. He could hit for power and drive in runs, but was not much of a fielder.

One day the A's were in Detroit for a doubleheader with the Tigers. Johnson, in a batting slump, was eating breakfast with Simmons at the hotel. When he finished, Simmons, a proud Catholic, excused himself from the table and said he was going to mass at a nearby Catholic church.

"Wait 'till I finish this coffee," Johnson told Simmons, "and I'll go with you. Can't do any harm." That afternoon, Simmons later recalled, Johnson went hitless in eight trips to the plate. "You know," Simmons said later in a serious tone, "the Lord could have won him over if he'd just got him three hits."[21]

The writer Red Smith recalled another game in Boston where Simmons was used as a pinch-hitter with one out in the ninth inning and a runner on third base. At his peak, it was a situation tailor-made for Simmons. But not anymore. He swung away, grounding meekly to the shortstop for an inning-ending double play. Simmons stalked away, visibly upset. When rookie dared to say, "What's the matter with you? You're white as a sheet," Simmons snapped, "Don't worry about me."

Red Smith: "If the rookie was so ignorant he had to be told that Al Simmons didn't choke in the clutch, then there was no use trying to explain. The fact that to Al baseball was so close to war it affected him as war affects some men — he didn't scare, but it filled him with a cold, bloodless fury that literally turned him pale."[22]

By the end of the season, Simmons had gotten into only 37 games, mostly as a pinch-hitter. When he did play, he hit well enough, posting a .309 average and collecting a precious 25 hits (only one home run) to put him just 109 hits shy of 3,000.

It was unsure how much more playing time Simmons would earn in the future. In that setting-sun period, players recalled the faded slugger's glory days. "When Simmons was at his peak," said pitcher Ted Lyons of Chicago, "you couldn't do anything with him. If you tried to waste a ball on him, he would reach out and hit it for two bases."[23]

Simmons also found that his world at home was changing. Both 3,000 hits and his family life seemed to slide farther out of his grasp.

CHAPTER EIGHTEEN

Twilight Times

"That's baseball, and it's my game. Y' know, you take your worries to the game, and you leave 'em there. You yell like crazy for your guys. It's good for your lungs, gives you a lift, and nobody calls the cops. Pretty girls, lots of 'em.
— *Humphrey Bogart*[1]

The country entered 1941 unsure of what might happen next. That summer Americans enjoyed historic seasons by Joe DiMaggio (56-game hit streak) and Ted Williams (.406 average), as baseball represented an innocent, joyous distraction before the coming storm of fury.

Later that year, Japan attacked the United States at its naval base in Pearl Harbor, immediately bringing the country into World War II, which was then raging throughout Europe, Russia and Asia. The die was cast, and people of most nations would be consumed in multiple ways by the largest conflict in world history for years to come — indeed, conflict was everywhere.

On the home front for Al Simmons, conflict came in the form of a divorce filing by his wife, Dores Lynn Reader, who was clearly fed up with his lifestyle. She charged "cruelty" in a February 13 filing, and maintained that Simmons had failed to provide a permanent home for her, due to his constant traveling as a ballplayer. There were serious money issues as well. A complaint was also served on the Milwaukee City Bank, which apparently operated as Simmons' investment agent. As a result, the bank was not allowed to sell or transfer any of his property.

Dores alleged the estate of Al Simmons exceeded $100,000, as she sought a property settlement. The address for Simmons was listed as 1972 S. 15th Place in Milwaukee. In the wake of the divorce filing, Dores and 5-year-old John Allen Simmons had moved back in with her parents in Racine, Wisconsin. In the paperwork, Dores said they had previously moved constantly from city to city, and even frequently stayed hotels when in Milwaukee. "She always had to live out of a trunk," one newspaper reported her as saying. The media

181

attention was extensive. The Associated Press ran a photo of the couple together under the headline, "They Were Happier Then."[2]

Simmons was not in Milwaukee when the filing was announced, but rather with the A's in Florida getting ready to leave for exhibition games in California. To the press, he complained that Dores was upset because he had refused to loan money to her father. As for his alleged failure to provide a home, he later told the court that his profession required so much travel that it was "impossible" to establish a permanent home.[3]

But it was more than just money and homes. According to one account, Al Simmons chased both women and alcohol, which deeply strained his marriage. Writing in the *Washingtonian* magazine in April 1997, Richard Willing told of Simmons' penchant for babes and booze. He quoted Joe Cascarella, a pitcher for the Washington Senators during 1937 when Simmons was with the team. Cascarella was 89 at the time of the interview. "I rode those benches for five seasons, and I heard two topics discussed to the exclusion of all others: women and alcohol. I'm no prude and I've been known to take a glass of bourbon, but you tell me: How many times can you listen to Al Simmons talk about drinking a case of beer and running off with some girl? After a while, it just isn't very stimulating."[4]

Divorce was not common in the 1940s, especially for Polish Catholics like Al Simmons. Still, as the writer Charles Alexander has noted, salacious stories about celebrity divorce actions made for big headlines. Players such as Waite Hoyt, Jimmie Foxx, Lefty Gomez and Paul Derringer all had their marital difficulties extensively publicized.

To be sure, club officials and baseball writers usually collaborated on keeping the really messy stuff from becoming public. "You could confide in a writer," player Dick Bartell said. "They weren't looking for scandal or gossip to print. Players' private lives were not considered fair game. The press was concerned with the game and what happened on the field. That was their beat."[5] Since teams usually paid the expenses of writers on road trips, the scribes weren't likely to do a great deal of derogatory reporting about the off-color behavior of players.

In any event, Simmons and his wife agreed to delay the divorce proceedings until they reached a settlement later in the year. They hoped to keep their differences out of court—and out of the public eye.[6]

As for the ever-roaming Simmons, he would not remarry. Perhaps he enjoyed his freedom, or perhaps his heart was never the same. The other spin was that his Catholic faith and "deep religious convictions" blocked that possibility, according to one writer who added that "the life of a bachelor was not suited to his nervous system." His whole world seemed upended that year.[7]

As for America's upcoming war, the 39-year-old Simmons was declared "overage" or 1-AH on his draft classification. He would not have to worry about heading off to the military. This gave him some more playing opportunities as many other younger ballplayers donned military uniforms.

Still, doubt clouded his mind during the spring of 1941 on all fronts — not an unusual characteristic for someone in the midst of a divorce. He felt a pull to return to his roots. That April he actually said he regretted having his surname changed from Szymanski. He blamed it on sportswriters, and he urged Felix Mackiewicz, a fellow Athletics outfielder of Eastern European origin, to keep his family name. He did. Apparently, some writers wanted to dub him "Mackie."[8]

After the 1941 season opened, Simmons seemed downbeat and he often lost his temper. In one game, Mack called Simmons in from his third-base coaching position to pinch-hit against Chicago left-hander Edgar Smith in the ninth inning. Simmons lined out to end a 1–0 loss to Chicago. Afterwards, the two had words, and then got into a fight before Chicago manager Jimmy Dykes pulled them apart.

Other than the occasional fight, Simmons cast a strong spell on some of the A's hitters, since he clearly understood how to hit a baseball.

Dick Siebert said, "Simmons watched me this spring and suggested I change my stance. Al said, 'Dick, did you ever see a picture of Ty Cobb batting?' I told him that I probably had, but that I had no clear recollection of it. Then Al pointed out how Cobb had a bend in his knees and a bend in his back. So I adopted a similar style and found that it loosened me up. Al put me on the right track."[9]

Right track indeed. In 1941, first baseman Siebert, 29, cranked out a career-high .334 average.

Connie Mack, who seemed to long for the old days, was effusive about Simmons' coaching — in fact, Bucketfoot Al was doing much more coaching than playing, thereby reducing his chances of ever reaching 3,000 hits. Mack said, "Yes, I wish I had Al playing in there. We've got some good ballplayers, some who want to win are out there hustling every day. But there isn't one like Mickey Cochrane whose spirit would set the whole club on fire. Only Simmons gives us that out on the third base coaching line."[10]

He was always ready to unleash the hardball barbs. Just before Ted Williams' two-game finale against the Philadelphia A's on September 28 — when the Boston player teetered on .400 heading into those games — Simmons sauntered into the Red Sox dugout, intent on planting doubts in Williams' mind with a few choice words.

Four times in his career, the free-swinging Simmons had averaged over .380, leading the American League in 1930 and 1931. Now, he and kindred

Philadelphia's Shibe Park during the 1940s when Al Simmons was a coach with the A's. Shibe Park was on the block bounded by Lehigh Avenue and 20th Street — where Al Simmons rented an apartment in his early days with the A's — and Somerset Street and 21st Street. It was renamed Connie Mack Stadium in 1953. *Philadelphia Athletics Historical Society*

spirit Ty Cobb routinely criticized Williams for being too selective at the plate. Maybe they didn't like that, or maybe they didn't like the kid's brashness, or both. According to the writers Bill Nowlin and Jim Prime, Simmons taunted Williams, reportedly saying, "How much you wanna bet you don't hit .400?" Lesser men would have wilted, perhaps. Not Williams, who was as cocky as anyone. If anything, it had the opposite effect, galvanizing the Boston outfielder to the challenge at hand.

Ted Williams: "The only guy who tried to put me down was Al Simmons. He came over to me in the dugout tunnel one day near the end. He was coaching for Philadelphia at the time. He had hit .390 one year for the A's, and he was another real big guy, but a different animal from Heilmann. Simmons had a kind of swaggering way about him. The kind of guy who when somebody else was in the batting cage, would say, 'Buy him a lunch, he's going to be in there all day.' Simmons wouldn't win any popularity contests. I'm sitting there on the bench and Simmons says, 'How much do you want to bet you don't hit .400?' Just like that. I said, 'Nuts to you, Simmons, I'm not going to bet I'll hit .400. I wouldn't bet a nickel on it.'"[11]

Williams would finish hitting over .400, pulling off the feat before a Philadelphia crowd of 10,000 that seemed to be rooting for the kid from Boston throughout the doubleheader. As he entered the batter's box, he heard home plate umpire Bill McGowan famously mutter, "To hit .400 a player has got to be loose."

Maybe Williams took the advice, as he singled sharply in his first at-bat, then homered to center field in his second appearance, and finished the game with two more singles and a walk. After game one, since there was no way he could fail to hit .400, many felt he would sit out the second game. Surprisingly, however, Williams jogged out to his position in left field for game two. At the end of the day, he had accumulated six hits in eight at-bats, raising his final average to .406.

Unfortunately, there was no report of Simmons' reaction after the game. He seemed to conveniently vanish, at least from the press. As a player-coach that season, Simmons had only seen action in nine games for three hits in 24 at-bats — putting him 103 hits away from 3,000.

After the season, Mack speculated that Simmons would probably not play again. But Japan's attack on Pearl Harbor on December 7 changed everything. Many young ballplayers were drafted or signed up for military service, creating opportunities for older players like Simmons. He signed on again as a player-coach for the A's, who had lost many players to the war cause.

Simmons coached exclusively in 1942, though, and did not even see action as a player in one game. His coaching responsibilities had grown, as he often filled in for the aging Mack when not serving as a third base coach.

Off the field, he and his wife were finally granted a divorce. Interestingly, around the time of the divorce ruling, a newspaper article claimed Simmons' "one crush of his life has been an eyeful he has never met, Paulette Goddard," an actress and a former child fashion model who starred in several Broadway productions as the "Ziegfeld Girl." She was a major star of the Paramount Studio in the 1940s, and married several notable men, including Charlie Chaplin and Burgess Meredith. The same story indicated that Simmons' favorite comic was Groucho Marx.

Back in Philadelphia, nostalgia was in the air for the increasingly woeful A's. Now 80, Mack reminisced about seasons past and players like Simmons. "Simmons was the best player in a pinch I ever had."[12]

The frustrations for the A's and Simmons heated up early in the spring of 1942. In a May 4 game against Detroit, Simmons was tossed out for arguing an umpire's ruling that a grounder hit by the A's Pete Suder was a fair ball. There was other trouble that day as well — a fan in the stands heaved a ball at umpire Art Passarella. The A's lost the game, 6–4.

Baseball during World War II was different — batting averages plummeted, many stars were overseas, and lesser mortals populated the teams. Not only was a "deader ball" being used due to rubber rationing, but playing at night had increased — both likely served to dampen offenses. Simmons, however, thought the game was more complex and required more discipline. "I'm not one to say we had it tougher than the present day players. We all know that night ball brings out the crowds and the financial angle is all important. That's as it should be. But you cannot expect players to hit .390 and pitchers to win 25 games now. This year is the first when we are really going in for night ball in a big way.... An athlete thrives on regular habits and regular hours. He doesn't have them now. His efficiency is impaired. I know you'll say that Ted Williams hit over .400 last year. True. But this year there are more night games. There are twilight games and all kinds of starting hours. We had it easier in the old days. Only single day games and occasional doubleheaders. We could keep regular hours."[13]

The acknowledgement of Williams hitting .400 was an ironic turnaround for Simmons, who had previously proclaimed his era the greatest for hitters.

In any event, Simmons had credibility on the subject of hitting. Through 1943, he ranked high in most of the major career records for right-handed batters. He was third in RBIs with 1,825 behind Rogers Hornsby and Cap Anson, and second with 307 home runs behind former teammate Jimmie Foxx.

The war would bring Simmons back into the game, give him a brief chance to add to his career totals as well as his chase for 3,000 hits — despite his blank line for the 1942 season.

Like many, Simmons understood that patriotism and helping out the war effort was the zeitgeist in America. So, in October after the 1942 season ended, Simmons took a job in a bomber factory at Ford Motors in Dearborn, Michigan. "Save my coaching job for me after the war," Simmons told Mack, who agreed. "I told him his job with the A's was here any time after the war," Mack told writers.[14]

That's about all there is to know about his wartime work; nothing else is written about it. We do know that a lot of people were working in such plants at the time. After America entered the war, the country became as efficient at producing war machines as it had been in making cars and trucks. Due to the number of men overseas fighting, plants used more women for manufacturing, as a total of 18 million women were employed in 1943.

Simmons' stint in the plant was short-lived and only an offseason situation, as he kept tabs on playing opportunities. In January, despite his request earlier to Mack to "save him a job," he signed with the Boston Red Sox. The Red Sox, depleted by the loss of Ted Williams and Dom DiMaggio to the military, sorely needed veteran outfielders.

And a veteran he was. At 41, Simmons hoped his legs could carry him in left field and through pinch-hitting assignments. But one newspaper described his ambitions as an "April Fool gag," and noted he had been "faltering downhill" the last couple of years.[15]

At any other time in baseball history, Simmons would probably not have a playing job, like other older players. "Under ordinary circumstances, their days of active competition would be considered finished," wrote one observer, citing Simmons, Lefty Grove, Freddie Fitzsimmons and Charlie Root.[16] But nostalgia mattered for some, as writer Jeff Moshier noted, "It's good to have him around, to bring back memories of his hey day." When he does smack a good hit, Moshier added, fans would likely say, "Boy, just like Simmons of old."[17]

Simmons spent the offseason, as usual, in Hot Springs, losing weight and trying to get into shape. He also attempted a new diet. "For breakfast," he said, "I have nothing but fruit, milk and coffee. At lunch I eat starches — baked beans, boiled or baked potato, spaghetti, etc. At night I can eat any kind of meat, except pork — but no fried food of any kind."

He said he weighed 217 pounds upon arriving in Arkansas, but was down to 200 by April. "I haven't had a drink in months, and I feel fine. I should have done this long ago." He eyed a regular job, not just pinch-hitting. That would help him crack 3,000 hits, he believed.

In April, Stan Baumgartner, a former relief pitcher for the Philadelphia A's who was now a newspaper writer, penned an account of Simmons' comeback bid that spring in 1943. Interestingly, Baumgartner was on the A's in 1924 when Simmons reported there as a rookie. "Ballplayers are human," wrote Baumgartner. "After five or ten years their nerves jangle. Suppose every time you sat down to your job, 10 million people peered over your shoulder to follow every move, and if you made the slightest mistake it was headlined through the nation."[18]

In the Red Sox workouts at Tufts College that April, Simmons wore an oilskin sweat jacket and a big Turkish towel around his neck so he could sweat more profusely. Red Sox manager Joe Cronin noticed his motivation. "Al's so enthusiastic that you've got to say he has a chance."[19]

Some accounts claimed he had "clinched" a regular outfield berth by the end of spring training. Cronin had apparently penciled him in as the team's starting left fielder for Opening Day.[20] But Simmons on April 14 pulled a ligament in his right calf while running out a home run in an exhibition game against Boston College. He missed Opening Day and several games after that. From there, it did not go so well.

That year New York gossip columnist Jeane Hofmann wrote about Al Simmons hitting the town at night. "Al Simmons, the Red Sox' post-deb starter, was all dressed up the other night, headed for the Ziegfeld Follies. Our Commodore Hotel Operator, Keyhole Kate, reports Al even stopped to have his shoes and teeth polished ... G'wan, Al, all the chorus girls are 4-Fs these days."[21]

Johnny Pesky was a rookie shortstop on the 1943 Boston Red Sox. He would play full-time that season, posting a .331 average and 205 hits, and then head off to serve in the war until 1946.

Pesky knew Simmons from his coaching days with the A's, and that he had a ruthless tongue. In one game back then, Simmons apparently had ribbed Pesky terribly, calling him — ironically — a "dumb Polack," according to author David Halberstam. This enraged Pesky, who was Croatian, not Polish.

Pesky "started screaming back at Simmons that he was not Polish, not a Polack," Halberstam wrote, "and a smart Croat at that. He would damn well fight Al Simmons right then and there, but Simmons started laughing and yelled back, 'Me fight you? You little son of a bitch. What a waste of my time. I'll send the batboy out, and he'll beat the shit out of you.'"[22]

Pesky aside, Simmons took an interest in other ballplayers of Eastern European origins. Stan Musial had begun playing full-time for the St. Louis Cardinals in 1942, the first step toward a Hall of Fame career. Then, Simmons reportedly counseled Musial to "stay in the lineup and bear down all the time." Musial was likely to do so regardless of Simmons' advice — he was that kind of ballplayer. By the end of his career, Musial had played in 3,026 games and collected 3,630 hits (setting then-National League records in both categories).[23]

Al Simmons: "If I'd ever imagined I could get as close as this, 3,000 hits would have been easy. When I think of the days I goofed off, the times I played sick or something and took myself out of the lineup because the game didn't mean anything, I could cut my throat. When I finally decided I had it made, I was never again the ballplayer I was when I was hungry. The only man I ever knew who never lost his fire when he got rich was Ty Cobb."[24]

It is a simplistic stretch to take this quote and find in it the answer of why Al Simmons did not make 3,000 hits, or play better in the second half of his career. To be fair, he was sometimes dogged by real injuries when younger. There is that gray area where a recovering player might feel good enough to get back in the lineup, but takes another day or so off. It sounds like Simmons may have done that occasionally — but perhaps taking an extra day to ensure he was fully healed actually prolonged his career.

When he did play that summer for the Red Sox, he was not good. By the end, he had managed 27 hits in 133 at-bats for a .203 average — he popped one home run, the last of his career. It came on August 29 against Tiny Bonham of the New York Yankees, a solo shot in the top of the ninth inning in a 6–4 loss in the first game of a doubleheader.

Al Simmons was now 76 hits away from 3,000. He would not get any more with the Red Sox, however. After the season ended, Boston announced that Simmons had been unconditionally released. The team had gone 68–84 for a seventh-place finish.

Still, Simmons was determined to stay close to the game, in whatever city, even if he had to "shine shoes at the ballpark," as he put it.[25] In December, he returned to the A's as a coach. Back to Philadelphia he went, with the presumed task of serving as Mack's de facto assistant manager.

Mack said Simmons could rejoin the team "any time he wants." He would turn 42 that season, and it was unclear if he could split time between coaching and playing. "I tried it last year and couldn't make the grade," admitted Simmons, saying he worked extremely hard to get into shape for the Red Sox. He acknowledged the lure of 3,000 hits propelled him on, yet he had little if anything left.[26]

Strangely, Mack threw cold water on the idea of "old-timers" making comebacks. "It's a joke to talk about such men as Ty Cobb, Tris Speaker, Eddie Collins, Babe Ruth, Walter Johnson and Al Simmons making comebacks."[27]

It was not odd that Mack made that statement about the other players — who were older than Simmons — but he wound up putting Simmons on the players' roster on April 15 anyway. The truth is, the team was desperate for some veteran talent, even if it was a bit over the hill.

Mack eyed Simmons exclusively as a pinch-hitter. In spring training, he had actually banged out six hits in seven at-bats, and felt a little more pep in his legs, enough to tempt him into thinking he could play the outfield again. But at this point, Mack would not commit to Simmons roaming the pastures. As for keeping him on the roster, he said, "What else can you do in these times and circumstances?"[28]

Simmons was in an ornery mood. He got into two fights on one day with a Washington Senators pitcher, whose name was never reported. "Three weeks after it happened," wrote Shirley Povich in the *Washington Post,* "it has leaked out that Al Simmons, coach of the Athletics, beat up a Washington pitcher twice on the day the two teams played an exhibition game at the Aberdeen, Md., Army camp." Povich wrote a fascinating column for the Post, complete with an assortment of juicy tidbits about sports, especially baseball. He noted that in 1925, Ty Cobb, then a player-manager for Detroit, paid out $525 to detectives and hotel staff for watching the hours the Detroit players kept. He also observed that 83-year-old Connie Mack had given up cocktails before dinner eight years ago due to indigestion.[29]

But the biggest news that season came on June 6, when the Allied forces launched the D-Day invasion of Europe. It signaled a turning point in the war against Germany — and for baseball, a light at the end of a long, dark tunnel. The sport longed for its boys to come back safely from the war to rejuvenate a rather stale wartime version of the game.

Seven days after the D-Day invasion, Simmons came to bat for the first time that 1944 season. He hit into a double play in the ninth inning of the Athletics' 7–2 loss to the Red Sox.

If he was not exactly fearsome at the plate anymore, Simmons the coach likely struck terror into the hearts of his players. He often advised the A's pitchers to stand up to hitters. Once he cited the case of Jesse Flores, who had taken a pounding from the Washington hitters: "How can a pitcher stand out there and take that kind of a beating and do nothing about it? Those batters are stealing his livelihood away from him. He (Flores) should have loosened those guys up by aiming some of those pitches at their heads."[30]

As his career wound down, Simmons, like Mack, reminisced about the players of yesteryear. Cobb was the "most demonizing combatant of all time," and Mickey Cochrane was a "spark for Philadelphia and later Detroit," and Lefty Grove was the finest pitcher he had ever seen.[31]

Memories — not hits — was about all he had left. When the season concluded, Simmons had played in but four games, mostly as a pinch-hitter, going 3-for-6 with one run scored and two RBIs.

As for the 3,000 hit milestone, he remained eternally 73 hits short. But missing that number should not distract from his broader accomplishments in the fundamental career yardsticks: .334 average, 2,927 hits, 307 home runs, and 1,827 RBIs.

In any era, those are top-of-the-chart numbers. Finally, after 20 seasons, Al Simmons — Bucketfoot Al of the ignoble stance and legion of critics — had finished a glorious, hard-fought career that defied expectations. He was now awaiting, many thought, a call from the Hall of Fame.

While his playing days had ended, Al Simmons still had some baseball life left in him.

CHAPTER NINETEEN

Coaching the A's and Indians

"A ballplayer doesn't spend ten years on the same team without developing an affection for the uniform, the city, the park and certain teammates."
— *Bob Feller*[1]

Charlie Metro was an outfielder for the Philadelphia A's in 1944 when Al Simmons was an A's coach. A journeyman player for the Detroit Tigers as well as a manager later on for the Chicago Cubs and the Kansas City Royals, Metro, like Simmons, had changed his name upon entering baseball. He borrowed "Metro" from his father, Metro Moreskonich, a Ukrainian immigrant.

Metro recalled his days with Simmons. "We roomed together in spring training on one road trip. Al was a tremendous hitter, and he would put on an exhibition in batting practice. He was a little heavy around the middle, but, oh, he'd hit that ball into those left-field stands. Then he'd rattle that ball over to right-field, right-center. Then he'd hit one nine miles, clear out in that deep left-centerfield stands. Once in awhile he'd hit one up there in the upper deck. I don't think I could even carry one that far."[2]

Metro said that Simmons, even in his coaching days, went to Hot Springs, Arkansas, a month before spring training started, where he "put on a pair of great big lumberjack boots, and walked and jogged for miles on those paths down there."

In Philadelphia, Simmons was the boss, more or less. As the A's manager Connie Mack got older, Simmons frequently disregarded Mack's signs and gave the team his own instructions. "You used better judgment than I did, Al," Mack once told Simmons.[3]

Ferris "Burrhead" Fain, 26, joined the A's as a rookie in 1947. A cranky sort, he quickly got impatient with the aging Mack, who was not truly running the club. Fain would go on to win batting titles in 1951 (.344) and 1952 (.327). He recalled frequently looked down at third base coach Simmons, who was flashing the signs for Mack.

Al Simmons was an aggressive third base coach for the A's, and in Mack's declining years virtually ran the team. *Philadelphia Athletics Historical Society*

According to Fain, once "I happened to look down to third base and I've got two strikes and Al Simmons is the third base coach and he gives me the take sign. It came from the bench." Unnerved, Fain made a few outs in such situations. After the last one, he stomped back to the dugout. "I got in the dugout and I pranced back and forth and finally stopped in front of Connie

Mack," Fain said. "Why don't you just take that take sign of yours and stick it in your ass?" Implored by the coaches, Fain apologized to Mack for his disrespect. In return, according to Fain, Mack told Fain not to worry about the signs. Fain was clear about who was running the team — it was Simmons, not Mack. "The lineup was always made by Simmons, (Earle) Brucker, and those guys," he said.[4]

But Simmons was actually using sound judgment for the good of the team. Many accounts exist of Simmons turning his back on a faulty Mack sign — one that would have made no sense — and giving the correct order on his own.[5]

The A's enjoyed a brief resurgence in 1947, posting a 78–76 record after suffering 105 losses the year before — they would also win 84 games in 1948 and 81 in 1949 before falling back into the second division for most of the 1950s (the team moved the Kansas City in 1955). Fain, shortstop Eddie Joost, third baseman Hank Majeski, and outfielders Elmer Valo, Barney McCosky and Sam Chapman led the offense while Phil Marchildon and Dick Fowler hurled gems from the mound.

One scribe described Simmons, now 45, as a "big, handsome gent, gray at the temples and with a little meat on him here and there where well-conditioned athletes don't carry meat." Still, he connected for mammoth strokes in batting practice, which he took frequently. One day, Simmons put "one clean out of the park, the only one who did."[6]

With the A's in those years, Simmons was candid to the press when the team played badly. During one game with the St. Louis Cardinals up 7–0 in the fifth inning, Simmons told a writer, "I said they looked bad because of the wind. I take it back. The wind had nothing to do with it."[7]

He showed admiration for pitcher Bob Feller of the Cleveland Indians, who was recovering his pre-war abilities. "His fastball has lost some of its old hop, but he is still Rapid Robert to me," said Simmons, calling Feller the best American League pitcher. On Larry Doby, the first black ballplayer in the American League when he came up in 1947, Simmons offered a positive review. "After he gains experience, Doby will be sensational. He did a great job for a first-year man last season."[8]

Despite his praise of Feller and Doby, Simmons made a crack that infuriated the Cleveland Indians in their pennant bid during 1948. Not only was he constantly needling opponents and umpires from the coaching lines, but he tweaked them in the sports pages. "Don't worry," Simmons said of the Indians, "they'll fold when the going gets rough. They always do." When told of the remark, Indians player manager Lou Boudreau said Simmons was just using a "little psychological warfare."[9]

Simmons might have been feeling his Hall of Fame oats. In 1948, he got a fair response on the question of his entering Cooperstown, receiving 49.6 percent of the vote, or 31 votes shy of the required number to equate to 75 percent of the vote. The next year would be even closer — 58.2 percent.

In 1949, Simmons showed up at spring training with a few extra pounds — a "big round man," as *New York Times* sportswriter Arthur Daley described the 47-year-old Simmons.

Though six years older than Simmons, White Sox manager Jimmy Dykes joked that he was the team's "junior coach" compared to the star slugger from Milwaukee. "Ignore me, fellas," Dykes was heard to say. "Ignore me."[10]

Dykes was one of the few people who could kid Simmons about his waistline. "Hey, fat stuff," Dykes one day called out to the former A's slugger. "We owe it to our public to be trim and svelte." Retorted Simmons, "Look who's talking," pointing to a likewise expanding Dykes. "I've been fighting excess weight all my life. It's a losing battle."

"Fat" was how Simmons viewed the salaries of ballplayers in the 1940s compared to what those in his period received. "This is the age of the $20,000 coach and the $100,000 ballplayer. You and I, Jimmy, just arrived on the scene too soon. There is no guy in the game I like better than Joe DiMaggio, but he hits .314 and gets a raise. I hit .331 for the White Sox and I'm asked to take a $7,500 pay cut."[11]

In his comments, he did not take inflation, nor the Great Depression, into account. (The year that Simmons hit .331 for the White Sox was 1933, three years before DiMaggio had entered the major leagues and in the middle of the nation's worst economic crisis. Simmons was likely referring to DiMaggio's .315 average in 1947, a far rosier economic time.)

But all was not well. After the last game of the 1949 season, the A's unexpectedly fired Simmons along with another coach, Earle Brucker. One newspaper account said Simmons and Brucker were dismissed for failing to "measure up to their jobs." Fans were shocked — they had little inkling of the Mack family machinations. Connie Mack told the newspapers he took the action "reluctantly," and indicated that the club's board of directors had overruled his desire to keep Simmons.

Connie Mack Jr., the A's treasurer, said the board of directors — not his father — voted to terminate the pair. Though the elderly Mack knew beforehand about the action, according to his son, the media learned about it before Simmons had. In fact, the A's front office had written to Simmons and Brucker, offering to let them resign rather than be fired. But once the press got wind of it, the damage was done. "The confusion was caused by the fact that dad just hated to part with his two old friends," said Connie Mack Jr.[12]

According to writer Bob Broeg, Simmons' maverick nature annoyed the A's front office run by Mack's sons. He was too outspoken for them. "Al could

The dapper-suited Connie Mack, with Al Simmons second from right, talks to his coaches in the dugout. Simmons was fired from his A's coaching position after the 1949 season. *Philadelphia Athletics Historical Society*

teach hitting as well as anyone and coach a smart and alert third base ... (But) his tendency to second guess cost him his last baseball job in 1950.[13]

Writer Red Smith described Brucker as a "darkly humorous gentleman of frightening candor" who finally reached the majors in his late 30s. A catcher, Brucker staged a holdout his first spring with the A's, writing Mack a letter in which he said he was too old to be a backstopper and, besides, did not want to take a pay cut from his minor league salary. Then, after agreeing to terms, he told reporters he would use his major league experience to become a manager. And, he constantly chided Mack to his face about the woeful A's. "If that's the way they play on this Chinese nine," he complained once to Mack.

Although Brucker's brashness sometimes annoyed Mack, the manager liked his forthrightness and his adroit handling of pitchers. In fact, Mack, who was not intimidated by headstrong players or coaches, told reporters he thought Brucker was the "smartest" player he had ever called up from the minors. And so, when Brucker was let go along with Simmons, it was clear that Earle Mack, not Connie Mack, was in charge of the franchise.[14]

"His impatient sons are starting to throw their weight around," wrote Arthur Daley of the *New York Times* who acknowledged being a "big fan of Al Simmons" who was "tops as a third base coach." Daley called the firing a "shabby trick." For his part, Simmons fired back, saying that what Philadelphia truly needed was a "new assistant manager," a direct slap at Earle Mack who had been filling that role under his father.[15]

The A's were mired in disruption and internal dissent. In 1950, faced with declining attendance and hefty expenses, the controlling interest of the club was sold to Earle and Roy Mack, Connie's sons from his first marriage. They also bought out the Shibe-McFarland interests as well as Connie's second wife and Connie, Jr., the half-brother of Earle and Roy.

To do so, Mack's sons then mortgaged the club to the Connecticut General Life Insurance Company. With Mack family tensions running high, it was only a matter of time that the Grand Old Man of Baseball would be replaced, and that is exactly what happened. Connie Mack resigned as manager, and the A's announced that his replacement would be Jimmie Dykes.

After 50 years of piloting the A's—from 1901 to 1950, the longest ever such tenure in major league baseball—Connie Mack was now idle. He still holds the all-time record for managerial wins (3,731) and most World Series wins (5) for an American League manager not with the Yankees.

It must have felt and looked odd as the A's took the field for the 1951 season under their new manager, Dykes.

Meanwhile, the seeds for a relocation to Kansas City were planted. The A's finished in seventh place in 1953, and the fire sale continued. After that season, Dykes and general manager Arthur Ehlers were let go by the Macks, and other high-salary players were sold and traded. In 1954, the A's finished with a 51–103 record, 60 games out of first place and farther behind than any other A's team had ever been.

Arnold Johnson, a Chicago real estate mogul, bought the team, despite a "Save the A's" drive in the city of Philadelphia. Pleas by Connie Mack and his sons went unheeded. The American League approved Johnson's request to relocate the Philadelphia Athletics to Kansas City.

In Kansas City, the Athletics never had a winning season. They became a de facto Yankee farm club, sending a flurry of good players like Roger Maris to the Bronx Bombers through the years. After the 1967 season, A's owner Charles O. Finley received permission to move the franchise to Oakland, California, where they won four World Series and have been occasional playoff contenders. But today, uncertainty exists about their future location.

Cut loose from the A's, Simmons, now 46, signed on with the Cleveland

Indians as a coach for the 1950 season. Cleveland general manager Hank Greenberg led the effort to bring Simmons aboard.

Cleveland's newspapers noted Simmons joined the Indians "less than two years after he needled them out of a pennant." But his antics seemed exactly what the docile Indians needed. Cleveland writers described him as a "loud talking veteran" and "burly Polish slugger" who would bring an "alert and aggressive brand of baseball" to the team.[16]

In announcing the move, Indians president Ellis Ryan said manager Lou Boudreau considered Simmons one of the best coaches around, and hoped he would give the team "much of the spark that was so badly needed in 1949" and help improve the Indians' hitting.[17]

With his coaching record held in such high esteem, one wonders why Simmons never managed.

Ira Thomas, the longtime A's scout, said that Simmons was too much of a "fun-loving sort" to be considered for a managerial job. His penchant for "sleeping late" and liking a "few drinks" amid the "night life," Thomas said, was not looked fondly upon by team owners when evaluating managerial prospects. "Believe me, that is the only fault they could find about Al Simmons. Baseball needs a man like Simmons," said Thomas.[18]

Sportswriter Bob Broeg wrote about Simmons' bouts with the bottle after his playing days. "Even when he began to spend more time with the sauce in his last professional baseball job, as a coach for Cleveland in 1950, Simmons took pride in proper techniques and methods," wrote Broeg in a backhanded compliment.

Broeg recalled Simmons and actor Bill Frawley partying in the Hollywood Plaza Hotel in Los Angeles during the spring of 1950. The Indians had come west for exhibition games against the Chicago Cubs, Pittsburgh Pirates, and Pacific Coast League teams. Frawley achieved his greatest fame playing landlord Fred Mertz in the hit TV comedy series *I Love Lucy*.

Bob Broeg: "Simmons and Frawley had started out to break bread together, but they had a liquid dinner and now sounded as if they would break each other's skull. Shouting at each other in the dark, semi-deserted bar, they would take turns scurrying the length of the mahogany. The reason for their argument? Trying to agree on the right way for an outfielder to go back on a fly ball."[19]

Broeg also wrote of Simmons' inner demons, especially his failed marriage: "Explaining to (sports columnist) McAuley his affection for Connie Mack, Al said, 'Mr. Mack seemed to look upon me as his son. He never stopped feeling sorry for me about the breakup of my marriage.' He told me, 'Al, you and Mrs. Simmons ought to patch things up. I stayed single for 18 years after the first Mrs. Mack died, and all the time I didn't know the meaning of the word happiness.'" Simmons had become a "restless, lonely man" after his marriage broke up, Broeg maintained. His reason for remaining single seemed to be his Roman Catholic faith. On top of his drinking, he gained weight and his diet worsened.[20]

"I like the loud-mouthed, positive-opinioned big lug," said Broeg, "but not when he was under the weather."[21]

As an Indians coach, Simmons got off to a rocky start. On May 23, he was suspended by the American League for using "excessive profanity" against umpire John Stevens in a game against the Yankees. "The third base coach charged at Stevens after the latter called Bob Kennedy (of the Indians) out" for leaving third base early after a fly ball out, a news report stated.[22]

Al Simmons: "I was suspended about four times when I was a player, but it's the first time since I've become a coach."

Contrary to his claim, the article noted that Simmons had been suspended a few times as a Philadelphia A's coach.[23]

Simmons, "one of the most effective bench jockeys in the business," continued his hard-talking ways for Cleveland that season. In one game he harangued Boston catcher Birdie Tebbetts when Tebbetts failed to block 235-pound Indian outfielder Luke Easter from sliding across the plate. Tebbetts accused Simmons of showboating for the TV cameras. "These Boston fellows are getting really tough," said Simmons, adding that Boston was a "choke up" team when the games truly mattered. "Maybe I shout a little bit louder. (The idea) is to talk people into making a couple of mistakes this season.[24]

Back with the Indians in 1951, an odd thing happened to Simmons that spring training. As the train carrying the Indians pulled out of the El Paso, Texas, station, a 22-caliber bullet shattered the compartment window of Simmons and coach Oscar Melillo. Neither coach was hurt, and no one was apprehended for the shot, which came from outside. That is all we know.

Meanwhile, Simmons was not feeling well that spring. He reported to training camp in terrible shape, even for a non-playing coach. His "broken heart" due to his marriage break-up was taking a physical toll as he continued to eat and drink too much.

On April 4, he suddenly resigned from the Indians, citing health reasons. Throughout camp, he had been avoiding the team's press conferences and was looking heavy and haggard. He had a talk with manager Al Lopez about his situation during training camp in Tucson, Arizona. "I'm no good to you, no good to the ball club in my condition, said Simmons. "I'm going to have to quit. I'm going home to Milwaukee to see my doctor. I'll stick with him until I feel better." Lopez told him they would keep his job open in case he returned. Simmons responded, "No, I appreciate everything you and Hank

(Greenberg, the general manager) have done. You've played fair with me. I've tried to play fair with you."[25]

That was one account. Another had it that Simmons had asked the Indians for permission to leave in order to see a physician. Simmons reportedly said, "I'm a sick man and I want to find out what the trouble is. I thought maybe if I felt better later on I could rejoin the club in Cleveland." According to this version, Lopez was startled by Simmons' request. "I can't understand it at all," he told reporters. "He came to me the other night and said he was terribly upset. He said, 'I'm quitting. I just can't go on like this any longer.'"[26]

Thus, the end of the baseball road for Simmons had truly come, after 27 years in the major leagues as a player and a coach.[27]

His spirit had cracked. Writer Ed McAuley told his readers that Simmons "isn't the same man. You wouldn't recognize him. He went to Hot Springs to take off all that blubber he was carrying, and he couldn't even summons the spirit to try. From the start, he kept telling manager Al Lopez he wanted to quit, but Lopez talked him out of it, hoping he'd snap out of it." And he reportedly could not even listen to baseball on the radio."[28]

As Simmons hung up his uniform for the very last time, there was one huge challenge awaiting him — gaining membership in the Hall of Fame.

CHAPTER TWENTY

Cooperstown Comes Calling

> "Lemmings head for the sea. The swallows come back to Capistrano. The buzzards somehow find their way to Hinckley, Ohio. The geese follow their instincts south. And baseball fans go to Cooperstown and the National Baseball Hall of Fame."
> — Dan Chabot, a writer for the Milwaukee Journal[1]

> "He was chesty and always said what he thought."
> — Bing Miller, on Al Simmons

By 1952, despite a sluggish war in Korea, most Americans considered the times good — wages rose, consumer choices abounded, and the doors to college swung wider open than ever before. Now, three out of five families owned a car, two out of three families had a telephone, and one in three homes had a television — the nation was changing, and sports were too. In the decade ahead, baseball would witness six team relocations as the landscape of the national pastime shifted, mostly westward.

For Al Simmons, the biggest issue was whether he would finally get into the Hall of Fame. He had been eligible for a decade now, but in 1951 received just 51 percent of the vote, short of the required 75 percent; the next year, he inched up to 60 percent.

Taking no chances, Simmons wrote a letter to the Hall of Fame, pleading his case for inclusion into the game's most hallowed halls. His friends in the media also chimed in. Writer Shirley Povich, a Hall of Fame voter, raised the question: "What's been keeping Al Simmons out of it all these years?"

Povich described the Hall's ignoring of Simmons as a "brutal brushoff." He emphasized that Simmons had crafted a .375 average over five consecutive seasons from 1927 to 1931. Only the likes of Ty Cobb, Rogers Hornsby, George Sisler and Harry Heilmann had ever topped that, he said. But for some, offense was the problem — so many players from his era boasted inflated numbers. By the 1950s, Hall of Fame voters were quite aware of the effects of the lively ball era on offensive statistics.

But the Duke of Milwaukee, observed Povich, was no ordinary player. "Simmons was a star among the great ones." Moreover, he was the complete ballplayer, an all-around athlete on the diamond. Povich continued, "They can't write Simmons off on account of his fielding. That, too, was superb, if not graceful. No left fielder ever guarded the left field line, holding potential extra base blows to singles, with the skill of Simmons. If he lacked a powerful throwing arm, he had the virtue of accuracy and he got his throws off smartly."[2]

Povich believed Simmons to be the greatest right-handed hitter ever in the American League—even better than Joe DiMaggio, who had just played his last season.

Former teammates also endorsed Simmons for baseball's pantheon. Bing Miller, the outfielder from the A's glory teams, said Cooperstown ought to "shut up shop" if Simmons was not elected. Like others, he thought that Simmons was not popular with the writers who held the votes to the Hall. Miller said, "Nobody can tell me he wasn't one of the greatest players of his era. Just look at his batting averages for about 15 years. I know there were a lot of people who didn't like Al. He was chesty and always said what he thought. But he was a great ballplayer, and that's all that ought to count. There were fellows on our club who didn't like him, but they liked to see him go to bat when there were men on base and we needed a couple of runs. I've heard Al pop off. He didn't mean to be nasty.... He was so confident in himself, and so proud of the things he could do that when he did say anything it sounded insulting, and the fellows thought he was swellheaded."[3]

In January 1953, a newspaper photographer spotted Simmons at the Hialeah horse racing track near Miami. Wearing a white suit with slicked back gray hair, Simmons smiled for the photo, which was contrasted alongside a more youthful photo—a wide-grinning, jet-black haired Simmons—from his Philadelphia A's days.[4]

Around this time, the lords of Cooperstown came calling. On January 21, 1953, the Hall of Fame announced the election of Al Simmons and Dizzy Dean—passing over Joe DiMaggio in his first year of eligibility. Simmons earned 75.4 percent of the votes, while Dean got 79.2 percent.

At first, Simmons did not believe it. When approached by a reporter at the horse track, he demanded that a wire service report be read to him. Finally, when he deemed it true, he said, "It's great news, well worth waiting for. I had begun to think the younger writers had forgotten about me." He added, "This must be my lucky day. I had three winners in the last four races."

The writer noted that Simmons seemed in better shape than when he resigned from the Indians coaching job two years ago. In fact, Simmons expressed a desire to return to baseball. "I'm completely recovered from the

A's outfielder Bing Miller on the temperament of Al Simmons: "I've heard Al pop off. He didn't mean to be nasty." *Philadelphia Athletics Historical Society*

sickness that made me quit at Cleveland." He also spoke fondly of his son, John Allen Simmons, now a teenager and living with his mother, Dores Reader. "My boy will get a kick out of this. He always wanted to see me make the Hall of Fame, and now I've made it. He'll be happy."[5]

Seven days later, Simmons spoke about his Hall of Fame selection at the annual Philadelphia Sportswriters Association banquet, where he was honored as one of the 10 greatest Philadelphia stars. Sportswriter Harold Eager of the *Lancaster Journal* captured the tribute with a touch of pathos: "Now, Al is not a polished speaker. He's no silver-tongued orator, but Monday night he was a spellbinder to his audience. Leaning casually, with his elbow propped on the dais and his face cradled in the palm of his hand, he spoke casually of the things he had to say. And you knew Al was speaking from his heart."

In a "chatty, informal manner," Simmons talked about his selection to the Hall of Fame — he admitted wondering if it would ever happen. And he was proud — "a guy had only to look at him to know that he was literally bustin' his vest with pride," wrote Eager. A candid Simmons credited Connie Mack, and acknowledged some regrets. "Records show I was a good player while playing for him, but only a fair one after I was traded to other clubs," he said.[6]

Again, he voiced his wish to return to the game. "I belong in baseball. I've been off too long," now three years. "I want to coach again or manage. I think I could run a big league club, but I'll take a job with a Triple A team just to get back."[7]

In the ensuing weeks, Dean, a colorful character beloved by the press and public, took the spotlight over Simmons, who was "never as popular or as talkative as Dizzy Dean," a writer said.[8]

Writer Arthur Daley noted that the fading star had grown "bitter" about being "overlooked" in recent years. Daley explained that while Simmons "never caught on with the fans," his fellow players had tremendous respect for his talent. "The fans only saw the outer shell and it was not so pleasing to the eye as others," he wrote. "The athletes themselves looked deeper and saw true greatness" in the "grim and relentless" slugger from Milwaukee.[9]

On July 27, Al Simmons and Dizzy Dean were enshrined into the Hall of Fame in Cooperstown, New York. Simmons opened his brief speech by describing his selection to the hall as "the greatest honor ever paid me," and then — as he had done so in Philadelphia — spoke mostly of Connie Mack and what he owed him. "I want to talk about the first nine years of my big league career. I want to pay my respects to the man who was responsible for me being here today. In the first nine years under Mr. Mack's guidance, I was a great ballplayer. In those nine years I hit .358. After I left Mr. Mack, I was just another ballplayer. He is the greatest man I ever met in my life."[10]

In the wake of his Hall of Fame selection, Simmons took a job in 1954 as the director of the *New York Journal-American's* sandlot program in New York City.

Late in the year, Simmons suffered two losses near and dear to him. On November 28, his 79-year-old mother, Agnes Szymanski, died back in Milwaukee. Then, a month later it was announced that the Philadelphia Athletics were moving to Kansas City for the 1955 season.

Strangely, there is no record of Simmons' reaction to the A's move — but he was likely upset at the relocation. How could he not be? There was little in it for him in Kansas City — he had no connections of substance with the A's anymore. More than this, it was the end of the Philadelphia Athletics, a team that he had spent parts of almost three decades with as a player and coach.

Early on, the A's of Kansas City attempted to reconnect with that past. Simmons, like a good trooper, showed up in 1955 for a pregame ceremony when the A's honored Mack and eight of his finest players — Foxx, Cochrane, Grove among them. It must have been a strange sight, to watch these old A's stand together one last time — but in a Kansas City ballpark.

Just a few months later, on February 8, 1956, Connie Mack died at the age of 93. Simmons was heartbroken at Mack's death; he was also not in good health. Ty Cobb reportedly cried at the news of Mack's passing. After Mack's death, one reporter revealed that the old A's manager had "wept for the loss" that had landed his team in Kansas City.[11]

Increasingly heavy-legged, Simmons was hospitalized in early 1956 for phlebitis, an inflammation of the lower leg. He was briefly hospitalized at the Sacred Heart Hospital in Milwaukee for treatment.

Bob Broeg: "The last time I saw him was in the spring of 1956 when he staggered out of a taxicab one midnight at the Milwaukee Athletic Club, arms loaded with bottled companionship."[12]

Barely a month after Mack's death on May 26, 1956, Simmons staggered out of another cab at the Milwaukee Athletic Club, at 753 N. Broadway Ave, and suddenly collapsed on the pavement. An ambulance whisked him to Milwaukee County Emergency Hospital, where he was pronounced dead upon arrival. According to Frank Esser, the cab driver, Simmons had been shopping and was returning to the club where he had lived for the past few years. Esser said he entered the club to find a bellhop to help Simmons carry his packages. When he returned to the cab, the Hall of Famer was laying on the sidewalk next to the cab.[13]

He was pronounced dead at 3:07 A.M. at the County Emergency Hospital. The death certificate listed acute coronary occlusion — or a heart attack — as the cause of his demise. His occupation was "baseball player and instructor," according to the document.[14]

Al Simmons was six days past his 54th birthday. His survivors included his ex-wife, Dores Lynn Reader, who lived in Miami; his son, John Allen, then attending college in Georgia; and two brothers, Walter and Anthony, and three sisters, Frances Nowak, Tille Mazurek and Anna Mischker, all of Milwaukee.

Funeral services for Simmons were held at the St. Hyacinth's Catholic Church at S. 15th and W. Becher Streets where Simmons had attended church as a boy under the name Alois Szymanski. There, Father Raymond Kurkiewicz delivered a high mass at his funeral services before hundreds of people.

"The south side, where Simmons played sandlot ball before he became one of the all-time great outfielders, turned out in large numbers for the funeral mass and all day Monday at the Rosolek funeral home on 1403 W. Hayes Avenue," according to a newspaper, which estimated the crowd at 600.

"Expensive floral wreaths arrived from all parts of the country," and flowers were sent by the Baseball Hall of Fame, Joe Cronin, Tom Yawkey, and Jimmy Dykes. Tom Neary, a friend of Simmons and a well-known Milwaukee boxer, brought a floral offering in the shape of a bat, a baseball and the figure of .334, Simmons' career batting average. Mickey Cochrane showed up, with "gray in his black hair and tears in his eyes."

That day, St. Hyacinth's Catholic Church was filled with "old south side friends" who knew Simmons as a neighborhood boy. These people had "followed with pride his diamond exploits and then picked up the old friendship when Simmons left baseball."

The choir that sang consisted of children from his old St. Hyacinth's school. Though born too late to know him as a baseball star, they understood him to be a local legend.

After the funeral procession formed, a police escort led the group toward St. Adalbert's Cemetery in south side Milwaukee. When the procession went north on S. 15th, it stopped briefly at the residence at 1972, "the cottage where Al Simmons and his family long lived," in a final gesture of farewell.

Simmons apparently left a "modest estate." In filing a petition for probate, his son, John, indicated that the estate amounted to only $1,000 in cash and $2,000 in insurance. This seems low, considering that Simmons once was reportedly worth $100,000 and kept working as a coach during his post-playing days. That is all we know.

Seventeen years before his death, a newspaper story claimed Simmons had $140,000 in annuities that would "start paying off in 1941" and that "Al saved his money when he was making big dough."[15]

When Simmons died, his longtime roommate and friend Jimmie Foxx said, "Al, Mickey Cochrane and I were inseparable when we played with the Athletics. Al was one of the great hitters."[16]

The writer Shirley Povich weighed in on Simmons' fatal heart attack. "With a bat in his hands, Simmons would have given it a battle, and you would have liked his chances."[17]

Just a few years after his death, in 1960, Povich imagined what Simmons would think about "modern" baseball and the decline of hitting through the

1960s. "Simmons once hit .391 and couldn't win the title." Povich said today's batters were swinging for home runs—which meant more money in salaries. But Simmons was a natural hitter, he said.[18]

Milwaukee sportswriters said Simmons displayed the same "flaming spirit that made Ty Cobb" unpopular, and that his hatred for pitchers was "cold, purely clinical." After all, he accepted, they wrote, the fact they should hate him, too.

Scribe Cleon Walfoort portrayed Simmons as a feared hitter, an outfielder who seldom misjudged the ball or threw to the wrong base, and he possessed a canny baseball instinct that made him a great baseball coach. Plus, he touched lives in his own quiet way, as he related in remarks by W.J. Szulakiewicz of the department of public welfare, who back in 1925 or 1926, had been a captain in the National Guard, overseeing about 150 young men, many of whom were troubled teens.

W.J Szulakiewicz: "One day in the offseason, Simmons came to me and offered to help by talking to the men and teaching them some baseball. Our problems seemed to solve themselves, and I've always given Al most of the credit. I understand he did the same kind of work with the police and fire departments."[19]

In his later years, Simmons was appreciative, in his tough-talking way, of the life that baseball had given him. "Baseball doesn't owe me a thing," he is quoted as saying. "It was wonderful to me, and I owe everything I've got to the game. No other business or fame could have given me so many happy years."[20]

He left his hometown a deep sense of pride. "Their pride is in the fact that an actual Hall of Famer was born in Milwaukee, Wisconsin," said Tom Rathkamp, a Milwaukee native, technical writer and Society for American Baseball Research member. "There is a heavy Polish ethnic pride from the old South Side of town, as Simmons himself was very proud of his hometown. Al Simmons is our claim to baseball fame. In Simmons' time, several players came from the Midwest, from ethnic enclaves such as Milwaukee, Chicago, and small towns in Iowa and Kansas. Today, we see an ethnic surge of players from Hispanic countries, Asian countries, and so on."

What is it about old-time ballplayers that fans today seek to understand? In a sense, fans may be trying to understand themselves, their cultures and where they come from, Rathkamp said. "I think fans like to discover that a player came from his or her hometown, or very near it. Today, it's probably more 'ethnic' than 'geographic,' as more and more players are foreign born. I don't know if many more players will make the majors who came from Milwaukee, but Al Simmons, Oscar "Happy" Felsch, Ken Keltner, Tony Kubek, Bob Uecker and others give us a lot to be proud of."

What became of Al Simmons' only son, John?

When Simmons died in 1956, his son was about 20 years old and enrolled as a student at Emory University in Georgia. He went on to graduate in 1958 with a business degree, and later became an Air Force helicopter rescue pilot in Vietnam during the 1960s, according to his son-in-law Patrick Graeber. In the 1970s, he was also the owner of a Gigi's Pizza franchise restaurant in the Atlanta area. As a captain in the Air Force, he lived all over the world at various points, and also worked as a tax accountant. John had three children with his wife, Joyce Bonner Simmons — Karen, to whom Patrick is married; Danny; and David. For the last 18 years of his life, John, divorced, lived in Chapal, Mexico, a popular U.S. military retirement area.[21]

"John did not talk about his father too much," said Patrick Graeber, "but he did say that he was able to travel with the team during his summer breaks when he was not attending military boarding school." John served as a batboy for the A's, and some of the players gave him autographs. "His relationship with his father was somewhat limited due to Al's hectic schedule as a player, and his travel requirements, though he did very much enjoy his time with his father," Graeber said.[22]

A great satisfaction exists in the family around his Hall of Fame accomplishments. "I think what is most amazing," Graeber said, "is that he was overshadowed by so many baseball greats like Ruth, DiMaggio, Foxx, Cobb, and Gehrig, yet still achieved so much with the A's and Connie Mack and kept a lower profile than they did."

On Mack, to this day that relationship rings loud. "He was Connie Mack's favorite and was close friends with Mack until his untimely death in 1956," said Graeber, noting that Mack wrote many letters to Simmons when he was coaching for the A's.

Al Simmons, the swaggering, shooting star, understood that baseball was about more than offensive accolades. It was also about relationships, and his with Connie Mack, the flinty-eyed patriarch who preached self-motivation, was paramount throughout his adult life. In many ways, Mack was the father that Simmons had lost at such a young age.

And in baseball, Simmons found the way to greatness out of the harsh world of the immigrant neighborhood. The game allowed him to make something of himself against all odds and all naysayers, and it gave him a chance to express himself by the fierce poetry of play he brought to the field. It is time we remember his unique place in the national pastime.

CHAPTER TWENTY-ONE

Analyzing Al Simmons

> "In the first version of this book, I compared Simmons to Al Oliver. I realize now that was harsh. Simmons was a better player than Al Oliver, and Al Oliver was a hell of a player."
> — Bill James, in the New Bill James Historical Abstract[1]

What are we to make of Al Simmons the ballplayer? It is not an easy answer.

Too much can be made of personality and extraneous issues. Most experts conclude that Simmons was among the best, though not at the top of the summit. In 1999, he ranked 43rd on *The Sporting News* list of the 100 Greatest Baseball Players. That's a subjective but seemingly fair assessment.

We know from the numbers that Simmons still holds the A's franchise records for most career RBI (1,178), total bases (2,998) as well as highest career batting average (.356). In 2000 he was voted to the Athletics' All Century Team outfield along with Rickey Henderson and Reggie Jackson. He is often considered to be the best athlete ever to come from the state of Wisconsin.

Simmons hit 307 home runs, a significant total for a player from the 1920s and 1930s when home runs were much less common than today. He also compiled more hits than any right-handed batter in American League history until surpassed by Detroit's Al Kaline.

Briefly, his achievements were:

- 2-time AL batting average leader (1930 and 1931)
- AL runs scored leader (1930)
- 2-time AL hits leader (1925 and 1932)
- 2-time AL total bases leader (1925 and 1929)
- AL RBI leader (1929)
- 20-home run seasons: 6 (1925, 1929–1932 and 1938)
- 30-home run seasons: 3 (1929, 1930 and 1932)
- 100 RBI seasons: 12 (1924–1934 and 1936)

- 100 runs scored seasons: 6 (1925, 1929–1932 and 1934)
- 200-hit seasons: 6 (1925 and 1929–1933)

For more complex analyses, let's examine what the experts say about Simmons.

Baseball historian Bill James' evaluation of Al Simmons is mixed. The sabermetrics guru ranks him as the 71st best player in baseball history, below what James claims most other experts would rate Bucketfoot. "Simmons played in a hitter's park in a big hitting era. He hit .334 but didn't walk; he had a lower career on-base percentage than Merv Rettenmund (.271), Earl Torgeson (.265), Bernie Carbo (.264), or Gene Tenace (.241)." (Note: the latter figures are batting averages.)

As James puts it, Simmons was an RBI man, and RBI men are usually "overrated, as opposed to lead-off type hitters, because a lot of people buy into payoff statistics without paying attention to the opportunities involved." James says Simmons piled up RBIs, in part, because A's leadoff hitter Max Bishop had a career .423 on-base percentage.

Fair enough. But many great players, like Joe DiMaggio and Willie Mays, did not take many bases on balls, and Lou Gehrig had the great advantage of batting behind Babe Ruth, who had an even higher lifetime on-base average (.474) than Bishop or anyone who ever played, except for Ted Williams. While it is true that Simmons did not expand on his offensive arsenal by taking many walks, he combined a high average with extra-base hits. As for the walks and OBP, yes, guilty as charged.

As for playing in an offensive park, there are problems with this analysis. Shibe Park was not an extreme hitter's park by any stretch of the imagination. Following are the *Baseball-Reference.com* Shibe Park Batting Park Factors during Simmons' tenure in Philadelphia (with 100 being neutral, and more than 100 favoring hitters, under 100 favoring pitchers):

1924	101
1925	107
1926	106
1927	106
1928	103
1929	104
1930	104
1931	106
1932	104

From 1933 to 1935, Simmons played home games in Chicago's Comiskey Park, which had run factors of 96, 103, and 102 respectively. In Detroit for 1936, the run factor was 100.

These are similar to the run factor for the so-called pitcher's haven, Forbes Field, in the National League:

1932	100
1931	99
1930	100
1929	102
1928	104
1927	107
1926	105
1925	107
1924	102

Shibe Park, during the years Simmons played there, offered a slight edge to hitters, but certainly not like Wrigley Field or Fenway Park. For left-handed pull hitters, Yankee Stadium was a home run paradise with its 295-foot right-field foul line; Ruth and Gehrig definitely benefited from this.

James himself does concede Simmons has grown on him over time. "In the first version of this book, I compared Simmons to Al Oliver. I realize now that was harsh. Simmons was a better player than Al Oliver, and Al Oliver was a hell of a player."[2]

Others evoke similarly mixed reviews. Historian Neal Pease said, "Looking at his career in retrospect, one suspects that Simmons' standing in the pantheon of baseball can be easily overrated. He had his best years and posted his gaudiest numbers in a hitter's park in a hitter's era in the limelight of national attention as a member of a storied championship team. He may have been the fourth best player on that A's juggernaut.... Still, in his prime, Simmons plainly ranked as one of the foremost hitters in the American league."[3]

"Fourth best" seems extreme — second best, perhaps, after Foxx, is more accurate. Cochrane was nowhere near the offensive force Simmons was, who put up a much higher OPS+ during the dynasty period of 1929–1931, and Grove was a different creature, a pitcher, so too hard to compare.

While Simmons may be overrated in some aspects, he may underrated in the narrative, if not the numbers, of baseball.

Simmons played for a fractured franchise. The A's franchise has weathered two dislocations — one moved them to Kansas City in 1955, and then another took them to Oakland in 1968. Contemporary A's fans in the Northern California region have little connection to the teams and stars of the Philadelphia version.

In Philadelphia, the fans' appreciation of Al Simmons — notwithstanding the great work done by the Philadelphia Athletics Historical Society in preserving the team's legacy — has suffered a great blow in recent decades. This dislocation makes it hard to appreciate Simmons, Foxx, Cochrane and Grove, for the team, of course, is no longer around.

Meanwhile, the great players in the Yankees franchise never had to confront this type of broken legacy. They enjoyed the additional benefit of playing in the world's media center where legends are grown, nurtured and cultivated for decades after playing careers end.

The break-up of the A's and the trading away of all the star players apparently affected Simmons—this is not to excuse him, but only to understand his context. After he left the A's, his performance was not as good, and it fell off badly in his later years, whether due to injuries, well-being woes or the psychological separation from his glorious days with Mack and the camaraderie of his fellow champion A's.

Again, excuses are not being made here—information is only being provided. It's hard to quantify this type of thing, and human beings are complex in how they process change and challenge. But suffice to say, baseball was simply never the same for Simmons, spoiled by his early success and that of the A's.

While this does not give him a "pass" on the full record of his career, it does lead us to look more closely at what kind of player he was in his *peak* years with the A's—and there, he excels, dramatically so. One may analyze players any number of ways, but two of the most common are peak and cumulative value. Players tend to be better in one than the other, and Simmons' strength is clearly in his peak years.

Through the age of 32, Simmons is most similar to a ballplayer named Stan Musial, according to *Baseballreference.com's* usage of Bill James' similarity scores. That speaks for itself, as Musial may be one of the top 10 or so players of all time. If Simmons had continued his offensive pace past age 32 the way he led up to it, he would have been one of the game's elite Hall of Famers. Consider that by age 32, DiMaggio, a right-handed outfielder like Simmons, had put up these statistics: .332 BA, .398 OBP and .588 SA. By comparison, Simmons had posted these numbers: .354 BA .398 OBP .574 SA.

For the first half of his career, Simmons hit like Joe DiMaggio. In the field, he was arguably every bit as good as DiMaggio. At the plate, Musial was a tad better than both (.345 BA, .432 OBP, .582 SA), though he did not have a good fielding reputation.

Simmons peaked brightly, early and enjoyed one of the greatest starts *ever* for a ballplayer.

His 11 consecutive seasons of 100-plus RBIs is proof of the hefty responsibility given to him by Mack for production in the cleanup hole. True, RBIs are products of opportunity, but to discount them entirely or too much, as is often done in sabermetrics, is to ignore the reality of production. Taking advantage of RBI opportunities is the role of a cleanup hitter like Simmons — if he was not getting the job done, Mack would have switched him to another spot. Clearly, he banged out big hits at the right time, and thrived in that context.

Cyril Morong, a leading sabermetrician and economics professor at San Antonio College, offers an elaborate analysis of Al Simmons. On his blog, *cybermetric.blogspot.com*, he delved into the issue in two separate evaluations in 2009, one on "How Good Was Al Simmons" and the other "Why Did Al Simmons Decline So Much in the Second Half of his Career?"

In the first article, Morong starts off by answering the question in the title of his column — Al Simmons "was very, very good. Great would work, too."

Morong notes that Ichiro Suzuki recently became the second quickest player to reach 2,000 hits. He did it in 1,402 games. Who was the fastest? Al Simmons. Simmons did it in 1,390 games. He points out that through 1931, Simmons' then-.363 overall average was second only to Ty Cobb for players with 4,500-plus plate appearances. Significantly, he was also third in isolated power (SA-BA) with .233, trailing only Ruth (.360) and Gehrig (.300). Other bright spots for him include:

Offensive winning percentage: Cyril Morong said, "He is one of 22 players to have at least three seasons with an .800-plus offensive winning percentage (the Bill James stat that says what your team's winning percentage would be with nine identical hitters when you give up an average number of runs). Ruth had 12, Cobb 11, and Ted Williams 10. So he is not close to them, but to be in that small a group is pretty good."

Win Shares: Cyril Morong said, "He had 375 Win Shares (the Bill James stat that includes all phases of the game). That was tied for 63rd through 2001 (including pitchers). Bill James ranked him as the 7th best left fielder of all time and gave him an A as a fielder. He played 1,377 games in LF and 771 in CF. He was 88th among position players in WS per PA. He led the league in Win Shares once (thanks to Ruth's 1925 stomach ache). But he had five other seasons in the top 10, including three in the top three (once losing to Foxx by a hair in 1929). He led all AL outfielders in fielding Win Shares twice and was third three times.

Wins Among Replacement: Simmons, Morong said, is ranked 85th (now 86th) among position players in Wins Among Replacement at Sean Smith's site *baseballprojection.com*. "Looks like he was one of the greatest players ever," Morong concludes.

The question begs, what happened? Morong examines the player's plunge in his latter years — Simmons batted .363 from ages 22 to 29, but only .309 from ages 30 to 37. "That is a very big drop-off," Morong wrote. "I wonder if he had nagging injuries that eventually caught up to him." Injuries were part of the problem, but there was more, as this book pointed out earlier — Simmons lost some of the fire in the belly, if not his lungs.

To determine how Simmons' decline compared to others in batting average, Morong found every player who had 4,000-plus plate appearances from ages 22 to 29 (390 players) and every one who had at least 3,230 plate appearances from ages 30 to 37 (also 390 players). He then compiled a list of all the players who were in both groups (143) and the difference between their "young" average and their "old" average and ranked them from highest to lowest.

Simmons ranked 141st out of those 143 players, with his huge decline of a minus .054 in batting average between the two chapters of his career. Morong said, "Simmons is very near the bottom. He did not have the biggest decline, but it was still very big."

Simmons' drop-off cannot be explained by a league-wide "low average" period — the league hit .288 compared to .293 in his two periods, not much of a difference. As for ballpark effects, they are not much different. Morong calculated the average park factor for the parks Simmons played in when he was "old" and it came out to about 101, which is just about average. Shibe Park had a park factor a little under 104 when Simmons was 22 to 29 years of age.

If Simmons had experienced just an "average" drop-off as an older player, Morong projects, he would have probably finished with a .360 average for his career. That would put him second to Cobb. Hornsby would be third, at .358 — which would have been extraordinary. But of course, he did not.

"I have not quite split (Simmons') career evenly in two, so I could have overestimated this by a couple of points," said Morong, who also found Simmons waned as well in OWP, or offensive winning percentage, when he got "old."

Morong sums up his findings: "Simmons finished with a career OWP of .644, which is now ranked 117th among players with 5,000-plus PAs. The typical drop-off when getting "old" was about .024. If Simmons had a .698 OWP when he was "old" that would give him a career OWP of about .710. That would currently rank 35th, a big improvement over 117."

There is potential, and there is performance — and a ballplayer's career is a mix of both. One is reminded of the quote by the Marlon Brando character, Terry, in the 1954 movie classic *On the Waterfront:* "You don't understand. I coulda had class. I coulda been a contender."

As a ballplayer, Simmons was criticized for not reaching his ultimate potential through a long, productive career. But this is not as easy as it may sound; and how many players do maximize the beginning, middle and end of their careers? They are all human beings, prone to this or that distraction or problem.

By today's sophisticated yardsticks of baseball analysis, Al Simmons may not have been the player he should have been. But he is close to it, and he was a winner, a champion.

If we judge Al Simmons by the baseball values of that day and age, we appreciate his all-around talents more deeply. Like his peers, Simmons viewed batting average as the arbiter of offensive success. In this context, he excelled famously, as he did with glove-work in the outfield.

In his prime, Al Simmons was a man and player full of color and controversy — always good for a hard hit or tough talk. He was enigmatic above all — charming in his confidence in overcoming opponents, powerfully candid in his baseball acumen, but touched with melancholy about what might have been in his life — if all the hits had fallen safely for him.

Appendix:
Al Simmons Statistics

Year	Team	G	AB	R	H	2B	3B	HR	RBI	SB	BB	SO	AVG	OBP	SLG	OPS	OPS+	RC/G
1924	Athletics	152	594	69	183	31	9	8	102	16	30	60	.308	.343	.431	.774	98	5.0
1925	Athletics	153	654	122	253	43	12	24	129	7	35	41	.387	.419	.599	1.018	149	10.0
1926	Athletics	147	583	90	199	53	10	19	109	11	48	49	.341	.392	.564	.957	142	8.7
1927	Athletics	106	406	86	159	36	11	15	108	10	31	30	.392	.436	.645	1.081	172	11.4
1928	Athletics	119	464	78	163	33	9	15	107	1	31	30	.351	.396	.558	.954	145	8.4
1929	Athletics	143	581	114	212	41	9	34	157	4	31	38	.365	.398	.642	1.040	159	10.1
1930	Athletics	138	554	152	211	41	16	36	165	9	39	34	.381	.423	.708	1.130	175	12.2
1931	Athletics	128	513	105	200	37	13	22	128	3	47	45	.390	.444	.641	1.085	175	12.2
1932	Athletics	154	670	144	216	28	9	35	151	4	47	76	.322	.368	.548	.915	130	7.9
1933	White Sox	146	605	85	200	29	10	14	119	5	39	49	.331	.373	.481	.854	130	7.2
1934	White Sox	138	558	102	192	36	7	18	104	3	53	58	.344	.403	.530	.933	136	8.5
1935	White Sox	128	525	68	140	22	7	16	79	4	33	43	.267	.313	.427	.739	88	4.6
1936	Tigers	143	568	96	186	38	6	13	112	6	49	35	.327	.383	.484	.867	113	7.1
1937	Senators	103	419	60	117	21	10	8	84	3	27	35	.279	.329	.434	.763	95	5.0
1938	Senators	125	470	79	142	23	6	21	95	2	38	40	.302	.357	.511	.868	121	6.8
1939	Bees	93	330	39	93	17	5	7	43	0	22	40	.282	.331	.427	.758	109	4.8
1939	Reds	9	21	0	3	0	0	0	1	0	2	3	.143	.217	.143	.360	-2	1.5
1940	Athletics	37	81	7	25	4	0	1	19	0	4	8	.309	.341	.395	.736	93	4.9
1941	Athletics	9	24	1	3	1	0	0	1	0	1	2	.125	.160	.167	.327	-13	1.2
1943	Red Sox	40	133	9	27	5	0	1	12	0	8	21	.203	.248	.263	.511	48	2.0
1944	Athletics	4	6	1	3	0	0	0	2	0	0	0	.500	.500	.500	1.000	190	13.5
Career		G	AB	R	H	2B	3B	HR	RBI	SB	BB	SO	AVG	OBP	SLG	OPS	OPS+	RC/G
20 years		2215	8759	1507	2927	539	149	307	1827	88	615	737	.334	.380	.535	.915	132	7.9

Career Splits

	G	AB	R	H	2B	3B	HR	RBI	SB	BB	SO	AVG	OBP	SLG	OPS
vs LH Starter	476	1901	351	694	137	32	77	416	20	131	100	.365	.408	.592	1.001
vs RH Starter	1739	6858	1156	2234	402	117	230	1414	68	487	637	.326	.372	.519	.891
Home	1118	4301	757	1488	274	80	162	994	42	350	330	.346	.397	.560	.957
Away	1097	4458	750	1440	265	69	145	836	46	268	407	.323	.364	.511	.875
First half	1144	4478	807	1488	280	74	174	970	52	346	405	.332	.382	.544	.927
Second half	1071	4281	700	1440	259	75	133	860	36	272	332	.336	.378	.525	.903
Team wins	1180	4873	1087	1834	368	100	212	1289	58	370	348	.376	.422	.623	1.045
Team losses	1026	3850	413	1083	170	49	94	537	29	246	387	.281	.327	.424	.751
Ties	9	36	7	11	1	0	1	4	1	2	2	.306	.342	.417	.759

Career Fielding

G in OF	Ch	PO	A	E	DP	Fld%	RF/G	lgFld%	lgRFG	LF-CF-RF
2142	5251	4988	169	94	37	.982	2.41	.968	2.37	1377-771-1

World Series

Year Team		G	AB	R	H	2B	3B	HR	RBI	SB	BB	SO	AVG	OBP	SLG	OPS
1929 Athletics	W	5	20	6	6	1	0	2	5	0	1	4	.300	.318	.650	.968
1930 Athletics	W	6	22	4	8	2	0	2	4	0	2	2	.364	.417	.727	1.144
1931 Athletics	L	7	27	4	9	2	0	2	8	0	3	3	.333	.400	.630	1.030
1939 Reds	L	1	4	1	1	1	0	0	0	0	0	0	.250	.250	.500	.750
Career	2-2	19	73	15	24	6	0	6	17	0	6	9	.329	.375	.658	1.033

Source: Baseball-Reference.com

Facts and Feats

- Al Simmons hit five home runs on May 22 during his career, the most by any batter on his own birthday.
- **Most Career RBIs, Right-handed Batters, through 1943:**
    1. Cap Anson: 2,076
    2. Rogers Hornsby: 1,882
    3. Al Simmons: 1,825
    4. Honus Wagner: 1,732
    5. Napolean Lajoie: 1,599
- **Most Career Homers, Right-handed Batters, through 1943**
    1. Jimmy Foxx: 527
    2. Al Simmons: 307
    3. Rogers Hornsby: 301
    4. Bob Johnson: 259
    5. Hank Greenberg: 249
- **Batting Feats (career)**
    Three-homer games: 1 (July 15, 1932)
    Two-run homer games: 19
    Five-hit games: 8
    Four-hit games: 52
    Three-double games: 3
    Two-triple games: 4
    Seven-RBI games: 1
    Six-RBI games: 9
    Five-RBI games: 11

    Source: Retrosheet

- **Hitting Streaks**
    27 games (1931)
    23 games (1925)
    22 games (1925)
    20 games (1929)

    Source: Retrosheet

- Led the AL in total bases — 392 — and runs created —157 — in 1925.
- At-bats per home run (career): 28.5
- At-bats per strikeout (career): 11.9
- At-bats per RBI (career): 4.8

    Sources: Baseball-Reference.com, Baseball Cube, Baseball Almanac

- **All-Star Selections**
    1933 AL
    1934 AL
    1935 AL

Notes

Introduction

1. Art Morrow, "Al Simmons, Two-Time Hit King of AL, Dies at 53," *The Sporting News*, June 6, 1956.
2. Ibid.
3. Bob Broeg, "Nothing Like Simmons," *The Sporting News*, April 8, 1978.
4. Dave Kindred, "Ted Williams Could Spin a Tale With the Same Skill That he Could Hit a Fastball," *The Sporting News*, July 6, 2002.
5. Ken Smith, unidentified newspaper clipping, August 13, 1976, Al Simmons Hall of Fame file.
6. John Kieran, undated newspaper clipping from *New York Times*, Al Simmons Hall of Fame file.
7. Shirley Povich, "This Morning," *Washington Post*, August 12, 1946.
8. Broeg, "Nothing Like Simmons."
9. Donald Honig, *Baseball America: The Heroes of the Game and the Times of their Glory* (New York: MacMillan, 1985), 173.
10. Donald Honig, *Baseball Between the Lines* (Lincoln: University of Nebraska Press, 1993), 69.
11. William Nack, "Lost in History," *Sports Illustrated*, August 19, 1996.

Chapter One

1. Tom Boswell, syndicated column, September 2, 1989, *Washington Post*, found at <www.baseball-almanac.com/quotes/quogiam.shtml>.
2. Al Simmons, as told to A.J. Schinner, *My Life*, unpublished manuscript provided to author by Tom Rathkamp and Craig and Laura Simmons-Larsen of Milwaukee.
3. George Reimann, "The Sandlot Duke," *Milwaukee Times*, January 26, 1967.
4. Vital Statistics of the Milwaukee Health Department, Wisconsin Board of Health, certificate of birth, state birth no. 148, signed September 19, 1974. The address change is noted in George Reimann's newspaper article, "Al Simmons: Pride of the South Side," *Milwaukee Journal*, 1983.
5. Reimann, "The Sandlot Duke."
6. Simmons, *My Life*.
7. Ibid.
8. Ibid.
9. Harry T. Brundidge, "Al Simmons' Rise Gripping Tale of Fight to Repay Toil-worn Mother," *St. Louis Star*, July 23, 1931.
10. Dale B. Smith, "Bucketfoot Al," Philadelphia Athletics Historical Society website, <www.philadelphiaathletics.org>.
11. Paul Dickson, *Baseball's Greatest Quotations* (New York: Harper Collins, 1991), xv.
12. John Kieran, undated newspaper clipping from *New York Times*, Al Simmons Hall of Fame file.
13. Simmons, *My Life*.
14. Brundidge, "Al Simmons' Rise."

15. Simmons, *My Life*.
16. Edward "Dutch" Doyle, *Al Simmons, the Best*, (Chicago: Adams, 1979), 4.
17. Brundidge, "Al Simmons' Rise."
18. Simmons, *My Life*.
19. "Aloysius Harry Symansky (*sic*)," unidentified and undated newspaper clipping, Al Simmons Hall of Fame file.
20. Brundidge, "Al Simmons' Rise."
21. Simmons, *My Life*.
22. Ibid.
23. George Reimann, "Al Simmons: Pride of the South Side," *Milwaukee Journal*, 1983.
24. Simmons, *My* Life.
25. Richard Crepeau, *Baseball: America's Diamond Mind* (Lincoln: University of Nebraska Press, 2000), 147–148.
26. Brundidge, "Al Simmons' Rise."
27. Reimann, "Pride of the South Side."
28. Simmons, *My Life*.

Chapter Two

1. William Shakespeare, *Romeo and Juliet*.
2. Marshall McLuhan, *Understanding Media* (New York: McGraw Hill, 1964).
3. "Al Simmons is Dead at 53: One of Baseball's Greats," Associated Press article, May 26, 1956.
4. Peter Morris, *A Game of Inches: The Stories Behind the Innovations That Shaped Baseball* (Chicago: Ivan R. Dee, 2006), 72.
5. Christy Mathewson, *Pitching in a Pinch* (Lincoln: University of Nebraska Press, 1994).
6. Paul Dickson, *The New Baseball Dictionary* (New York: Harcourt Brace, 1999), 202.
7. Ibid.
8. Reimann, "The Sandlot Duke."
9. Arthur Daley, "The Duke of Milwaukee," *New York Times*, May 28, 1956.
10. Doyle, *Al Simmons, the Best*.
11. Ibid.
12. Brundidge, "Al Simmons' Rise."
13. Ibid.
14. Simmons, *My Life*.
15. Document from the American League Service Bureau, December 2, 1928.
16. Westbrook Pegler, "Al Szymanski, Alias Al Simmons, Always Said He'd be a Star," *Chicago Daily Tribune*, September 22, 1932.
17. Ibid.
18. Neal Pease, "Diamonds Out of the Coal Mines," in *The American Game: Baseball and Ethnicity*, ed. Lawrence Baldasarro and Richard Johnson (Carbondale, IL: Southern Illinois University Press, 2002), 147–149.
19. Ibid.
20. Ibid.
21. C. William Duncan, "Simmons Will Knock Home Run for White Sox on Opening Day if Tradition Runs True to Form," *Philadelphia Public Ledger*, April 1933.
22. Daley, "Duke of Milwaukee."
23. Ibid.
24. Arthur Daley, "Refugee from the Polo Grounds," undated clipping from *New York Times*, Al Simmons Hall of Fame file.
25. Daley, "Duke of Milwaukee."

Chapter Three

1. Brundidge, "Al Simmons' Rise."
2. R.D. Laing, *The Politics of Experience* (New York; Pantheon: 1967), introduction.
3. Doyle, *Al Simmons, the Best*.

4. Brundidge, "Al Simmons' Rise."
5. Reimann, "Pride of the South Side."
6. Reimann, "Pride of the South Side"; Bob Broeg, "Bucketfoot Never Lost That Swagger," *Sport Guide,* July 11, 1971.
7. Morrow, "Al Simmons, Two-Time Hit King."
8. *Any More Questions: Al Simmons was Briefly a Pro Boxer,* unidentified newspaper clipping dated May 29, 1956, Al Simmons Hall of Fame file.
9. "Writers Were Right, Borchert Was Wrong When Simmons Reported to the Brewers in 1922," unidentified newspaper clipping dated January 1953, Al Simmons Hall of Fame file.
10. Brundidge, "Al Simmons' Rise."
11. Doyle, *Al Simmons, the Best.*
12. "Writers Were Right, Borchert Was Wrong."
13. Broeg, "Bucketfoot Never Lost That Swagger."
14. "Writers Were Right, Borchert Was Wrong."
15. Ernest Lanigan, National Baseball Hall of Fame historian, 1953, Al Simmons Hall of Fame file.
16. Brundidge, "Al Simmons' Rise."
17. Broeg, "Bucketfoot Never Lost That Swagger."
18. "Aloysius Harry Symansky (*sic*)."
19. Document from the American League Service Bureau, December 2, 1928.
20. Larry Desautels letter to Ernest Lanigan of the National Baseball Hall of Fame. Desautels was the sports editor of the *Aberdeen American News.*
21. Larry Desautels, "Batting Around," *Aberdeen American News,* undated newspaper clipping, Al Simmons Hall of Fame file.
22. Doyle, *Al Simmons, the Best.*
23. "Aloysius Harry Symansky (*sic*)."
24. Brundidge, "Al Simmons' Rise."
25. Ibid.
26. Broeg, "Bucketfoot Never Lost That Swagger."
27. Doyle, *Al Simmons, the Best.*
28. Brundidge, "Al Simmons' Rise."
29. Ira Thomas letter to Ernest Lanigan, dated March 9, 1953, Al Simmons Hall of Fame file.
30. Ibid.
31. Brundidge, "Al Simmons' Rise."
32. Ibid.
33. Ibid.
34. John Kieran, unidentified and undated newspaper clipping from *New York Times,* Al Simmons Hall of Fame file.
35. Doyle, *Al Simmons, the Best.*
36. "Looking Good, Looking Bad," unidentified newspaper clipping dated August 20, 1927, Al Simmons Hall of Fame file.
37. Ibid.
38. John Kieran, *New York Times.*
39. "Writers Were Right, Borchert Was Wrong."
40. John Kieran, *New York Times.*
41. Thomas letter to Lanigan.
42. Ibid.
43. "Connie Mack Buys Outfielder Simmons from Milwaukee," *Reading Eagle,* December 16, 1923.

Chapter Four

1. Bill James, *Sport,* July 1984.
2. John P. Carmichael, "My Greatest Diamond Thrill," *Chicago Daily News,* reprinted in *The Sporting News,* June 22, 1944.
3. Charles Alexander, *Breaking the Slump: Baseball in the Depression Era* (New York: Columbia University Press, 2004), 1–13.
4. Jerome Romanowski, *The Mackmen* (Camden, NJ: Graphic, 1979), 74,

5. Broeg, "Bucketfoot Never Lost That Swagger."
6. Thomas letter to Lanigan.
7. Joe Williams, "Connie Mack Banks on These Star Recruits," *Southeast Missourian*, March 22, 1924.
8. Connie Mack, *Connie Mack's Baseball Book* (New York: Alfred A. Knopf, 1950), 75.
9. Ed Pollock, "Mack Almost Gave Up on Simmons as a Rookie," *Philadelphia Sunday Bulletin*, May 27, 1956.
10. Bruce Kuklick, *To Every Thing a Season: Shibe Park and Urban Philadelphia, 1909–1976* (Princeton: Princeton University Press, 1993).
11. Barra Foundation, *Philadelphia: A 300-Year History* (New York: W.W. Norton, 1982), 535.
12. Document from the American League Service Bureau, December 2, 1928.
13. Sam Levy, "Al Simmons Well Deserves His Niche in Hall of Fame," *Milwaukee Journal*, July 26, 1953.
14. Frank Graham, "Graham's Corner," *New York Journal-American*, January 22, 1953.
15. Document from the American League Service Bureau, December 2, 1928.
16. Morrow, "Al Simmons, Two-Time Hit King."
17. William Kashatus, *Connie Mack's '29 Triumph: The Rise and Fall of the Philadelphia Athletics Dynasty* (Jefferson, NC: McFarland, 1999), 41.
18. Ray Kelly, "Simmons Hitting .380, Still Wanted to Learn, but Dykes, .200, Brushed Off Cobb's Tips," *Philadelphia Bulletin*, January 1953.
19. Arch Ward, "Talking It Over," *Chicago Tribune*, April 30, 1935.
20. Henry W. Thomas, *Walter Johnson: Baseball's Big Train* (Lincoln: University of Nebraska Press, 1998), 196,
21. Document from the American League Service Bureau, December 2, 1928.
22. C. William Duncan, "Former Socker Simmons Filled Family Sock Well," *The Sporting News*, October 28, 1943.
23. Reed Browning, *Baseball's Greatest Season: 1924* (Amherst: University of Massachusetts Press, 2003), 89,
24. John Carmichael, "100 Percent for Sox, Says Al," *Chicago Daily News*, 1933, Al Simmons Hall of Fame file.
25. Babe Ruth, *Babe Ruth's Own Book of Baseball* (Lincoln: University of Nebraska Press, 1992), 167.
26. Morrow, "Al Simmons, Two-Time Hit King."
27. Stephen Riess, "Baseball and Ethnicity," in *Baseball as America: Seeing Ourselves Through Our National Game*, ed. National Geographic Society and National Baseball Hall of Fame and Museum (Washington: National Geographic, 2002), 88–89.
28. Pease, "Diamonds Out of the Coal Mines."
29. Lawrence Ritter, *The Glory of their Times* (New York: HarperCollins, 1992), 101–110.

Chapter Five

1. "Athletics Appear Strengthened for 1925 Season," *Eugene Register-Guard*, January 28, 1925.
2. Stuart Schimler, "Ben Shibe," SABR Baseball Biography Project, <bioproj.sabr.org.>
3. "Al Simmons Runs Rough Shod Over Bat Leaders," *Lewiston Evening Journal*, June 6, 1925.
4. "Simmons Justifies Big Purchase Price," *Ludington Daily News*, June 9, 1925.
5. Untitled newspaper clipping from *New York Times*, June 14, 1925, Al Simmons Hall of Fame file.
6. Broeg, "Bucketfoot Never Lost That Swagger."
7. Billy Evans, "Simmons Proves Sensation at Bat Though He Has Odd Style," *Lewiston Evening Journal*, July 2, 1925.
8. John P. Carmichael, *My Greatest Day in Baseball* (Lincoln: University of Nebraska Press, 1996), 78.
9. "Simmons in a Batting Spurt," Associated Press story in the *Los Angeles Times*, August 23, 1925.
10. "Youth Shares Clout Throne with Veterans," Associated Press story in the *St. Petersburg Times*, September 7, 1925.
11. "American League Bat Records; Hitting Much Higher than in 1924," *Berkeley Daily Gazette*, November 30, 1925.

12. "Simmons, Only American Leaguer to Play Full Time at One Position," *Pittsburgh Press,* November 29, 1925.

Chapter Six

1. Honig, *Baseball America,* 173.
2. "Al Simmons is Praised by Manager Connie Mack," *Deseret News,* January 11, 1926.
3. Billy Evans, "Stars in the Pinch, Gets Job," syndicated column published in *Southeastern Missourian,* January 22, 1926.
4. Neil Baldwin, *Edison: Inventing the Century* (Chicago: University of Chicago Press, 2001), 369; Bob Broeg, "Nothing Like Simmons," *The Sporting News,* April 8, 1978.
5. Shirley Povich, "This Morning," *Washington Post,* January 10, 1952.
6. N.W. Baxter, "Al Simmons Poles Out Homer," *Washington Post,* May 24, 1936.
7. Billy Evans, "Sheely, Hornsby and Meusel, Best Batsmen in Big Crisis," syndicated column published in *The Evening Independent,* July 1, 1926.
8. Morris, *A Game of Inches,* 73.
9. Donald Honig, *Baseball When the Grass Was Real: Baseball from the Twenties to the Forties, Told by the Men Who Played It* (Lincoln: University of Nebraska Press, 1993), 49–50.
10. Billy Evans, "Seriousness in Game Necessary, Evans Finds, Citing Instances," syndicated column published in *The Evening Independent,* August 3, 1926.
11. Thomas letter to Lanigan.
12. Joe Paprocki, *Bringing Catechesis and Liturgy Together* (New London, CT: Twenty-Third, 2002), 31.
13. Cleon Walfoort, "Simmons' Hatred for Hurlers Made Baseball Legends," *Milwaukee Journal,* May 26, 1956.
14. Billy Evans, "Present Season to be Off-Year for Many Former Leading Stars," syndicated column published in *The Evening Independent,* August 30, 1926.
15. "Al Simmons' Bat Work Penalized Athletic Hopes," *Miami News,* November 7, 1926.
16. "Landis Holds Testimony Against Two Old Stars, Says They Knew of Bets," *Associated Press* story in the (Syracuse) *Herald Journal,* December 22, 1926.
17. "Fight for Cobb Grows Furious," *Victoria Advocate,* February 6, 1927.
18. "Ty Cobb Accepts Offer from Mack," *Chicago Tribune,* February 9, 1927.
19. "Connie Mack Says Team Will Enter this Year's Play with Fine Spirits," *St. Petersburg Times,* February 27, 1927.
20. Feg Murray, "A Rampaging Elephant," *Los Angeles Times,* March 6, 1927.
21. Jack Gallagher, "Cobb, Collins to Aid Macks," *Los Angeles Times,* February 20, 1927.

Chapter Seven

1. Philip Roth, "My Baseball Years," *New York Times,* April 2, 1973.
2. William Curran, *Big Sticks: The Batting Revolution of the Twenties* (New York: William Morrow, 1990), quoted from *The Sporting News* (12 July 1950); as actually published in *The Sporting News,* "prick" was replaced by "[censored]"—elsewhere, including *Field of Screams: The Dark Underside of America's National Pastime* (1994) the quote has appeared as "Ty Cobb is a prick," or sometimes "Cobb is a prick. But he sure can hit. God Almighty, that man can hit."
3. John Kieran, "Sports of the Times," *New York Times,* March 21, 1927.
4. John Kieran, "Sports of the Times," *New York Times,* April 25, 1927.
5. Broeg, "Bucketfoot Never Lost That Swagger."
6. Arthur Daley, "Listening to Jimmy Dykes and Al Simmons," *New York Times,* March 8, 1949.
7. Simmons, *My Life.*
8. Vincent X. Flaherty, "Straight from the Shoulder," *Los Angeles Examiner,* October 24, 1939.
9. Al Stump, *My Life in Baseball: Ty Cobb* (Lincoln: University of Nebraska Press, 1993), 252–253.
10. Arthur Daley, "Jimmy Dykes and Al Simmons."
11. Charles Bevis, *Mickey Cochran: The Life of a Baseball Hall of Fame Catcher* (Jefferson, NC: McFarland, 1998), 45.

12. Stump, *Ty Cobb*, 252–253.
13. Kashatus, *Connie Mack's '29 Triumph*, 41.
14. "Johnson Censures Mack, Fines Cobb," *New York Times*, May 12, 1927.
15. Stump, *Ty Cobb*, 255
16. Ibid., 253.
17. "Looking Good, Looking Bad," unidentified newspaper clipping dated August 20, 1927, Al Simmons Hall of Fame file.
18. Arthur Daley, "Jimmy Dykes and Al Simmons."
19. Ibid.
20. "Murderers' Row," Wikipedia website, <http://en.wikipedia.org/wiki/Murderers%27_Row>
21. "Al Simmons Out for Season: Mack," Associated Press story in *Atlanta Constitution*, July 30, 1927.
22. Billy Evans, "Billy Evans Says" syndicated column published in *Pittsburgh Press*, September 12, 1927.
23. Babe Ruth, "Batting Form Differs With Ballplayers," *Pittsburgh Press*, September 5, 1927.
24. Adolph Hitler, 1927 Nuremberg Rally speech, <http://www.calvin.edu/academic/cas/gpa/rpt27c.htm>

Chapter Eight

1. John J. Rooney, "Bleachers in the Bedroom," *Elysian Fields Quarterly*, Summer 2000.
2. Dickson, *Baseball's Greatest Quotations*, 85; quoted also in *The Tiger Wore Spikes* by John McCallum (New York: A.S. Barnes, 1956).
3. "Al Simmons Turns Scout," *Milwaukee Journal*, January 14, 1928.
4. "Speaker, with Simmons and Miller, Gives A's Strong Outfield Array," *Reading Eagle*, February 13, 1928.
5. "High-Salaried Speaker and Cobb May Cause Dissension in Athletics Clubhouse," *Los Angeles Times*, March 11, 1928.
6. John Kieran, "Sports of the Times," *New York Times*, March 9, 1928.
7. "Waite Hoyt is Latest Player to Join Team," *Miami News*, March 16, 1928.
8. Henry Farrell, "Athletics Giving Yankees Chance to Display Class," *The Evening Independent*, May 22, 1928.
9. Bevis, *Mickey Cochrane*, 61.
10. Bill Brandt, "75,000 Storm Park as Athletics Win and Lose to N.Y.," *Philadelphia Public Ledger*, May 25, 1928.
11. Joe Dittmar, *Baseball Records Registry: The Best and Worst Single-Day Performances and the Stories Behind Them* (Jefferson, NC: McFarland, 1997).
12. Andrew Johnson, Al Simmons biography, <www.pabook.libraries.psu.edu/palitmap/bios/Simmons__Al.html>
13. Rooney, "Bleachers in the Bedroom."
14. James Isaminger, untitled article dated 1928 in *Philadelphia Inquirer*, Al Simmons Hall of Fame file.
15. "Athletics Crush Red Sox, 14–2," *New York Times*, September 2, 1928.
16. Babe Ruth, "Babe Ruth Names His 1928 All-American Ball Team," *Pittsburgh Press*, September 9, 1928.
17. Dixon Stewart, "Athletics Star Gets 53 Votes," *Pittsburgh Press*, October 16, 1928.
18. C. William Duncan, "Wide Open Spaces, Golf and Ice Cream Are Big Moments in Life of Simmons," *Philadelphia Public Ledger*, September 16, 1929.
19. Ralph Davis, untitled column, *Pittsburgh Press*, February 1, 1929.

Chapter Nine

1. George Kirksey, "All Is Not Well with Mackmen," *Pittsburgh Press*, March 21, 1929.
2. "Simmons Expects Big Year," *Los Angeles Times*, February 10, 1929.
3. "Al Simmons, Star Outfielder, Lost to Macks for Opener," *Pittsburgh Post-Gazette*, April 9, 1929.

Notes — Chapter Nine

4. Ed Pollock, "Macks' Pennant Hopes Struck Blow by Lack of Strong Starting Lineup," *Philadelphia Evening Ledger*, April 11, 1929.
5. Sam Murphy, "Al Simmons to Be Back Soon," *The Sporting News*, undated 1929 clipping, Al Simmons Hall of Fame file.
6. Shirley Povich, "This Morning," *Washington Post*, May 2, 1956.
7. Jack Barry, "Late, Great Simmons Always Idolized Cobb," *Boston Globe*, May 5, 1956.
8. "Marauding Men of Mack Go Down Before Big Ed Morris," *Hartford Courant*, May 1, 1929.
9. Kashatus, *Connie Mack's '29 Triumph*, 107.
10. "Scribbled by Scribes," unidentified newspaper clipping dated July 4, 1929, Al Simmons Hall of Fame file.
11. Kashatus, *Connie Mack's '29 Triumph*, 108.
12. Jack Sords, "Sords Point," *Sarasota Herald*, July 25, 1929.
13. Al Simmons, "A's Three in Row Over Yankees Decide Issue," North American Newspaper Alliance article in *Los Angeles Times*, September 8, 1929.
14. "A's Give Connie Mack Credit," North American Newspaper Alliance article, September 21, 1929.
15. "Al Simmons of Athletics Named the Most Valuable American League Player in '29," *The Sporting News*, December 26, 1929.
16. Westbrook Pegler, "Al Simmons is Hitting 'Em Wronger and Better Than Ever," *Chicago Tribune*, September 24, 1929.
17. Brian Bell, "Ty to Watch World Series as a Scribe," Associated Press story in *Palm Beach Post*, September 25, 1929.
18. "Connie Mack Tells of Struggle to Mold Another Pennant Winner," *The Evening Independent*, October 1, 1929.
19. Brian Bell, "Jimmy Foxx Will be the Baby of the 1929 World Series," Associated Press story in *Ludington Daily News*, September 24, 1929.
20. Bell, "Ty to Watch World Series."
21. Lou Wollen, "Sports from All Angles," *Pittsburgh Press*, October 4, 1929.
22. "George Earnshaw," Wikipedia website, <http://en.wikipedia.org/wiki/George_Earnshaw>, attributed to a Babe Ruth quote on page 255 of a book only identified as *Play Ball*.
23. Westbrook Pegler, "A's Resent Arrogance of Malone," *Chicago Tribune* article reprinted in *Pittsburgh Post-Gazette*, October 10, 1929.
24. Terry Stephan, "A Justice For All," *Northwestern Magazine*, Spring 2009, 17.
25. Al Simmons, "A's Flawless in First Game, Says Simmons," ghostwritten column by North American Newspaper Alliance in *Atlanta Constitution*, October 9, 1929.
26. John Kieran, "The Odd Game of Baseball," *New York Times*, May 14, 1934.
27. Bert Demby, "Athletics Favorites Over Cubs in Series," UPI story in *Berkeley Daily Gazette*, October 7, 1929.
28. John Kieran, "Sports of the Times," *New York Times*, October 10, 1929.
29. Ibid.
30. Pegler, "A's Resent Arrogance."
31. Roscoe McGowen, "Athletics Jaunty Leaving for Home," *New York Times*, October 10, 1929.
32. "Radio Crowds Here Thrilled by Homers," *New York Times*, October 10, 1929.
33. Al Simmons, "Simmons Says He's Awful," ghostwritten column by North American Newspaper Alliance in *Los Angeles Times*, October 12, 1929.
34. John P. Carmichael, "Al Hears of Airing Over the Air," *Chicago Daily News*, undated 1933 article, Al Simmons Hall of Fame file.
35. Nack, "Lost in History."
36. "Cubs Routed by A's in Lucky Seventh," Associated Press story in *Sarasota Herald*, October 13, 1929.
37. Ibid.
38. Al Simmons, "Al Simmons Says A's Will End Series Today," ghostwritten column by North American Newspaper Alliance in *Atlanta Constitution*, October 14, 1929.
39. "Sidelights," Associated Press story in *Palm Beach Post*, October 14, 1929.
40. Nack, "Lost in History."
41. Al Simmons, "Simmons Dazed by Mack Rally," ghostwritten column by North American Newspaper Alliance in *Los Angeles Times*, October 15, 1929.
42. Al Simmons, "Al Simmons Praises Mack for A's Victory," ghostwritten column in *Milwaukee Journal*, October 16, 1929.

Chapter Ten

1. Andrew Mellon, widely quoted; Mark Kramer entry in Dickson, *Baseball's Greatest Quotations*, 230.
2. Jonathan Eig, *Luckiest Man: The Life and Death of Lou Gehrig* (New York: Simon and Schuster, 2005), 145.
3. Unidentified newspaper clipping dated December 12, 1929, Al Simmons Hall of Fame file.
4. "Al Simmons' Kid Brother is Star with Cleveland," Associated Press story in *St. Petersburg Times*, April 1, 1930.
5. Westbrook Pegler, "Al Simmons is Hitting 'Em Wronger and Better Than Ever," *Chicago Tribune*, September 24, 1929.
6. "Simmons Holdout, Athletics Reveal," Associated Press story in *New York Times*, April 15, 1930.
7. "Simmons Puts Away War Club," *The Evening Independent*, April 15, 1930.
8. "Simmons a Holdout as A's Start Season," unidentified newspaper clipping dated April 17, 1930, Al Simmons Hall of Fame file.
9. Unidentified newspaper clipping dated April 24, 1930, Al Simmons Hall of Fame file.
10. Broeg, "Nothing Like Simmons."
11. Ibid.
12. Unidentified April 24, 1930, clipping.
13. Will Wedge, "Fans Back Up Galloway," unidentified newspaper clipping dated April 17, 1930, Al Simmons Hall of Fame file.
14. John Kieran, "Sports of the Times," *New York Times*, April 25, 1930.
15. Bob Warrington, speech tribute to the 1930 World Champion Philadelphia Athletics delivered at the 2005 Philadelphia Athletics Historical Society Reunion Weekend Breakfast.
16. C. William Duncan, "Former Socker Simmons Filled Family Sock Well," *The Sporting News*, October 28, 1943.
17. "Questions and Answers," *The Evening Independent*, November 13, 1929.
18. Carmichael, "My Greatest Diamond Thrill."
19. "A's Slump but Cling to Lead in Hot Race," unidentified newspaper clipping dated June 19, 1930, Al Simmons Hall of Fame file.
20. Orlo Robertson, "20 Home Runs and 256 Hits Day's Record," Associated Press story in *Sarasota Herald*, June 24, 1930.
21. Walter Trumbull, "Chuck Klein Praised," North American Newspaper Alliance story in *Los Angeles Times*, July 15, 1930.
22. Hub Miller, *Baseball Magazine*, December 1950, as portrayed on page 655 in *The New Bill James Historical Abstract*.
23. Unidentified newspaper clipping dated September 11, 1930, Al Simmons Hall of Fame file.
24. Alan Gould, "Al Simmons Rated as the Best in the Outfield," Associated Press story in *Free Lance-Star*, September 30, 1930.
25. Al Munro Elias, "World Series Dope," *Reading Eagle*, September 22, 1930.
26. Jimmie Dykes, as told to Charles Dexter, *You Can't Steal First Base* (Philadelphia: J.B. Lippincott, 1967), 18–19.
27. John Kieran, "Al Simmons, the Climbing Pole," *New York Times*, December 2, 1930.
28. "Mackmen Favorites Over St. Louis," *Pittsburgh Press*, October 1, 1930.
29. Carmichael, "My Greatest Diamond Thrill."
30. Daniel Okrent and Harris Lewine, *The Ultimate Baseball Book* (Boston: Houghton Mifflin, 2000), 164.
31. "Daniel, Ray Blades and Gelbert are Goats," *Pittsburgh Press*, October 2, 1930.
32. "Series Sidelights," *Pittsburgh Post-Gazette*, October 7, 1930.
33. "Mack Still Smiles Over World Series," UPI story in *Pittsburgh Press*, December 27, 1930.
34. Edward Neil, "Connie Says A's Great Ball Team," Associated Press story in *Lewiston Daily Sun*, October 9, 1930.
35. "Series Sidelights," *Pittsburgh Post-Gazette*, October 7, 1930.
36. Kashatus, *Connie Mack's '29 Triumph*, 145.
37. W. Harrison Daniel, *Jimmie Foxx: The Life and Times of a Baseball Hall of Famer* (Jefferson, NC: McFarland, 2004), 48.
38. Jules Tygiel, *Baseball's Great Experiment: Jackie Robinson and his Legacy* (New York: Oxford University Press, 1997), 33.

Chapter Eleven

1. Dickson, *Baseball's Greatest Quotations*, 133.
2. Unidentified newspaper clipping dated January 15, 1931, Al Simmons Hall of Fame file.
3. "Al Simmons and Fiance Break Engagement," *Chicago Daily Tribune*, February 7, 1931.
4. "Simmons' Engagement to Marry Broken," Associated Press story in the *Reading Eagle*, February 7, 1931.
5. Alexander, *Breaking the Slump*, 37.
6. Unidentified newspaper clipping dated January 1, 1931, Al Simmons Hall of Fame file.
7. Ibid.
8. Simmons, *My Life*.
9. "Simmons Not with Athletics," (Syracuse) *Herald Journal*, March 11, 1931.
10. Manning Vaughan, "Al Simmons Wants $100,000 from Mack," *Milwaukee Journal*, March 21, 1931.
11. Broeg, "Bucketfoot Never Lost that Swagger."
12. "Athletics are All Signed for the Season," Associated Press story in *Palm Beach Post*, April 10, 1931.
13. "Hooks and Slides," *Florence Times Daily*, April 20, 1931.
14. Alan Gould, "Four Other Teams Assume Role of Flag Contenders," Associated Press story in *The Evening Independent*, March 25, 1931.
15. Paul Mickelson, "Al Simmons Credits Mack for Comeback of Team," *Washington Post*, May 14, 1931.
16. Morris, *A Game of Inches*, 73.
17. "Al Simmons Hero as A's Win," Associated Press article, May 7, 1931.
18. Nack, "Lost in History."
19. Mickelson, "Al Simmons Credits."
20. Manning Vaughan, "Putting 'Em on the Pan," *Milwaukee Journal*, May 4, 1931.
21. Ibid.
22. "Players Separated by Umpire, Al Charges Dusting to Firpo," *Washington Post*, July 14, 1931.
23. Unidentified newspaper clipping dated July 23, 1931, Al Simmons Hall of Fame file.
24. Ed Pollock, "Playing the Game," *Philadelphia Public Evening Ledger*, January 1953.
25. Jim Kaplan, *Lefty Grove: American Original* (Cleveland: Society for American Baseball Research, 2000), 150, 156, 268.
26. Ibid., 115–116.
27. Bevis, *Mickey Cochrane*, 81.
28. Shirley Povich, "This Morning," *Washington Post*, August 12, 1946.
29. Alan Gould, "Athletics Take Series Opener from Cards, 6–2," Associated Press story in *Montreal Gazette*, October 2, 1931.
30. John McGraw, "John McGraw Explains Big Plays of the Last World Series," syndicated column in *Los Angeles Times*, February 27, 1932.
31. Brian Mulligan, *1940 Cincinnati Reds: A World Championship and Baseball's Only In-Season Suicide* (Jefferson, NC: McFarland, 2005), 65.
32. Red Smith, *The Book: Red Smith on Baseball* (Chicago: Ivan R. Dee, 2000).
33. Alan Gould, "Wild Bill Blanks Champions 2–0 by Great Hurling," Associated Press story in the (Syracuse) *Herald Journal*, October 3, 1931.
34. "Series Notes," *Reading Eagle*, October 5, 1931.
35. "Al Simmons Clouts Home Run in Ninth," Associated Press story in *Milwaukee Journal*, October 5, 1931.
36. Alexander, *Breaking the Slump*, 45.
37. "One Weakness," Associated Press story in *The Evening Independent*, October 14, 1931.
38. "Mack Plans No Shake Up," *Ellensburg Daily Record*, October 12, 1931.
39. Alexander, *Breaking the Slump*, 45.
40. Daniel, *Jimmie Foxx*, 48.
41. Bevis, *Mickey Cochrane*, 92
42. "Japanese Much Better Fielders Than Batters, Says Bob Grove After Baseball Tour of Orient," Associated Press story, January 1, 1932.
43. Document from the American League Service Bureau, January 31, 1932.
44. "Al Simmons Dances Jig as Bat He Lost in Japan is Returned," *Washington Post*, April 7, 1937.

Chapter Twelve

1. Dykes, *Steal First Base*, 52.
2. Nack, "Lost in History."
3. "Mackies Can Set a Record for American," Associated Press story in the *Schenectady Gazette*, March 26, 1932.
4. Aloysious Harry Simmons, June 2, 1932, player bio in Al Simmons Hall of Fame file.
5. Document from the American League Service Bureau, February 7, 1932.
6. John Kieran, unidentified and undated article in *New York Times*, Al Simmons Hall of Fame file.
7. John P. Carmichael, "Al Hears of Airing Over the Air," *Chicago Daily News*, 1933, Al Simmons Hall of Fame file.
8. Dick Axman, "It Really Happened," unidentified publication, December 1932, Al Simmons Hall of Fame file.
9. Simmons biography in Al Simmons Hall of Fame file.
10. Morrow, "Al Simmons, Two-Time Hit King."
11. Dom Forker, Wayne Stewart and Robert Obojski, *Big Book of Baseball Brainteasers* (New York: Sterling, 2004), 76.
12. Bevis, *Mickey Cochrane*, 100.
13. William Braucher, "Hooks and Slides," *Florence Times Daily*, August, 23, 1932.
14. Chuck Voorhis, "Thinks Mack Won't Make Many Trades," *The Observer*, 1932, Al Simmons Hall of Fame file.
15. George Kirksey, "Blame Placed for Hornsby's Demise," UPI article in *Berkeley Daily Gazette*, August 6, 1931.
16. "Ruth Not in Shape," *Milwaukee Journal*, September 28, 1932.
17. "Simmons Picks Yankees to Win Series," *The Star and Sentinel*, October 1, 1932.
18. Al Simmons, "Al Simmons as a Pinch-writer Hits a Three-bagger," ghostwritten column in *Chicago Daily News*, September 7, 1933.
19. Carmichael, "Al Hears of Airing."
20. Simmons, "Pinch-writer."
21. Carmichael, "Al Hears of Airing."
22. Simmons, "Pinch-writer."
23. Dykes, *Steal First Base*, 52.
24. "Moves Closer to Home," unidentified newspaper clipping dated October 6, 1932, Al Simmons Hall of Fame file.
25. "White Sox Hopes High, Claims Harry Grabiner," *Los Angeles Times*, October 12, 1932.
26. Unidentified newspaper clipping dated October 16, 1932, Al Simmons Hall of Fame file.
27. "Al Simmons Already Busy Shedding Surplus Weight," Associated Press story in *Los Angeles Times*, November 16, 1932.
28. Kuklick, *Shibe Park*, 72.
29. Kashatus, *Connie Mack's '29 Triumph*, 163.
30. Nack, "Lost in History."

Chapter Thirteen

1. Leonard Levinson, radio writer, widely quoted.
2. Ken Belson, "Apples for a Nickel, and Plenty of Empty Seats," *New York Times*, January 6, 2009.
3. Ed Bang, "Just Between You and Me," *Cleveland News*, April 28, 1933.
4. John Carmichael, "100 Percent for Sox, Says Al," *Chicago Daily News*, undated clipping from 1933, Al Simmons Hall of Fame file.
5. "Simmons, Haas, Dykes Sold to Chisox by Connie Mack," *Washington Post*, September 29, 1932.
6. "Al Simmons Takes Policy for $100,000," Associated Press story, November 2, 1932.
7. "New Socks for White Sox," photo caption in story "Al Simmons Picks Yankees in Walk-Away Pennant Race," Associated Press, January 12, 1933.
8. Ibid.
9. Carmichael, "100 Percent for Sox."

10. Henry Edwards, American League Service Bureau article, February 12, 1933.
11. Edward Neil, "Practically Everything Wrong with Simmons," Associated Press story, March 2, 1933.
12. Arch Ward, "Talking It Over," *Chicago Daily Tribune*, January 18, 1934.
13. Alan Gould, "Good Start Helpful to Young Pilot," *The Evening Independent*, April 18, 1933.
14. Frank Yeutter, "Al Simmons Confesses All," *Philadelphia Bulletin*, August 1953.
15. "Al Simmons, Ballplayer, Dead," *New York Times*, May 27, 1956.
16. Jerome Holtzman, *Baseball, Chicago Style* (Los Angeles: Bonus, 2001), 100; UPI story in *Berkeley Daily Gazette*, "All-Star Game Adds New Thrill," July 6, 1933.
17. Arch Ward, "Al Leads Ruth, Klein in Total for Star Game," *Chicago Daily Tribune*, June 25, 1933.
18. John Drohan, "Al Like Cobb in Having Fun with Razzers," *The Sporting News*, September 15, 1933.
19. "Al Simmons Believes Yankees Will Repeat," Associated Press story in the (Syracuse) *Herald Journal*, July 18, 1933.
20. Nick Altrock, "Simmons Total Loss as Baseball Prophet," *Ottawa Citizen*, August 26, 1933.
21. Simmons, "Pinch-writer."
22. Ibid.
23. Edward Burns, "Sox Shift Diamond to Aid Simmons' Batting," *Chicago Daily Tribune*, November 2, 1933.
24. Edward Burns, "Hard to Satisfy," *Chicago Daily Tribune*, November 14, 1933.
25. "Close Sox Fences Not Simmons Idea," Associated Press story, November 13, 1933.
26. "Comiskey Park to be Made Over to Suit Simmons," *Los Angeles Times*, November 2, 1933.
27. Edward Burns, "Seems Sox Done Wrong by Simmons in Shrinking Park," *Chicago Daily Tribune*, November 14, 1933.
28. Edward Burns, "Hard to Satisfy," *Chicago Daily Tribune*, November 14, 1933.
29. Burns, "Seems Sox Done."

Chapter Fourteen

1. "Simmons Joins in Kids' Game, and It Costs Him Puh-lenty," *Washington Post*, February 14, 1934.
2. Bob Ray, "Al Simmons Here: Thumb in Bad Shape," *Los Angeles Times*, February 16, 1934.
3. Paul Zimmerman, "Simmons, Dykes and Haas Look for Banner Chisox Season," Associated Press story, February 17, 1934.
4. Broeg, "Bucketfoot Never Lost that Swagger."
5. "Simmons; X-Rays Shows No Skull Fracture," *Chicago Daily Tribune*, May 9, 1934.
6. John Kieran, "The Man Who Was Hit on the Head," *New York Times*, May 11, 1934.
7. "Chisox May Leave Al Simmons Here," *The Washington Post*, May 9, 1934.
8. William Weekes, "Jimmy Dykes Takes Helm of White Sox After Ragged Start," Associated Press story in *The Evening Independent*, May 9, 1934.
9. "Sports Stew: Served Hot," *Pittsburgh Press*, May 19, 1934.
10. "Sox Stopped by Rowe," *Chicago Daily Tribune*, June 2, 1934.
11. "You're Telling Me," *Owosso Argus-Press*, May 5, 1934.
12. "Dykes to Clean House for 1935: May Ship Simmons," *Gazette and Bulletin*, July 14, 1934.
13. "Simmons Weds; On Honeymoon in Wisconsin," *Chicago Daily Tribune*, Aug. 10, 1934.
14. Arch Ward, "Talking It Over," *Chicago Daily Tribune*, August 1, 1934.
15. "Simmons Weds; On Honeymoon in Wisconsin," *Chicago Daily Tribune*, August 10, 1934.
16. Unidentified newspaper clipping dated 1934, Al Simmons Hall of Fame.
17. Edward Burns, "Simmons Says He's Glad He is Still a Sox," *Chicago Daily Tribune*, December 8, 1934.
18. Edward Burns, "Here's the American League Batting Leader: Al Simmons," *Chicago Daily Tribune*, January 31, 1935.
19. Ibid.
20. "Simmons Gets Early Start in Year's Worrying," *Chicago Daily Tribune*, February 28, 1935.
21. *The Sporting News*, June 6, 1935; David M. Jordan, *The Athletics of Philadelphia* (Jefferson, NC: McFarland, 1999), 88.
22. Jeff Mosier, "Playing Square," *The Evening Independent*, April 19, 1935.

23. Arch Ward, "Talking It Over," *Chicago Daily Tribune,* July 10, 1935.
24. Unidentified newspaper clipping dated August 8, 1935, Al Simmons Hall of Fame file.
25. "Batting Slump Grips Big Guns of Last Season," Associated Press story in *Sarasota Herald,* July 18, 1935.
26. "Blames Hawaii and Its Waters," *Spokane Daily Chronicle,* July 12, 1935.
27. "International News and Gossip," *Montreal Gazette,* July 16, 1935.
28. Sam Levy, "Sports Chatter," *Milwaukee Journal,* July 10, 1935.
29. Shirley Povich, "This Morning," *Washington Post,* November 26, 1935.
30. Broeg, "Bucketfoot Never Lost That Swagger."
31. Edward Burns, "Foxx Sold to Boston, Simmons to Detroit," *Chicago Daily Tribune,* December 11, 1935.
32. H.G. Salsinger, "Can Al Simmons Hit .325 for Detroit?" *Detroit News,* December 18, 1935.
33. Edward Burns, "Simmons Ready to Prove Tigers Bought Wisely," *Chicago Daily Tribune,* January 5, 1936.
34. Burns, "Foxx Sold."

Chapter Fifteen

1. Both quotes drawn from Donald Honig's *Baseball Between the Lines,* 69–71.
2. Al Abrams, "Sidelights on Sports," *Pittsburgh Post-Gazette,* March 2, 1936.
3. Dick Farrington, "On the Spot in 1936," *The Sporting News,* March 12, 1936.
4. "Higher Pays Likely from Owners," *Pittsburgh Press,* January 12, 1936.
5. Unidentified newspaper clipping dated March 16, 1936, Al Simmons Hall of Fame file.
6. Unidentified newspaper clipping dated March 26, 1936, Al Simmons Hall of Fame file.
7. Morrow, "Al Simmons, Two-Time Hit King."
8. "Al Simmons Given 4 Slot Assignment," unidentified and undated newspaper clipping, Al Simmons Hall of Fame file.
9. "Schoolboy Rowe sees Tigers as Champs Again," Associated Press story in *Palm Beach Post,* February 13, 1936.
10. "Al Simmons' Hitting Improves; Tigers See Another Pennant," Associated Press story in the *Southeast Missourian,* March 14, 1936.
11. "Cochrane Says Tigers Will Repeat," Associated Press story in the (Syracuse) *Herald Journal,* March 29, 1936.
12. "Trosky, Simmons Again Display Power at Bat," Associated Press story in *Milwaukee Journal,* April 21, 1936.
13. "Dykes Warns Mickey," Associated Press story in the (Syracuse) *Herald Journal,* April 14, 1936.
14. "Al Simmons' $75,000 Claw Scratches Detroit Tigers Out of Losing Ways," unidentified newspaper clipping dated July 2, 1936, Al Simmons Hall of Fame file.
15. Charlie Bevis, "Mickey Cochrane," SABR Baseball Biography Project, <http://bioproj.sabr.org>.
16. "Del Baker Claims Tigers are Going to do Better," Associated Press story in *Ludington Daily News,* June 30, 1936.
17. Bevis, *Mickey Cochrane,* 140.
18. Paul Mickelson, "Mickey Cochrane Declares Tigers are Not Through," (Syracuse) *Herald Journal,* July 17, 1936.
19. "Facts and Rumors from the Montreal Meeting," *Pittsburgh Post-Gazette,* December 2, 1936.
20. "Rowe Hopes for 25 Victories," Associated Press story in *Ludington Daily News,* March 8, 1937.
21. H.G. Salsinger, "Simmons is Fading," *Detroit News,* March 31, 1937.
22. "Let's Go," *Deseret News,* April 16, 1937.
23. Bill Braucher, "Cardinals and Pirates Picked to Wage Fight for Bunting This Year," (Syracuse) *Herald Journal,* April 16, 1937.
24. "Detroit Tigers Sell Simmons to Washington," *Chicago Daily Tribune,* April 5, 1937.
25. Bevis, *Mickey Cochrane,* 139.
26. "Al Simmons Is Sold to Solons," Associated Press story in the *Prescott Evening Courier,* April 5, 1937.
27. "Al Simmons Goes Out on Flyer on Atlas Tack Stock," Associated Press story, April 20, 1937.

28. "Al Simmons Dances Jig as Bat He Lost in Japan is Returned," *Washington Post,* April 7, 1937.
29. "Trailing Sports Events," *The Southeast Missourian,* April 16, 1937.
30. Joe Williams, "They'll Never Die," *Pittsburgh Press,* April 21, 1937.
31. Al Abrams, "Sidelights on Sports," *Pittsburgh Post-Gazette,* April 6, 1937.
32. "Training Camp Notes," Associated Press story in *Ludington Daily News,* April 14, 1937.
33. Shirley Povich, "Al Simmons Resumes Place in Left Field," *Washington Post,* May 4, 1937.
34. "Simmons Fights Knickerbocker, Browns Win, 6–0," Associated Press story, June 19, 1937.
35. "Broken Bone in Hand to Bench Simmons," Associated Press, June 20, 1937.
36. Honig, *Baseball Between the Lines,* 69–71.
37. Marc McNeil, "Casual Close-ups," *Montreal Gazette,* July 10, 1937.

Chapter Sixteen

1. "Al Simmons Signs Contract After Conference with Griffith," *Washington Post,* February 26, 1938.
2. Shirley Povich, "This Morning," *Washington Post,* April 2, 1939.
3. Shirley Povich, "Al Simmons Pinch Double Settles Issue," *Washington Post,* May 26, 1938.
4. Sid Feder, "Al Simmons' Comeback Features American League," Associated Press story, June 27, 1938.
5. "Nats Hurdle Southpaw Jinx," Associated Press story in the (Syracuse) *Herald Journal,* July 12, 1938.
6. Jack Cuddy, "Al Simmons Laughs Off the Years," United Press story, July 7, 1938.
7. Shirley Povich, "This Morning," *Washington Post,* April 2, 1938.
8. Vincent X. Flaherty, "Griffith Angry Over Language Used by Player," *Washington Herald,* October 3, 1938.
9. "Simmons is Through," *Washington Post,* October 4, 1938.
10. Vincent X. Flaherty, "Griffith Angry Over Language Used by Player," *Washington Herald,* October 3, 1938.
11. "Simmons is Through."
12. Letter from Elizabeth and Peter Huidekoper, dated October 5, 1938, in the Al Simmons Hall of Fame file.
13. Letter from Clark Griffith to American League President William Harridge, dated October 3, 1938, in the Al Simmons Hall of Fame file.
14. Western Union telegram from William McGowan to American League President William Harridge, dated October 5, 1938, in the Al Simmons Hall of Fame file.
15. Transcript of an October 4, 1938, interview between Kenesaw Landis, Al Simmons, Clark Griffith and Arch McDonald, in the Al Simmons Hall of Fame file.
16. Letter from Naomi Craver, 801 Mt. Vernon Ave. in Alexandria, Virginia, dated October 10, 1938, in the Al Simmons Hall of Fame file.
17. Letter from Kenesaw Mountain Landis, dated October 28, 1938, in the Al Simmons Hall of Fame file.
18. "Al Simmons Swings Deal for Self; Goes to Boston Bees for $5,000," *Washington Post,* December 30, 1935.

Chapter Seventeen

1. Red Smith, "Views of Sports," *New York Herald-Tribune,* May 28, 1956.
2. Mark Schraf, *Cooperstown Verses: Poems about Each Hall of Famer* (Jefferson, NC: McFarland, 2001), 118.
3. "15-year-Veteran, Al Simmons Enters NL as Happy Rookie," Associated Press story, February 9, 1939.
4. William J. Marshall, *Baseball's Pivotal Era: 1945–1951* (Lexington: University Press of Kentucky, 1999), 329.
5. Shirley Povich, "Al Simmons Sizes Up Ted," *Washington Post,* August 28, 1946.
6. George Kirksey and Al Todd, "Al Simmons Trying for Comebacks with Bees," United Press International story, March 25, 1939.

7. Shirley Povich, "This Morning," *Washington Post,* April 2, 1939.
8. Ibid.
9. Ibid.
10. Sam Levy, "Al Has Changed," *Milwaukee Journal,* May 8, 1939.
11. C. William Duncan, "Former Socker Simmons Filled Family Sock Well," *The Sporting News,* October 28, 1943.
12. Wes Singletary, *Al Lopez: The Life of Baseball's El Señor* (Jefferson, NC: McFarland, 1999), 98.
13. "Al Simmons Struck Down by a Pitched Ball," Associated Press story, April 25, 1939.
14. "Veteran Al Simmons Sold to League-Leading Cincinnati," Associated Press story, August 31, 1939.
15. Unidentified newspaper clipping dated September 30, 1939, Al Simmons Hall of Fame file.
16. "Baseball Hall of Fame Beckoning Al Simmons," Associated Press story in *Milwaukee Journal,* October 20, 1939.
17. Shirley Povich, undated 1939 clipping from *Washington Post,* Al Simmons Hall of Fame file.
18. Vincent X. Flaherty, "Straight from the Shoulder," *Los Angeles Examiner,* October 24, 1939.
19. "Al Simmons Returns to Athletics," Associated Press story, December 10, 1939.
20. Bill M'Adams, "Al Simmons Through? Nonsense, Says Mack," unidentified publication, March 4, 1940.
21. Red Smith, "Views of Sport," *New York Herald Tribune,* February 3, 1952.
22. Red Smith, "Views of Sport," *New York Herald Tribune,* May 28, 1956.
23. Harry Ferguson, "McLemore's Sports Parade," UPI story in *Philadelphia Bulletin,* August 27, 1940.

Chapter Eighteen

1. From Quote Garden website, <www.quotegarden.com>.
2. "Al Simmons' Wife Plans to Seek Divorce," *Chicago Daily Tribune,* February 14, 1941.
3. "Al Simmons Replies to Divorce Action," Associated Press story, September 30, 1941.
4. Richard Willing, "Throwing a Curve," *The Washingtonian,* April 1997.
5. Dick Bartell and Norman L. Macht, *Rowdy Richard* (Berkeley, CA: North Atlantic, 1987), 156.
6. "Al Simmons' Divorce Proceedings Delayed," *Chicago Tribune,* December 2, 1941.
7. "Ed McCauley, Tribe Lost True Baseball Man When Simmons' Spirit Cracked," unidentified newspaper clipping dated 1951, Al Simmons Hall of Fame file.
8. Arch Ward, "In the Wake of the News," *Chicago Daily Tribune,* April 3, 1941.
9. George Kirksey, "Siebert Says Al Simmons Helped Him," UPI story in *The Sunday Morning,* August 17, 1941.
10. Jeff Moshier, "Playing Square," *The Evening Independent,* August 5, 1941.
11. Ted Williams, as told to John Underwood, *My Turn at Bat: The Story of My Life* (New York: Simon & Schuster, 1988).
12. "Mack Recalls Former Glory," World Wide News Service story in *Milwaukee Journal,* April 11, 1942.
13. "It's the Nights: Simmons," unidentified clipping from August 27, 1942, Al Simmons Hall of Fame file.
14. "Al Simmons Takes War Job," Associated Press story, October 16, 1942.
15. Unidentified Chicago newspaper clipping dated April 1, 1943, Al Simmons Hall of Fame file.
16. Whitney Martin, "Sports Trail," Associated Press story in *Schenectady Gazette,* February 17, 1943.
17. Jeff Moshier, "Playing Square," *The Evening Independent,* March 24, 1943.
18. Stan Baumgartner, "Baseball Love Forced Simmons Comeback," *Philadelphia Inquirer,* April 20, 1943.
19. "Al Simmons, 40 and Determined to be a Regular, Adopts New Diet," Associated Press story in *Milwaukee Journal,* April 2, 1943.
20. "Veteran Looks like Cinch for Red Sox Team," *Sarasota Herald Tribune,* April 7, 1943.
21. Jean Hastings Ardell, *Breaking into Baseball: Women and the National Pastime* (Carbondale, IL: Southern Illinois University Press, 2005), 195–196.

22. David Halberstam, *The Teammates* (New York: Hyperion, 2003), 35–36.
23. Broeg, "Nothing Like Simmons."
24. Red Smith, "The Duke of Milwaukee," *New York Herald Tribune,* May 1956.
25. C. William Duncan, "Former Socker Simmons Filled Family Sock Well," *The Sporting News,* October 28, 1943.
26. "Old-Timers to Find Comeback Tough, Says Al Simmons," *Milwaukee Journal,* February 21, 1944.
27. "Oldtime Players Said Not Wanted," Associated Press story in *Montreal Gazette,* February 15, 1944.
28. Art Morrow, "Simmons to Play, Army Calls Northy," *Philadelphia Inquirer,* April 16, 1944.
29. Shirley Povich, "This Morning," *Washington Post,* July 16, 1944.
30. Shirley Povich, "This Morning ," *Washington Post,* January 10, 1952.
31. Jeff Moshier, "Playing Square," *The Evening Independent,* April 29, 1944.

Chapter Nineteen

1. Bob Feller entry in Dickson's *Baseball's Greatest Quotations,* 131.
2. Charlie Metro and Tom Altherr, *Safe By A Mile* (Lincoln: University of Nebraska Press, 2002), 90.
3. David Kaiser, *Epic Season: The 1948 American League Pennant Race* (Amherst: University of Massachusetts Press, 1998), 140.
4. Brent Kelley, *The San Francisco Seals, 1946–1957: Interviews with 25 Baseballers* (Jefferson, NC: McFarland, 2002).
5. Bob Considine, "The Connie Mack Story," INS story in *Milwaukee Sentinel,* February 11, 1956.
6. Whitney Martin, "Spirit Has Helped Macks, Explains Coach Simmons," Associated Press story in *Milwaukee Journal,* July 8, 1947.
7. "A's Prove Wind Blows Man, but Good," *Chicago Daily Tribune,* April 9, 1948.
8. Sam Levy, "On the First Bounce," *Milwaukee Journal,* 1948.
9. "Cleveland Signs Simmons to Put Fire Into Team," Associated Press story, January 20, 1950.
10. Arthur Daley, "Listening to Jimmy Dykes and Al Simmons," *New York Times,* March 7, 1949.
11. Arthur Daley, "Out of the Time," *New York Times,* April 9, 1951.
12. "Connie Still Running A's, Son Avers," Associated Press story, October 21, 1949.
13. Broeg, "Nothing Like Simmons."
14. Red Smith, "Views of Sport," *New York Herald Tribune,* October 19, 1949.
15. Arthur Daley, "Ominous Portent," *New York Times,* October 20, 1949.
16. Cleveland Indians yearbook, 1950.
17. "Cleveland Signs Simmons to Put Fire Into Team," Associated Press story, January 20, 1950.
18. Thomas letter to Lanigan.
19. Broeg, "Bucketfoot Never Lost That Swagger."
20. Ibid.
21. Broeg, "Nothing Like Simmons."
22. "Al Simmons Suspended," *Associated Press* story in *St. Petersburg Times,* May 23, 1950.
23. "Simmons Suspended for Indefinite Period," unidentified 1950 clipping, Al Simmons Hall of Fame File.
24. Ed McAuley, "Simmons Tells How Heckling Beats Bosox," *Cleveland News,* 1951.
25. "Ruffing Replaces Al Simmons as Coach for Tribe," *Washington Post,* April 6, 1951.
26. "Simmons Denies Quitting Indians," *New York Times,* April 5, 1951.
27. Hal Lebovitz, "Bucketfoot Al Leaves as Tribe Aide," *Cleveland News,* April 11, 1951.
28. Ed McAuley, "Tribe Lost True Baseball Man When Simmons' Spirit Cracked," *Cleveland News,* 1951.

Chapter Twenty

1. Dan Chabot entry in Dickson's *Baseball's Greatest Quotations,* 78.
2. Shirley Povich, "This Morning," *Washington Post,* January 10, 1952.

3. Frank Yeutter, "Bing Miller Boosts Al Simmons for Place in Hall of Fame," *Philadelphia Bulletin*, January 12, 1952.
4. "Now and Then," January 22, 1953, photos from an unidentified publication in Al Simmons Hall of Fame file.
5. Whitey Kelley, "Simmons Thought Younger Writers 'Had Forgotten Me,'" *Miami Herald*, February 4, 1953.
6. Daniel, *Jimmie Foxx*, 186.
7. "Al Simmons Itches for Baseball Play," Associated Press story in *Spokane Daily Chronicle*, January 29, 1953.
8. Hi Nelson, "New Names in the Hall of Fame," *Current Events*, February 16–20, 1953.
9. Arthur Daley, "The Duke of Milwaukee," *New York Times*, January 26, 1953.
10. "Diz Dean and Al Simmons in Baseball Hall of Fame," Associated Press story in *Toledo Blade*, July 28, 1953.
11. "Big, Little Pay Homage to Mack," Associated Press story in *Spokane Daily Chronicle*, February 9, 1956.
12. Broeg, "Bucketfoot Never Lost That Swagger."
13. "Al Simmons Dies at 54 of Heart Attack," Associated Press story, May 26, 1956.
14. Death certificate from the Wisconsin Board of Health, filed June 11, 1956.
15. "Al Simmons Still the Duke," unidentified newspaper clipping dated April 13, 1939, Al Simmons Hall of Fame file.
16. Daniel, *Jimmie Foxx*, 194.
17. Shirley Povich, "This Morning," *Washington Post*, May 1956.
18. Shirley Povich, "This Morning," *Washington Post*, December 12, 1960.
19. Cleon Walfoort, "Simmons' Hatred for Hurler Made Him Baseball Legend," *Milwaukee Journal*, May 26, 1956.
20. "Al Simmons," National Baseball Hall of Fame website, <baseballhall.org/hof/simmons-al>.
21. Obituary published in *Atlanta Journal-Constitution*, February 1, 2010.
22. E-mail interview with Patrick Graeber, August 9, 2010.

Chapter Twenty-One

1. Bill James, *The New Bill James Historical Baseball Abstract*, revised edition (New York: Free Press, 2003), 656.
2. Ibid., 366.
3. Ibid.
4. Pease, "Diamonds Out of the Coal Mines."
5. Cyril Morong's blog, <cybermetric.blogspot.com>

Bibliography

Books

Alexander, Charles. *Breaking the Slump: Baseball in the Depression Era.* New York: Columbia University Press, 2004.
Ardell, Jean Hastings. *Breaking into Baseball: Women and the National Pastime.* Carbondale: Southern Illinois University Press, 2005.
Baldasarro, Lawrence, and Richard Johnson, eds. *The American Game: Baseball and Ethnicity.* Carbondale: Southern Illinois University Press, 2002.
Baldwin, Neil. *Edison: Inventing the Century.* Chicago: University of Chicago Press, 2001.
Barra Foundation. *Philadelphia: A 300-Year History.* New York: W.W. Norton, 1982.
Bartell, Dick, and Norman L. Macht. *Rowdy Richard.* Berkeley, CA: North Atlantic, 1987.
Bevis, Charles. *Mickey Cochrane: The Life of a Baseball Hall of Fame Catcher.* Jefferson, NC: McFarland, 1998.
Browning, Reed. *Baseball's Greatest Season: 1924.* Amherst: University of Massachusetts Press, 2003.
Carmichael, John P. *My Greatest Day in Baseball.* Lincoln: University of Nebraska Press, 1996.
Crepeau, Richard. *Baseball: America's Diamond Mind.* Lincoln: University of Nebraska Press, 2000.
Curran, William. *Big Sticks: The Batting Revolution of the Twenties.* New York: William Morrow, 1990.
Daniel, W. Harrison. *Jimmie Foxx: Life and Times of a Baseball Hall of Famer.* Jefferson, NC: McFarland, 2004.
Dickson, Paul. *Baseball's Greatest Quotations.* New York: HarperCollins, 1991.
_____. *The New Baseball Dictionary.* New York: Harcourt Brace, 1999.
Dittmar, Joe. *Baseball Records Registry: The Best and Worst Single-Day Performances and the Stories Behind Them.* Jefferson, NC: McFarland, 1997.
Doyle, Edward "Dutch." *Al Simmons, the Best.* Chicago: Adams, 1979.
Dykes, Jimmie, and Charles Dexter. *You Can't Steal First Base.* Philadelphia: J.B. Lippincott, 1967.
Forker, Dom, Wayne Stewart, and Robert Obojski. *Big Book of Baseball Brainteasers.* New York: Sterling, 2004.
Honig, Donald. *Baseball America: The Heroes of the Game and the Times of their Glory.* New York: MacMillan, 1985.
_____. *Baseball Between the Lines.* Lincoln: University of Nebraska Press, 1993.
_____. *Baseball When the Grass Was Real: Baseball from the Twenties to the Forties, Told by the Men Who Played It.* Lincoln: University of Nebraska Press, 1993.
Holtzman, Jerome. *Baseball, Chicago Style.* Los Angeles: Bonus, 2001.
James, Bill. *The New Bill James Historical Abstract.* Revised ed. New York: Free Press, 2003.
Jordan, David M. *The Athletics of Philadelphia.* Jefferson, NC: McFarland, 1999.
Kaiser, David. *Epic Season: The 1948 American League Pennant Race.* Amherst: University of Massachusetts Press, 1998.
Kaplan, Jim. *Lefty Grove: American Original.* Cleveland: Society for American Baseball Research, 2000.
Kashatus, William. *Connie Mack's '29 Triumph: The Rise and Fall of the Philadelphia Athletics Dynasty.* Jefferson, NC: McFarland, 1999.
Kelley, Brent. *The San Francisco Seals, 1946–1957: Interviews with 25 Baseballers.* Jefferson, NC: McFarland, 2002.

Kuklick, Bruce. *To Everything a Season: Shibe Park and Urban Philadelphia, 1909–1976.* Princeton: Princeton University Press, 1993.
Laing, R.D. *The Politics of Experience.* New York: Pantheon, 1967.
Mack, Connie. *Connie Mack's Baseball Book.* New York: Alfred A. Knopf, 1950.
Marshall, William J. *Baseball's Pivotal Era: 1945–1951.* Lexington: University Press of Kentucky, 1999.
Mathewson, Christy. *Pitching in a Pinch.* Reprint. Lincoln: University of Nebraska Press, 1994.
McCallum, John. *The Tiger Wore Spikes.* New York: A.S. Barnes, 1956.
McLuhan, Marshall. *Understanding Media.* New York: McGraw Hill, 1964.
Metro, Charlie, and Tom Altherr. *Safe By a Mile.* Lincoln: University of Nebraska Press, 2002.
Morris, Peter. *A Game of Inches: The Stories Behind the Innovations That Shaped Baseball.* Chicago: Ivan R. Dee, 2006.
Mulligan, Brian. *1940 Cincinnati Reds: A World Championship and Baseball's Only In-Season Suicide.* Jefferson, NC: McFarland, 2005.
National Geographic Society and National Baseball Hall of Fame and Museum. *Baseball as America: Seeing Ourselves Through Our National Game.* Washington: National Geographic Society, 2002.
Okrent, Daniel, and Harris Lewine. *The Ultimate Baseball Book.* Boston: Houghton Mifflin, 2000.
Paprocki, Joe. *Bringing Catechesis and Liturgy Together.* New London, CT: Twenty-Third, 2002.
Ritter, Lawrence. *The Glory of Their Times.* New York: HarperCollins, 1992.
Romanowski, Jerome. *The Mackmen.* Camden, NJ: Graphic, 1979.
Ruth, Babe. *Babe Ruth's Own Book of Baseball.* Reprint. Lincoln: University of Nebraska Press, 1992.
Schraf, Mark. *Cooperstown Verses: Poems About Each Hall of Famer.* Jefferson, NC: McFarland, 2001.
Singletary, Wes. *Al Lopez: The Life of Baseball's El Señor.* Jefferson, NC: McFarland, 1999.
Smith, Red. *The Book: Red Smith on Baseball.* Chicago: Ivan R. Dee, 2000.
Stump, Al. *My Life in Baseball: Ty Cobb.* Lincoln: University of Nebraska Press, 1993.
Thomas, Henry W. *Walter Johnson: Baseball's Big Train.* Lincoln: University of Nebraska Press, 1998.
Tygiel, Jules. *Baseball's Great Experiment: Jackie Robinson and his Legacy.* New York: Oxford University Press, 1997.
Williams, Ted, and John Underwood. *My Turn at Bat: The Story of My Life.* New York: Simon & Schuster, 1988.

Newspapers, Magazines, and Websites

Atlanta Constitution, 1927–2010
Baseball Magazine, 1950
Berkeley Daily Gazette, 1925–1933
Boston Globe, 1956
Chicago Daily News, 1933–1944
Chicago Tribune, 1927–1948
Cleveland News, 1933–1951
Current Events, 1953
Cybermetrics
Deseret News, 1926
Detroit News, 1935–1937
Ellensburg Daily Record, 1931
Elysian Fields Quarterly, Summer 2000
Eugene Register-Guard, 1925
Evening Independent, 1926–1943
Florence Times Daily, 1931–1932
Free Lance-Star, 1930
Gazette and Bulletin, 1934
Hartford Courant, 1929
Lewiston Daily Sun, 1930
Lewiston Evening Journal, 1925
Los Angeles Examiner, 1939
Los Angeles Times, 1927–1933
Ludington Daily News, 1925–1937
Miami Herald, 1953

Miami News, 1926–1928
Milwaukee Journal, 1928–1983
Milwaukee Sentinel, 1956
Milwaukee Times, 1967
Montreal Gazette, 1931–1937
New York Herald-Tribune, 1952–1956
New York Journal-American, 1953
New York Times, 1927–2009
Northwestern Magazine, Spring 2009
The Observer, 1932
Owosso Argus-Press, 1934
Palm Beach Post, 1929–1936
Philadelphia Athletics Historical Society
Philadelphia Evening Ledger, 1929–1953
Philadelphia Inquirer, 1928–1944
Philadelphia Public Ledger, 1928–1953
Philadelphia Sunday Bulletin, 1940–1956
Pittsburgh Press, 1925–1937
Pittsburgh Post-Gazette, 1930–1937
Prescott Evening Courier, 1937
Reading Eagle, 1923–1931
SABR Baseball Biography Project
St. Louis Star, 1931
St. Petersburg Times, 1927–1930
Sarasota Herald, 1929–1943
Schenectady Gazette, 1932–1943
Southeast Missourian, 1924–1936
Spokane Daily Chronicle, 1935–1953
Sport Magazine, 1984
Sports Guide, 1971
Sports Illustrated, 1996
(Syracuse) *Herald Journal*, 1926–1936
The Sporting News, 1929–1978
Star and Sentinel, 1932
Sunday Morning, 1941
Toledo Blade, 1953
Victoria Advocate, 1927
Washington Post, 1931–1989
The Washingtonian, April 1997

Archival Documents

American League Service Bureau, documents dated December 2, 1928, February 7, 1932, and February 12, 1933.
My Life, unpublished manuscript by Al Simmons as told to A.J. Schinner, provided to author by Tom Rathkamp and Craig and Laura Simmons-Larsen of Milwaukee.
National Baseball Hall of Fame, A. Bartlett Giamatti Research Center, Al Simmons file.
Wisconsin Board of Health, Al Simmons' death certificate filed June 11, 1956, and certificate of birth, state birth no. 148, signed September 19, 1974.
Personal Interview
Patrick Graeber, e-mail interview with author on August 9, 2010.

Index

Aberdeen 23–25
Alger, Horatio 10–11
Allen, Woody 45
Auker, Eldon 23

Bartell, Dick 182
Baumgartner, Stan 33, 187
Bell, Brian 77
Bevis, Charles 158
Bogart, Humphrey 181
Boley, Joe 52
Borchert, Otto 20–25
Brandt, Bill 64
Braucher, William 120
Bresnahan, Roger 18
Broeg, Bob 3, 15, 24, 31, 53, 138, 194, 197
Brucker, Earle 194–195
Brundidge, Harry 25
Burns, Edward 144–145, 149

Campanella, Roy 13
Cangelosi, Carmen 83
Carmichael, John 91
Cascarella, Joe 182
Case, George 3, 151, 161–162
Chabot, Dan 200
Chicago Cubs 77–85
Clark, Harry 23, 24
Cobb, Ty 3, 8, 27, 41, 51–52, 53–62, 70, 77
Cochrane, Mickey 4, 35, 44, 68, 74, 108–109, 144, 149–150, 152 163
Collins, Eddie 33
Comiskey, Lou 127, 134–135, 139, 149
Conwell, Arthur 41, 66
Coolidge, Calvin 34
Coover, Robert 1
Coveleski, Stan 37
Crepeau, Richard 10
Cronin, Joe 187
Cuddy, Jack 166

Daley, Arthur 15, 19, 203
Davis, Harry "Jaspar" 27

Davis, Ralph 69
Dickson, Paul 8, 13
Dittmar, Joe 65
Doby, Larry 193
Doyle, Edward "Dutch" 8, 15
Drohan, John 132
Duncan, William 68
Dykes, Jimmy 54, 115, 139, 141, 148, 194

Eager, Harold 203
Earnshaw, George 35, 140
Edison, Thomas 46
Ehmke, Howard 78–80
Evans, Billy 42, 48–49, 59

Fain, Ferriss 191–193
Farrington, Dick 151
Feller, Bob 193
Felsch, Happy 8
Ferber, Edna 101
Flaherty, Vincent X. 178
Fonseca, Lou 134–136, 139
Foxx, Jimmie 4, 71–72, 74–76, 78–85, 118–121
Foxx, Nanci 71
Frawley, Bill 197

Gallagher, Joe 52
Galloway, Chick 89–90
Gehrig, Lou 3, 4, 94–95, 163
Gehringer, Charlie 48
Gould, Alan 95, 104, 129
Grabiner, Harry 127
Graeber, Karen 207
Graeber, Patrick 207
Greenberg, Hank 152, 154, 158
Griffith, Clark 160, 167–171
Grove, Lefty 39, 113–114, 107–108, 113

Halberstam, David 188
Harkin, E.B. 23
Honig, Donald 45, 48, 161–162, 176
Hornsby, Rogers 4, 22, 43
Hubbell, Carl 141

239

Index

Isaminger, James 64, 174

James, Bill 2, 29, 209–210
Johnson, Arnold 196
Johnson, Ban 56
Johnson, Bob 179–180
Johnson, Walter 47–48
Juneau 13, 14

Kashatus, William 34, 56, 73, 90
Kieran, John 2, 8, 53, 80, 89, 95
Klein, Chuck 92–93, 104
Kramer, Mark 86
Kuhn, Dorothy 101
Kuhn, John 101
Kuklick, Bruce 32, 124

Laabs, Chet 157
Laing, R.D. 20
Lane, F.C. 35
Levinson, Leonard 126
Lopez, Al 176, 198–199

Mack, Connie 2, 18, 19, 20, 25–28, 29–33, 36, 42, 45, 49–52, 58, 62–63, 77–85, 88–89, 95–100, 109–113, 122–125, 129, 137, 146, 178–179, 184–186, 189, 191–199, 204
Marciano, Rocky 2
Martin, Pepper 110–114
Mathewson, Christy 13
Matsui, Hideki 49
McAuley, Ed 198–199
McCarthy, Joe 79–83
McFarlane, Todd 4
McGowan, Bill 168–169
McGraw, John 18–19, 110
McLuhan, Marshall 12
McQuillan, George 13
Melillo, Oscar "Ski" 22–23
Mellon, Andrew 86
Metro, Charlie 191
Miller, Bing 200–201
Milwaukee 5–11
Milwaukee Brewers 20–28
Morong, Cyril 212–213
Murphy, Johnny 36
Musial, Stan 188

Nack, William 4, 115, 125
Neil, Edward 128

Ott, Mel 4

Paprocki, Joe 50
Pardon, George 24
Pease, Neal 17, 210
Peckinpaugh, Roger 44
Pegler, Westbrook 17, 77, 81, 87
Perkins, Cy 33

Pesky, Johnny 188
Phelon, William 40
Philadelphia 32–33
Philadelphia Athletics 32–33, 47, 115–116, 122–125
Pollock, Ed 31, 72
Povich, Shirley 46, 115, 148, 166, 173, 178, 189, 200–201, 205

Rathkamp, Thomas 206
Reader, Dores Lynn 142, 181–183
Reimann, George 21
Riess, Steven 37
Ritter, Lawrence 38
Robinson, Ray 126
Romanowski, Jerome 31
Rooney, John 62, 66–67
Roth, Phillip 53
Ruth, Babe 3, 4, 5, 36, 40, 53, 60, 68, 145

St. Hyacinth 7, 8
St. Louis Cardinals 96–100, 110–114
Salsinger, H.G. 156
Schinner, A.J. 16
Schraf, Mark 172
Schwender, Anton "Butch" 13
Shakespeare, William 12
Shibe, Benjamin 40
Shinners, Ralph 68, 152
Shreveport Gassers 25–26
Siebert, Dick 183
Simmons, Al 5–13, 16–18, 20–45, 53–61, 71–100, 106–107, 118–136, 142–143, 148–163, 167–171, 173, 181–183, 187–199, 202–206
Simmons, John Allen "Duke" 150, 173, 181, 202, 207
Sisler, George 43
Slavic emergence in baseball 16–18
Smith, Ken 2
Smith, Red 172, 180, 195
Sords, Jack 75
"Spawn" 4
Speaker, Tris 43, 62–63
Spencer, Jack 16
Stengel, Casey 174
Stephens, Vern 13
Stevens, John Paul 79
Stevens Point Teachers College 15
Stumpf, Eddie 21
Suzuki, Sotaro 113
Szulakiewicz, W.J. 206
Szymanski, Agnes (Czarnecki) 6–11, 203
Szymanski, Anna 7
Szymanski, Anthony 7, 87
Szymanski, Frances 7
Szymanski, John 6–11, 203
Szymanski, Steven 87
Szymanski, Tillie 7
Szymanski, Walter 7, 87

Thomas, Ira 23, 25, 152
Tincup, Ben 27
Trumbull, Walter 93
Tygiel, Jules 99

Vaughan, Arky 13
Vaughan, Manning 102, 105, 107
Voorhis, Chuck 120

Walfoort, Cleon 206
Ward, Arch 34, 126, 130, 142, 146

Warrington, Bob 90
Wedge, William 89
Wilde, Oscar 137
Williams, Ted 2, 173, 183–184
Wilson Hack 82–85
Wisconsin State League 15
Wollen, Lou 78

www.ingramcontent.com/pod-product-compliance
Ingram Content Group UK Ltd.
Pitfield, Milton Keynes, MK11 3LW, UK
UKHW041939140426
5217IPUK00014B/554